Preparation Guide: Redesigned SAT 2016

Yellow Writing

Version 1.0

Printed in the United States of America
International Standard Book Number:
978-0-9906704-8-3

Published by Reetiforp, LLC Publishing, a division of Reetiforp, LLC Reetiforp

Publishing books are available at special quantity discounts to use for sales promotions, employee premiums, or educational purposes. Please email our Marketing Department to order or for more information at workbooks@c2educate.com. Please report any errors or corrections to corrections@c2educate.com.

Letter to Students and Parents

To Students and Parents

C2 Education's Redesigned SAT workbooks focus on curriculum that will help students build key foundation skills and learn problem-solving methods to tackle the new SAT to be released in 2016. We strongly recommend that students use these workbooks aligned with instructions and guidance from our tutors at a C2 Education center.

This book contains a number of exercises designed to guide the student through a careful, progressive process that will build layers of understanding and present problems with an increasing degree of difficulty. Each colored (belt) level will confront a variety of topics within the realms of Writing, Essay, Reading, and Math; some topics may re-appear in other workbooks of different difficulties while some topics may only appear once. The ultimate goal of C2 Education's workbooks is to cover the academic content in a comprehensive manner with sufficient practice sets and homework review.

Students will obtain the greatest benefit and improvement from these workbooks by following the workbooks from Lesson 1 to the end. Each lesson will contain the following:

- A diagnostic assessment designed to help our C2 tutors gauge the student's understanding prior to the lesson
- Instructional text and information focused on methodology and problem-solving thought processes
- Practice problems about the concepts presented and any connecting concepts from other lessons
- Test-like practice problems geared to emulate the real exam
- Homework problems to review academic information covered in class and the workbook

We wish you the best of luck in your academic endeavors and we hope that our workbooks will provide you with strong improvements, facilitated understanding, and expanded problem-solving skills. Thank you for being a part of the C2 family; we hope that you enjoy your time learning with us!

- C2 Education's Curriculum Team

SAT Yellow Writing
Table of Contents

Lesson wY1
Fragments, Run-Ons, and Comma Splices
Getting Your Feet Wet

1. The little girl jumped for <u>joy, she was so excited</u>.

    A) NO CHANGE
    B) joy; she was so excited.
    C) joy, so excited was she.
    D) joy she was so excited

2. Depending on what happens in the next <u>few hours, a major news story</u> on our hands.

    A) NO CHANGE
    B) few hours may give a major news story
    C) few hours, we have a major news story
    D) few hours, a major news story to be

3. <u>Having been replaced by</u> newer, more powerful computers that are capable of many more calculations per second.

    A) NO CHANGE
    B) They have been replaced by
    C) The old computer stations have been replaced by
    D) The old computer stations, replaced by

4. Although many people have disputed his theories, the scientist ultimately vindicated himself with his <u>latest experiment, it proved that the</u> basis of his research had broad consequences.

    A) NO CHANGE
    B) latest experiment, with proving the
    C) latest experiment, it was proving that
    D) latest experiment, which proved that the

Lesson wY1
Fragments, Run-Ons, and Comma Splices
Getting Your Feet Wet

TOPIC OVERVIEW: SENTENCES

Sentences are sometimes hard to keep track of. Do they have all the required pieces, or are they overstuffed with too many words? A quick grammar review about sentence structure should clear things up.

Sentences are made of **clauses**. A clause is a part of a sentence that has both a subject and a verb. The subject is who or what the sentence is about. The verb is the action that the subject is performing.

Example 1: The dog barked.

Example 1 is a single clause. What is the subject? What is the verb?

Exercise 1

After reading the following sentences, underline the **subject** once and the **verb** twice.

1. The rowdy boys played baseball every day.

2. The lightning flashed in the sky.

3. The cheese has an interesting smell.

4. The children on the swingset laugh happily.

5. Jake always gets into trouble with his friends.

We'll learn more about subjects and verbs in Lesson 3.

Clauses can be separated into two classes, **independent** and **dependent.** An independent clause can stand by itself with no other parts of the sentence, as with Example 1.

Clauses are often connected with words called **conjunctions**. Some conjunctions, known as coordinating conjunctions, can connect independent clauses:

Example 2: The dog barked, and the boy laughed.

Other conjunctions (subordinating conjunctions) create dependent clauses.

Example 3: Because we were hungry.

Example 3 is a dependent clause, and a **sentence fragment**. It cannot be a sentence by itself. Why? The sentence starts with the subordinating conjunction "because." Words like *although, because, before, after, when, while,* are subordinating conjunctions. They make it so that the clause does not make a complete sentence. A dependent clause always needs an independent clause with it.

Example 4: Because we were hungry, we went to the store.

Example 5: We went to the store because we were hungry.

Note that if the dependent clause comes first, use a comma. If it comes after the independent clause, no comma is necessary. We'll learn more about conjunctions and their uses in the next lesson.

Clauses can also be connected by a **semicolon**, as shown by Example 6:

Example 6: The farmer wiped sweat from his brow; the day had been hot and dry.

A semicolon connects two independent clauses that relate to the same idea. (We'll learn more about semicolons in lesson 4.)

Some sentences can have more than two clauses. Read the sentence below. How many clauses does it have?

Example 7: Though he was told he would never be a boxer, Arturo practiced every day; years later he became the middleweight boxing champion of the world.

The sentence has two independent clauses ("Arturo practiced every day" AND "years later he became…") and one dependent clause ("Though he was told…") for a total of three clauses. Some sentences may have even more, but as long as the correct conjunctions and punctuation is used, they are grammatically correct.

Exercise 2

After reading the following sentences, circle the independent clauses and underline the dependent clauses.

1. When I studied ancient history, I could imagine the people of the past.

2. The dog eagerly wagged its tail.

3. He thought he could never be scared, but he was proven wrong when his friends took him to the haunted house.

4. The sports hero was known for his generosity and friendliness.

5. After her cat ran away, Ali could not be consoled.

WRAP-UP: SENTENCES

1. Sentences are made up of clauses, which each have a subject and a verb. Clauses are connected by conjunctions. Independent clauses can stand on their own, but dependent clauses need another clause for the sentence to be complete.
2. Independent clauses can be connected by semicolons or coordinating conjunctions; dependent clauses use subordinating conjunctions.

TOPIC OVERVIEW: SENTENCE FRAGMENTS

Sentence Fragments are incomplete sentences that lack something important in their structure. There are two main types of fragments.

The first is a <u>sentence missing a subject or verb</u>. Remember, every independent clause needs a subject and a verb. Take a look at the sentence fragments below:

<u>Example 8</u>: Standing alone by a phone booth with change in his hand.

This sentence consists entirely of a verb phrase – there's no subject. Who is standing alone?

<u>Example 9</u>: The general, decorated with medals and honors displayed proudly on his uniform.

This sentence is only describing the subject – there's no verb phrase. (Words in this sentence such as "decorated" and "displayed" are not acting as the verb phrase – they don't say what the general is doing. They only act to tell us about what the general's medals and awards are like.)

These sentences are incomplete, because every complete sentence must have at least one independent clause. If the independent clause in the sentence is missing its subject or verb, then the sentence is a fragment—even if it has multiple dependent clauses.

<u>Example 10</u>: Peter met his brother Irwin at the burger restaurant; a place filled with the smell of grease, charred meat, and fries.

As the second part of the sentence ("a place filled…") lacks a verb, the whole sentence is a fragment. (This is also an illustration of a semicolon error, which we will discuss more in Lesson 4).

The second type of sentence fragment is a <u>dependent clause that is standing alone</u>.

<u>Example 11</u>: Although I want to go.

The best way to fix a fragment like this is either to remove the subordinating conjunction:

<u>Example 12</u>: I want to go.

Or add an independent clause to the sentence:

<u>Example 13</u>: Although I want to go, I have work to do.

Exercise 3

Read the sentences. On the line below, write what kind of fragment the sentence is – "missing subject," "missing verb," or "dependent clause." Then write a corrected version of the sentence.

1. The gentleman with the winning smile and jaunty cap.

   _____

   _____

   _____

   _____

2. Before the war ripped families apart and destroyed much of the city.

   _____

   _____

   _____

   _____

3. Running past the beautiful fountain by the side of the wide plaza.

   _____

   _____

   _____

   _____

TOPIC OVERVIEW: RUN-ON SENTENCES

Run-on sentences are sentences that have too many clauses and not enough connection between the clauses. Most errors with run-on sentences occur due to faulty coordination or subordination between clauses.

Example 14: The patient thanked the doctor profusely, the doctor had cured his psoriasis.

Here we have a sentence with two clauses; however, these two clauses are connected only by a comma. This is what we call a **comma splice**. How do you fix a comma splice? You need to connect the two parts of the sentence in a grammatically correct way. Take a look at the fixes below.

Example 15: The patient thanked the doctor profusely; the doctor had cured his psoriasis.

Example 16: The patient thanked the doctor profusely, for the doctor had cured his psoriasis.

In Example 15, the clauses are connected by a semicolon instead of a comma; in Example 16, we added a conjunction after the comma. Both fix the comma splice in the sentence.

Some run-on sentences simply lack anything to connect multiple clauses:

Example 17: I don't trust the neighbors across the street my sister doesn't either.

There are two distinct clauses in that sentence, but they're all mashed together. Where should the split be made? What would you do to fix it?

_____

_____

_____

To determine if a sentence is a run-on sentence, **count the number of subjects and verbs**. If there are two or more subjects and two or more verbs, but no conjunctions or semicolons, you may have a run-on sentence.

Exercise 4

In the sentences below, circle the subjects and verbs. Using the information you have gathered from these clues, determine if the sentence is a fragment, a run-on sentence, a comma splice, or a correct sentence.

1. Expecting his friends to show up to the concert, but Patrick soon realized he was alone when the band appeared on stage.

   _____

2. Please stop speaking, I have a headache.

   _____

3. Alison and her coworkers rarely speaking, for their work required them to spend much of their time at their computers.

   _____

4. The dog yapped loudly it was really getting on my nerves.

   _____

WRAP-UP: SENTENCE FRAGMENTS AND RUN-ONS

1. Sentence fragments are incomplete sentences. When trying to find sentence fragments, look for dependent clauses standing by themselves without independent clauses, or clauses missing either a subject or verb.
2. Run-on sentences have multiple subjects and verbs, but do not have the correct punctuation or conjunctions to connect the clauses of the sentence. Look for sentences with two or more subjects/verbs, and make sure that these clauses are separated by semicolons or conjunctions.

Lesson wY1
Run-Ons and Fragments
Learning to Swim

CONCEPT EXERCISE:

Directions: Find and correct errors in the following sentences. Some sentences will not have any errors.

1. The idea that entertainment affects our politics might seem ludicrous to some; many would doubt that the *Star Wars* saga might have influenced the ideas of Generation X.

2. Additionally, the idea that the music that the baby boomers listened to played a supporting role in the development of that generation's politics.

3. A new theory, J.K. Rowling's immensely popular *Harry Potter* series may have played a role in the political development of the millennials.

4. Some might say it even affected election results, and recent research has indicated this is possibly true.

5. The *Harry Potter* series influenced the perspectives of the generation that came of age with these books; reading the books correlated with greater support for equality, and greater opposition to the use of torture.

6. As *Harry Potter* fans may note, these are major themes throughout the series; these correlations remained significant even when applying more sophisticated analyses.

7. Although some might interpret this as "*Harry Potter* books brainwashed millennials."

8. The actual research presents a much more nuanced picture.

9. People consume more and more entertainment media; less news coverage and more sitcoms, books, and action movies.

10. Our entertainment consumption may play a large role in how we see the world; after all, many political and social views are not acquired in a purely rational way.

11. Research has demonstrated that we do not process ideas in entertainment the same way we process information; reacting on a more emotional level distant from real world facts.

12. Although the scornful retort is that people's choice of entertainment will reflect their pre-existing views.

13. While the argument of selective exposure—that we only consume media that agrees with our existing beliefs—is less applicable to entertainment than it is to political media.

14. We're often drawn to stories for reasons that may have nothing to do with our views.

15. For example, the stories' popularity, attention given to them in the media, critical reviews, special effects, advertising, boredom, or exposure when we have little choice.

16. Once we're immersed in the book, TV program, or film, we internalize the lessons of the narrative, and emulate the qualities of those characters with whom we identify.

17. Selective exposure is also complicated by the fact that the lessons of a narrative or the qualities of fictional characters are not always evident early on in the story. Because they may evolve throughout it.

18. Take the case of Darth Vader, a cultural icon of evil who turns out to still have some good in him.

19. A separate experiment that found that exposure to different types of fictional villains affected attitudes about justice.

20. It may seem odd to believe that entertainment shapes our politics, but a great volume of research has already examined the effects of entertainment on other behaviors, such as violence or the development of unhealthy habits.

Lesson wY1
Run-Ons and Fragments
Diving Into the Deep End

PRACTICE EXERCISE:

Directions: Answer the questions that accompany the following passages.

The Beginnings of American Football

American football finds its roots in rugby football, in which two teams vie for possession of a **(1)** ball. That they then attempt to kick or carry into an opponent's goal zone. In the late 1800s, American football began to become a popular collegiate **(2)** sport. Eventually the Intercollegiate Football Association was created.

As the years went by, new concepts were **(3)** introduced and existing ones were altered significantly. The "snap" was instituted to replace the inconsistent and dangerous "scrum," a sort of "dog pile" that began each series and determined which team gained initial possession of the game ball. The introduction of the snap resulted in unexpected strategy changes. Originally, the strategy had been to "punt" if a scrum resulted in poor field position. Players from Princeton realized that, because the snap was uncontested, they now could hold on to the ball **(4)** indefinitely. Thus preventing their opponent from scoring. In 1881, both teams in a Yale-Princeton game used this strategy to maintain their perfect records. Each team held the ball, gaining no ground, for an entire period. This "block game" strategy proved extremely unpopular with spectators.

A reversion to the scrum was **(5)** considered. Until Walter Camp, a Yale player, proposed a rule in 1882 that gave a team three downs, or tackles, to advance the ball five yards. Failure to do so would forfeit control of the ball. This change made American football a separate sport from rugby, and the resulting yard lines added to the field made it resemble a gridiron. Other major rule changes included a reduction of the field **(6)** size, and the adoption

1.
   A) NO CHANGE
   B) ball; that they
   C) ball that they
   D) ball that, they

2. A) NO CHANGE
   B) sport eventually
   C) sport. And eventually
   D) sport; and eventually

3. A) NO CHANGE
   B) introduced,
   C) introduced, while
   D) introduced. And

4. A) NO CHANGE
   B) indefinitely; thus preventing
   C) indefinitely, thus a prevention of
   D) indefinitely. This prevented

5. A) NO CHANGE
   B) considered, until
   C) considered and
   D) considered until

6. A) NO CHANGE
   B) size. The
   C) size and the
   D) size, the

of a scoring system that awarded four points for a touchdown, two for a safety, and five for a field goal. In 1888 tackling below the waist was legalized.

Football remained a violent **(7)** <u>sport. Despite</u> innovations to promote players' safety. Dangerous mass-formations like the flying wedge resulted in serious **(8)** <u>injuries. Even occasional</u> deaths. Following a record 19 fatalities in **(9)** <u>1905 President</u> Theodore Roosevelt threatened to abolish the game unless major changes were made. Sixty-two schools met in New York City to discuss rule changes in December of 1905. These proceedings resulted in the formation of the Intercollegiate Athletic Association of the United **(10)** <u>States later</u> renamed the National Collegiate Athletic Association.

The forward pass was introduced in 1906 after it was suggested by John Heisman. At first, its impact was limited due to restrictions placed on its use. The time of play was reduced from 70 to 60 minutes, and the requirement for a first down was increased to 10 yards. To reduce altercations between plays, the neutral zone was created along the width of the football. Field goals were lowered to three points in 1909, and touchdowns were raised to six in 1912. The field length was also reduced to 100 yards, but two 10-yard end zones were inserted. Teams were also given four downs instead of three to advance the ball 10 yards. The "roughing-the-passer" penalty was implemented in 1914 to prevent unnecessary **(11)** <u>contact, players</u> were first allowed to catch the ball anywhere on the field in 1918.

7. A) NO CHANGE
    B) sport despite
    C) sport; despite
    D) sport, and despite

8. A) NO CHANGE
    B) injuries and occasional
    C) injuries; also occasional
    D) injuries, while also with occasional

9. A) NO CHANGE
    B) 1905. President
    C) 1905, President
    D) 1905; President

10. A) NO CHANGE
    B) States. Later
    C) States and later
    D) States; this was later

11. A) NO CHANGE
    B) contact; players
    C) contact; and players
    D) contact and players

TEST EXERCISE:

Personalized Medicine

The right patient. The right drug. The right dose. Bringing this trio together is the mission of personalized medicine, an evolving field of medicine in which treatments **(1)** were tailored to individual patients. You may have a condition, for example, that is caused by a mutation in **(2)** one's genes. With advances in personalized medicine, you might be prescribed a medication that targets that specific mutation.

[1] Scientists advanced the cause of personalized medicine with the decoding of the human genome, a genetic map of our DNA. [2] "The human genome allowed us to learn and discuss a lot more," says Elizabeth Mansfield, Ph.D., director of personalized medicine in the Office of In Vitro Diagnostics Device Evaluation and Safety in FDA's Center for Devices and Radiological Health. [3] "This is one person's genome, and this is another's. [4] What is abnormal and should be targeted? [5] You can use the difference to assess how to treat a disease. [6] What particular kind of drug will make a difference?" [7] Researchers identified 20,000-25,000 human genes and the sequences of billions of chemical pairings. {3}

When developing personalized treatments, researchers must work to identify the problem at the molecular level, **(4)** develop a medicine that targets that specific problem, and to identify patients with this mutation to participate in the clinical trial. To learn which patients would benefit from a particular drug therapy, doctors use companion **(5)** diagnostics because companion diagnostics are medical devices that help doctors decide which treatments to offer patients and which dosages to give.

Mansfield **(6)** gives cancer treatment as a model of how personalized medicine functions. Cancer centers across the country perform molecular profiling to look for genetic mutations in their **(7)** patients, when mutations are found that are common in a certain kind

1. A) NO CHANGE
    B) are tailored
    C) had been tailored
    D) will be tailored

2.   A) NO CHANGE
    B) you're
    C) their
    D) your

3. To improve the cohesion of the paragraph, sentence 7 should be placed

    A) where it is now.
    B) between sentences 1 and 2.
    C) between sentences 2 and 3.
    D) between sentences 3 and 4.

4. A) NO CHANGE
    B) developing a medicine that targets that specific problem and identify patients
    C) to develop a medicine that targets that specific problem and identifying patients
    D) develop a medicine that targets that specific problem, and identify patients

5. A) NO CHANGE
    B) diagnostics, which
    C) companion diagnostics, and these
    D) diagnostics, although these

6.   A) NO CHANGE
    B) recalls
    C) alludes to
    D) cites

7. A) NO CHANGE
    B) patients when
    C) patients. When
    D) patients; for when

of cancer, researchers work to develop a targeted treatment. Most drugs with a companion diagnostic test have been cancer treatments that target specific mutations.

[1] **(8)** <u>Likewise,</u> the FDA recently approved a melanoma drug **(9)** <u>intended</u> for patients with tumors that have a mutation in a gene known as BRAF. [2] This mutation is also associated with other types of cancers, including some types of lung cancer. [3] Alongside the drug, FDA approved a genetic test to detect the gene mutation in patients.   [4] This test will identify those patients most likely to benefit from the drug, **{10}**

{11} With the advent of more drugs that target particular genetic mutations, there has been increasing acceptance from drug manufacturers that these diagnostic tests can greatly increase the clinical success of certain medications. Mansfield says it has become apparent over the last 10 years that producing "blockbuster" drugs that are approved for everyone, but may only benefit some patients, may not be as useful as creating more specifically targeted therapies.

"Nothing happens quickly," she notes. "But progress is coming."

8. A) NO CHANGE
    B) Moreover,
    C) However,
    D) For example,

9. A) NO CHANGE
    B) destined
    C) predetermined
    D) ordered

10. Which of the following sentences should be removed in order to improve the focus of the paragraph?

    A) NO CHANGE
    B) Sentence 2
    C) Sentence 3
    D) Sentence 4

11. Which of the following most effectively establishes the main topic of the paragraph?

    A) Drug manufacturers are skeptical of targeted therapies because the added cost of companion diagnostics creates an undue burden.
    B) Drugs should no longer be produced for the general population because these drugs are less useful than more personalized treatments.
    C) In some cases, pursuing personalized treatments is more effective than developing drugs for a wide population.
    D) Personalized medicine allows researchers and drug manufacturers to tailor drugs to patients.

Lesson wY1
Run-Ons and Fragments
Race to the Finish

HOMEWORK EXERCISE 1:

Directions: Identify and correct any run-ons, sentence fragments, or comma splices in the following sentences.

1. Theodore Roosevelt was an American politician, author, naturalist, explorer, and historian; serving as the 26th President of the United States.

2. Born into a wealthy family in New York City, Roosevelt was a sickly child who suffered from asthma.

3. Though he attempted to move the GOP toward progressive policies, including trust busting and increased regulation of businesses.

4. By 1907 he propounded more radical reforms, these were blocked by his enemies in Congress.

5. Roosevelt then launched the Progressive ("Bull Moose") Party that called for progressive reforms; splitting the Republican vote, it allowed Democrat Woodrow Wilson to win the White House.

6. During his first administration Woodrow Wilson enacted a sweeping raft of progressive legislation it was called The New Freedom.

7. The New Freedom continued the anti-trust and anti-monopoly policies of Theodore Roosevelt, in some ways Wilson took these policies considerably further.

8. Narrowly re-elected in 1916 around the slogan *He kept us out of war*; Wilson then spent most of his second term navigating America's entry into World War I.

9. The United States conducted military operations with the Allies without a formal alliance, Wilson focused on diplomacy and financial considerations.

10. In 1918, after years of opposition, Wilson was pressured to change his position on women's suffrage; being claimed as a wartime provision.

11. In 1919 he went to Paris to negotiate the Treaty of Versailles, Wilson then suffered a severe stroke and was unable to secure Senate ratification of the Treaty.

12. The Paris Peace Conference was the meeting of the Allied victors, following the end of World War I, to set terms of peace for the defeated Central Powers.

13. The "Big Four" participants of the Conference, the President of the United States, Woodrow Wilson; the Prime Minister of Great Britain, David Lloyd George; the Prime Minister of France, Georges Clemenceau; and the Prime Minister of Italy, Vittorio Orlando.

14. The main result was the Treaty of Versailles with Germany; in section 231 laid the guilt for the war on "the aggression of Germany and her allies."

15. Although many Germans deeply resented this clause, feeling it was a slander and a humiliation of their country.

16. The Treaty of Versailles also stripped Germany of its overseas colonies, these were later awarded to Britain and France as "mandates."

17. The most significant provision of the Treaty forced Germany to pay high economic reparations to the Allies these would significantly damage the German economy in the decade to come.

18. While President Wilson managed to convince the rest of the Big Four at the Conference to help create his vision of an international peacekeeping organization, the League of Nations.

19. American opposition to the League of Nations was led by Massachusetts Senator Henry Cabot Lodge; a close personal friend of Theodore Roosevelt and a longtime opponent of Woodrow Wilson.

20. Before he died, historians speculate, Theodore Roosevelt schemed with Lodge as to how they might sabotage the Treaty.

HOMEWORK EXERCISE 2:

Going Back to the Source

It is an exciting time to be developing and directing programs for teaching with primary sources. **(1)** Educators can now bring authentic learning materials to the classroom in ways we could only dream of a few decades ago.

[1] As a student teacher at Casey Junior High School in Boulder, Colorado, in 1989, **(2)** teaching a unit about World War I to a class of eighth-graders. [2] I was disappointed by the minimal information contained in the **(3)** students textbook's. [3] With the encouragement of my cooperating teacher, I searched the school's library for additional resources. [4] I was thrilled when I found a hefty, bound compilation volume that featured a transcription of President Woodrow Wilson's speech of January 8, 1918, in which he described his Fourteen Points. [5] This speech would serve as the basis for peace in November 1918. [6] I made photocopies of the speech and designed classroom activities to engage my students with the elements of Wilson's proposed program for world peace. **{4}**

At that time, it never occurred to me that the original draft of Wilson's speech might still exist, or that it would be 13 pages long—in shorthand—or that one day the pages would be "scanned" and made available "online" via the "Internet," for free. To think that I would have access to them anytime, day or night, on any number of devices—including my phone—was truly **(5)** unimaginable.

1. Which version of the underlined sentence best states the passage's main idea?

   A) NO CHANGE
   B) The Internet allows students to find reliable help for their homework assignments.
   C) Textbooks today are printed with full-color photographs and helpful graphics.
   D) Teachers now have the ability to easily learn all about Woodrow Wilson.

2. A) NO CHANGE
   B) because teaching
   C) taught
   D) because I taught

3. A) NO CHANGE
   B) students' textbooks
   C) students' textbook's
   D) students textbooks'

4. Which sentence should be eliminated in order to improve the focus of the paragraph?

   A) Sentence 3
   B) Sentence 4
   C) Sentence 5
   D) Sentence 6

5. Which of the following provides the most precise replacement for the underlined word?

   A) NO CHANGE
   B) insurmountable
   C) awesome
   D) unique

(6) I shared the photocopied transcription of Wilson's speech with my students, I sought to connect them with **(7)** the words that Wilson had actually said. I wanted to provide them with context so that they would come to understand that The Fourteen Points mentioned in **(8)** their textbooks were actually outlined in a speech that the president had delivered to Congress in the midst of the conflict. I was teaching with the original primary sources—nearly, anyway. {9}

Wilson's speech helped my students better understand the context surrounding the events included in their textbooks. Today, however, the digital images of the shorthand draft would help students learn lessons well beyond those of historical context. The images would introduce powerful lessons related to human connections over time, **(10)** inspire wonder in a new generation.

[1] I would encourage my students to see connections between shorthand and the texting language that they have become expert with. [2] If I were back in the classroom, sharing scans of the president's own shorthand, I would expect complaints about the illegibility of the text. [3] I would smile when they realized that even presidents have to make rough drafts. [4] Most of all, I would encourage them to conduct research and find the information they need on their own—because they can. {11}

6. A) NO CHANGE
   B) The sharing of my
   C) My shared
   D) By sharing the

7. Which choice is most concise and effective in the context of the passage?

   A) NO CHANGE
   B) Wilson's actual words that he had spoken
   C) Wilson's actual words
   D) some words

8. A) NO CHANGE
   B) their textbook was
   C) its textbook was
   D) its textbook were

9. Which sentence, if added here, would most clearly support the points made in the passage?

   A) Afterward, the students came to believe that their textbooks were worthless.
   B) Unfortunately, much digital information is difficult to find on the Internet.
   C) The only better source would be the original, shorthand draft that Wilson wrote.
   D) No student would be able to read Wilson's notoriously illegible handwriting, anyway.

10. A) NO CHANGE
    B) inspired
    C) would inspire
    D) inspiring

11. To improve the cohesion of the paragraph, in what order should the sentences be arranged?

    A) NO CHANGE
    B) 2, 1, 3, 4
    C) 1, 3, 4, 2
    D) 3, 1, 2, 4

C2 education
be smarter

Lesson wY2
Coordination and Subordination
Getting Your Feet Wet

1. Tyler called Sarah. She met him at the park.

   A) NO CHANGE
   B) While Tyler called Sarah, she
   C) Tyler called Sarah, or she
   D) After Tyler called Sarah, she

2. The movie was sold out, and we went to the arcade instead.

   A) NO CHANGE
   B) out, so we
   C) out so we
   D) out and we

3. Mom wouldn't let me go to the sleepover, unless I cleaned my room.

   A) NO CHANGE
   B) sleepover because
   C) sleepover, and
   D) sleepover unless

Lesson wY2
Coordination and Subordination
Wading In

TOPIC OVERVIEW: COORDINATION AND SUBORDINATION

Before we learn about coordination and subordination, you should review the concepts you learned in the last lesson, which discussed run-on sentences, comma splices, and fragments. In that lesson, we learned that one way to address these errors is by using conjunctions.

There are two kinds of conjunctions: coordinating conjunctions, which combine two independent clauses of equal importance, and subordinating conjunctions, which combine a dependent clause and an independent clause.

WHEN TO USE COORDINATION AND SUBORDINATION

Coordination and subordination are incredibly useful writing tools that can be used to:

- Correct run-ons, comma splices, and sentence fragments
- Vary the sentence structure by combining sentences
- Combine sentences to show that two ideas are closely linked or of equal importance (using coordination)
- Combine sentences to emphasize the more important of two ideas (using subordination)

CORRECTING RUN-ONS, COMMA SPLICES, AND SENTENCE FRAGMENTS

In the last lesson, we learned about run-ons, commas splices, and sentence fragments. Let's take just a moment to review:

1. In your own words, what is a run-on sentence?

   _____

   _____

   _____

2. Use the space below to write an example of a run-on sentence.

   _____

   _____

   _____

3. In your own words, what is a comma splice?

   _____

   _____

   _____

4. Use the space below to write an example of a comma splice.

   _____

   _____

   _____

5. In your own words, what is a sentence fragment?

   _____

   _____

   _____

6. Use the space below to write an example of a sentence fragment.

   _____

   _____

   _____

One of the strategies used to correct these types of errors is to use a conjunction – either a coordinating conjunction or a subordinating conjunction – to combine two clauses or sentences. In the rest of this lesson, we'll explore the rules for combining sentences using coordination and subordination.

COMBINING SENTENCES WITH COORDINATION

We use coordinating conjunctions to combine two independent clauses or complete sentences – independent clauses have a subject and a verb and can stand on their own as complete sentences.

Which conjunctions are coordinating conjunctions? You can remember these conjunctions using the mnemonic FANBOYS:

For

And

Nor

But

Or

Yet

So

When a writer uses several simple sentences – sentences that contain just one independent clause – the final product can seem choppy and poorly written. For example:

<u>Example 1:</u> I wanted candy. Shea wanted soda.

These sentences are grammatically correct, but when we read them back to back, they sound overly simplistic and choppy. Instead, we can use coordination to combine them:

<u>Example 2:</u> I wanted candy**, but** Shea wanted soda.

Now the sentences flow more smoothly. The addition of the coordinating conjunction also helps to clarify the relationship between the two ideas. Instead of seeming like two random thoughts, the ideas are closely linked. This is one benefit of coordination.

If we look at example 2, we can also see how to properly punctuate a sentence with a coordinating conjunction: Always use a comma before the coordinating conjunction.

It's important to choose a coordinating conjunction that best shows the relationship between the two sentences or clauses. Sometimes one conjunction works better than another. For example:

Example 3: They didn't want to be late, or they hurried.

The word "or" doesn't really describe the relationship between the two ideas. Let's fix it:

Example 4: They didn't want to be late, **so** they hurried.

"So" more clearly explains the relationship between these two thoughts by explaining that they hurried *because* they didn't want to be late.

Let's practice. Use a coordinating conjunction to combine each of the following pairs of sentences:

1. The baseball game was cancelled. We will have to do something else.

    _____

    _____

    _____

2. We can go to the movies. We can go to the beach.

    _____

    _____

    _____

3. Dave rides his old bike. He doesn't like his new one.

    _____

    _____

    _____

WRAP UP: COORDINATION

Let's review the rules we've learned in this part of the lesson:

1. Coordinating conjunctions (FANBOYS) are used to combine two independent clauses or sentences.
2. Coordinating conjunctions show the reader that the information in each clause is equally important.
3. We must use the coordinating conjunction that best describes the relationship between the two clauses.
4. When we use coordinating conjunctions, we always put a comma before the conjunction.

COMBINING SENTENCES WITH SUBORDINATION

Like coordinating conjunctions, subordinating conjunctions can be used to combine clauses or sentences. However, these conjunctions serve a slightly different purpose. Let's look at the main differences between the two types of conjunctions:

Coordinating Conjunctions	Subordinating Conjunctions
Combine two independent clauses	Combine an independent clause and a dependent clause
Show that two ideas are equally important	Show that the ideas in the independent clause are more important than those in the dependent clause
Only 7 coordinating conjunctions (FANBOYS)	Many subordinating conjunctions

Unlike coordinating conjunctions, which are easy to remember, subordinating conjunctions are much harder to memorize. Since they are used to show much more detailed relationships, there are a lot more options to choose from. Some of the most commonly used subordinating conjunctions include:

Relationship	Subordinating Conjunction
Time	When
	Whenever
	While
	After
	Until
	Before
	Once
	Since
Place	Where
	Wherever
Cause/Effect	Because
	Since
	So that
	In order to
Condition	If
	Unless
	If only
	Even if
Contrast	Although
	Even though
	While

Even though subordinating conjunctions combine an independent clause and a dependent clause, we can still use subordination to combine whole sentences. First, we need to make one of the sentences a dependent clause by adding a subordinating conjunction. For example, let's look at these two sentences:

Example 4: I stayed up all night studying for my Algebra test. I am very tired.

To combine the sentences, we need to figure out the relationship between the two sentences so that we can choose a good conjunction. In this case, we know that the first sentence is the reason that the second sentence is true, so let's use "because."

Example 5: **Because** I stayed up all night studying for my Algebra test**,** I am very tired.

Adding "because" to the first sentence makes it a dependent clause. "Because I stayed up all night studying for my Algebra test" can no longer stand on its own as a sentence because it no longer expresses a complete thought.

Notice the use of the comma after the word "test." When we use subordination, there are slightly different rules for punctuation: Place a comma *after* but not *before* a dependent clause. Since the dependent clause came at the beginning of the sentence, we used a comma at the end of the clause. If the dependent clause comes at the end of the sentence, we don't use a comma:

Example 6: I am very tired **because** I stayed up all night studying for my Algebra test.

Just as with coordinating conjunctions, we must be sure to choose the subordinating conjunction that best describes the relationship between the two clauses. For example:

Example 7: Until I have to study for tomorrow's test, I can't go out tonight.

This is another example of a sentence that is technically grammatically correct, but it still doesn't make sense. The use of the conjunction "until" does not properly describe the relationship between the two ideas. Why would I be unable to go out *until* I have to study? Instead, we should use a subordinating conjunction that describes the cause and effect relationship between the ideas:

Example 8: **Since** I have to study for tomorrow's test, I can't go out tonight.

In addition to the relationship that the conjunction establishes, subordination also creates a relationship that is harder to see: By making one of the two clauses a dependent clause, we are sending the message that one of the ideas in the sentence is more important than the other. In example 8, the fact that I can't go out tonight is the main idea of the sentence; the reason why I can't go out tonight is less important information.

Let's practice. Use subordination to combine each of the following sentences:

1. He enjoys long walks. He often goes on hikes while on vacation.

    _____

    _____

    _____

2. I already have a cat. I adopted a puppy.

    _____

    _____

    _____

3. I missed a really exciting part of the movie. I was in the bathroom.

    _____

    _____

    _____

WRAP UP: SUBORDINATION

Let's review the rules we've learned in this part of the lesson:

1. Subordinating conjunctions combine a dependent clause and an independent clause.
2. To use subordination to combine sentences, you must use a subordinating conjunction to make one of the sentences a dependent clause.
3. When the dependent clause comes first, use a comma after it.
4. Do not use a comma when the dependent clause comes second.
5. Be sure to choose the conjunction that best describes the relationship between the two ideas.
6. Subordination suggests to the reader that the information in the dependent clause is less important than the information in the independent clause.

Lesson wY2
Coordination and Subordination
Learning to Swim

CONCEPT EXERCISE:

Directions: Correct any subordination or coordination errors in the following sentences. If a sentence has no error, write "NO ERROR."

1. But we were having a great time at the party, we had to leave early.

2. Our flight was canceled at the last minute, the plane had an engine malfunction.

3. I bought two tickets to the concert as a token of appreciation for I could not have finished this project without you.

4. If an entertainer of Diana Ross' stature asks for a favor, you would be foolish not to agree to whatever she asks.

5. This sunscreen claims to be waterproof, but my skin began to burn, I had spent only twenty minutes in the ocean.

6. Global warming continues at its current pace, coastal cities like New York and Miami may be flooded.

7. I went to the farmer's market to buy vegetables while my wife stopped by Mackenzie's Butcher Shop, the meat there is the freshest in town.

8. So my friend's poetry class is having a group reading at a local coffee shop, we should all go and support her.

9. The blue whale, the heaviest animal that has ever lived on Earth, weighs over 170 tons, and its tongue alone weighs more than 5,000 pounds.

10. And the rest of the world seems even more excited about American action movies than Americans themselves, since many blockbusters earn more money overseas than domestically.

Directions: Combine each pair of sentences using subordination or coordination.

11. That is a highly unusual request. I will do my best to honor it.

12. Birds are much more susceptible than humans to poisoning from carbon monoxide. In the 19th century, miners used birds to determine when underground gases reached dangerous levels.

13. The actor was primarily known for his comic roles. He was also capable of impressive dramatic range.

14. Many shoppers prefer reusable fabric bags. They are easier to carry than paper bags. They are less likely to break than plastic bags.

15. The English won the Battle of Crecy against France in 1346. The English troops had longbows, which could fire farther and more quickly than the French crossbows.

16. Roger came down with the flu the day before the test. His teacher let him make up the test the following week.

17. The Hawaiian Islands are extremely isolated. Polynesian sailors needed only small canoes to navigate there from hundreds of miles away.

18. Bernadette does not believe in ghosts. She still gets frightened when she listens to a well-told ghost story.

19. Mitchell is taking a short vacation. If he does not use his vacation days by the end of the year, he will lose them.

20. You have likely seen "neon" lights in many store windows. Most of these lights contain argon or a mixture of gases rather than neon.

Lesson wY2
Coordination and Subordination
Diving into the Deep End

PRACTICE EXERCISE:

Directions: Answer the questions that accompany the following passages.

The Future of Farming, adapted from "A Five-Step Plan to Feed the World," by Jonathan Foley, National Geographic May 2014

(1) We think about threats to the environment, we tend to picture cars and smokestacks, not dinner. But the truth is, our need for food poses one of the biggest dangers to the planet.

Agriculture is among the greatest contributors to global warming, emitting more greenhouse gases than all our cars, trucks, trains, and airplanes combined. Farming is the thirstiest user of our precious water supplies and a major polluter, as runoff from fertilizers and manure disrupts fragile lakes, rivers, and coastal ecosystems across (2) the globe. Agriculture also accelerates the loss of biodiversity. (3) Even though we've cleared areas of grassland and forest for farms, we've lost crucial habitat, making agriculture a major driver of wildlife extinction. The environmental challenges posed by agriculture are (4) huge, they'll only become more pressing as we try to meet the growing need for food worldwide. Along with population growth, the spread of prosperity across the world, especially in China and India, is driving an increased demand for meat, eggs, and dairy, boosting pressure to grow more corn and soybeans to feed more livestock. (5) If these trends continue, the double whammy of population growth and richer diets will require us to roughly double the amount of crops we grow by 2050.

1. A) NO CHANGE
    B) We think about threats to the environment; we
    C) Each and every time we think about threats to the environment, we
    D) When we think about threats to the environment, we

2. A) NO CHANGE
    B) the globe, agriculture
    C) the globe, besides that agriculture
    D) the globe. In addition, agriculture

3. A) NO CHANGE
    B) As we've cleared areas of grassland and forest for farms, we've lost crucial habitat
    C) At the same time that we've been clearing areas of grassland and forest for farms, we've been losing crucial habitat
    D) We've cleared areas of grassland and forest for farms, and we've lost crucial habitat

4. A) NO CHANGE
    B) huge, and
    C) huge, because
    D) huge; and

5. A) NO CHANGE
    B) If and when these trends continue,
    C) When these trends continue
    D) These trends will continue, and

Unfortunately the debate over how to address the global food challenge has become **(6)** <u>polarized. It pits</u> conventional agriculture and global commerce against local food systems and organic farms. Those who favor conventional agriculture talk about how modern mechanization, irrigation, fertilizers, and improved genetics can increase yields to help meet demand. And they're right. Meanwhile proponents of local and organic farms counter that the world's small farmers could increase yields plenty—and help themselves out of poverty—by adopting techniques that improve fertility without synthetic fertilizers and **(7)** <u>pesticides. They're</u> also right.

But it needn't be an either-or proposition. Both approaches offer badly needed **(8)** <u>solutions: neither one</u> alone gets us there. We would be wise to explore all of the good ideas, whether from organic and local farms or high-tech and conventional farms, and blend the best of both.

We are facing unprecedented challenges to food security and the preservation of our global environment. The good news is that we already know what we have **(9)** <u>to do, now we</u> need to figure out how to do it. **(10)** <u>If we address our global food challenges; all</u> of us must become more thoughtful about the food we put on our plates. We need to make connections between our food and the farmers who grow it, and between our food and the land, watersheds, and climate that sustain us. **(11)** <u>We</u> steer our grocery carts down the aisles of our supermarkets, the choices we make will help decide the future.

6. A) NO CHANGE
   B) polarized; it is pitting
   C) polarized because it pits
   D) polarized, and it pits

7. A) NO CHANGE
   B) pesticides, and they're
   C) pesticides, they're
   D) pesticides, but they're

8. A) NO CHANGE
   B) solutions; but neither one
   C) solutions although neither
   D) solutions, neither one

9. A) NO CHANGE
   B) to do, for now we
   C) to do since now we
   D) to do, so now we

10. A) NO CHANGE
    B) We address our global good challenges, and all
    C) Because addressing our global food challenges, all
    D) In order to address our global food challenges, all

11. A) NO CHANGE
    B) As we
    C) Because we
    D) At the same time that we

TEST EXERCISE:

Two Ways to Fly

When people find out that I work at NASA and fly trapeze, **(1)** their surprised that I have such diverse interests. I don't see it that way, however. **(2)** While the "rockets" are different, the sky is the same. Plus, the concepts involved overlap quite a bit.

"If you release the fly bar too early," explains Richie Gaona, fourth-generation trapeze artist turned trainer, "your trick will go long and you risk banging into the catcher." We are standing near the net talking about timing. He tosses a gardening glove into the air. It spins and lands **(3)** a few feet away.

[1] "If you hold on too long, then your trick is short and you'll miss." [2] Someone brings back the glove and he throws it again. [3] **(4)** He goes up spinning, but this time it travels backwards. [4] "If you let go at just the right moment, however, you get vertical lift and end up a perfect arm's distance from the catcher." **{5}**

Richie's "timing" explanation uses the same principles of physics **(6)** that are the ones used by NASA to deploy many of its spacecraft. Satellites must be launched within a tight, 30-second window in order to leave Earth's atmosphere. Even more precise is the timing needed to ensure that a spacecraft can safely meet up with the International Space Station, which travels thousands of miles an hour at an orbit 200 miles above the Earth's surface.

1. A) NO CHANGE
    B) they're
    C) there
    D) there are

2. A) NO CHANGE
    B) Yet
    C) But
    D) Despite

3. Which choice provides the most effective support for the point that the author (and Gaona) are making?

    A) NO CHANGE
    B) on a table
    C) with its palm facing up
    D) far from its target

4. A) NO CHANGE
    B) They go
    C) It goes
    D) You go

5. Where in the preceding paragraph would the following sentence be most logically added?

    The glove goes up, spins twice, and lands squarely where he intended with a satisfying plunk.

    A) Before Sentence 1
    B) After Sentence 1
    C) After Sentence 2
    D) After Sentence 4

6. A) NO CHANGE
    B) for the using of NASA
    C) that NASA considers to be useful
    D) that NASA uses

(7) Despite my love of the trapeze, I never ran away to join the circus. Kristin Finley, the girl I stood next to for so many years on the trapeze platform (just another term for "launch pad"), made it all the way to the (big) top, though. As part of the Tuniziani Trapeze Troupe, she has traveled all around the globe, just like one of NASA's Earth-orbiting satellites. **(8)** Our journeys seem worlds apart. They're really more like parallel universes. To me, working for NASA is enough like soaring through the air, shooting for the sky, and flirting with the forces of gravity.

Why do trapeze artists do what they **(9)** do. They have the same reasons that we have at NASA. It's the attraction to what seems impossible; the excellent pay and benefits; the chance to leave the ground and go upward, as high as you can; the desire to push boundaries; and the unbeatable combination of physics and sheer determination. **{10}**

7. Which version of the underlined sentence most effectively introduces the paragraph's topic?

 A) NO CHANGE
 B) As long as you're not an astronaut, working for NASA is a lot safer than being a trapeze artist.
 C) These days, computers do most of the calculations at NASA.
 D) My job at NASA is to monitor these spacecraft to ensure they stay on course.

8. Which choice best combines the two sentences?

 A) Our journeys seem worlds apart, they're really more like parallel universes, however.
 B) Our journeys seem worlds apart but they're really more like parallel universes.
 C) Although our journeys seem worlds apart, they're really more like parallel universes.
 D) But our journeys seem worlds apart, they're really more like parallel universes.

9. A) NO CHANGE
 B) do! They
 C) do? They
 D) do, they

10. Which of the items in the preceding list should be deleted to improve the focus of the passage?

 A) the attraction to what seems impossible;
 B) the excellent pay and benefits;
 C) the chance to leave the ground and go upward, as high as you can;
 D) the desire to push boundaries;

We push ourselves for the pure joy of pushing, in the hope that those who watch will be moved and inspired—that someone, somewhere, might see what we're doing and consider pushing beyond their **(11)** witnessed limits.

11. Which version of the underlined word fits best in the context of the passage?

A) NO CHANGE
B) perceived
C) seized
D) distinguished

Lesson wY2
Coordination and Subordination
Race to the Finish

HOMEWORK EXERCISE 1:

Directions: Find and correct errors in the following sentences. Some sentences may have no errors.

1. During World War II, several Major League Baseball executives, led by Philip K. Wrigley, were concerned that the league would have to shut down although so many men were away at war.

2. They wanted to keep interest in the sport alive, but they formed a women's league that could continue to play in spite of the war.

3. Although the fears about the men's league shutting down proved to be unfounded, the women's league flourished alongside the men's league for about a decade.

4. Since the women's league was officially considered to be a professional baseball league, it did not play according to the standard rules of baseball.

5. Initially the play closely resembled softball, for over the years the rules were changed to become more like men's professional baseball.

6. After scouts went out to many major cities across the United States, 280 women were invited to the final tryouts in Chicago where they vied for just 60 roster spots.

7. Wrigley did not want the women to appear too masculine, but the players were required to attend "charm school" in order to learn proper feminine etiquette.

8. Unless a woman wanted to maintain her spot on a team, she had to obey the league's 'Rules of Conduct.'

9. People across the country were impressed by the talent the women displayed, yet interest in the league grew quickly.

10. The league's highest attendance was reached in 1948 though the teams attracted a total of 910,000 fans.

Directions: Combine the following pairs of sentences using coordination or subordination.

11. In the 1992 film *A League of Their Own,* Dottie does not want to leave her family farm to join the baseball league. Her younger sister Kit convinces her to go.

12. Both Dottie and Kit impress the scouts. They earn spots on the same team, the Rockford Peaches.

13. The girls are excited to meet their manager, Jimmy Dugan, a former star player for the Chicago Cubs. He turns out to be rude and completely uninterested in the women's league.

14. Dugan makes no effort to lead his team. Dottie takes the responsibility upon herself.

15. Dugan begins to realize that the girls have a lot of talent. He slowly starts to take an interest in the team.

16. At one point, Dottie tells the manager to take Kit out of the game. Dottie can tell that Kit is too tired to continue pitching effectively.

17. Dottie was trying to do what was best for the team. Kit is upset and thinks that Dottie is trying to hold her back.

18. Kit continues to quarrel with Dottie. Dottie asks to be removed from the team.

19. Dottie is the star of the Rockford Peaches. Management decides to trade Kit to the Racine Belles instead of letting Dottie go.

20. The Belles defeat the Peaches in the League Championship. Kit finally feels independent of her older sister, and the two are reconciled.

HOMEWORK EXERCISE 2:

Do Sugar Taxes Work?

Two out of three adults and one out of three children in the United States **(1)** <u>is</u> overweight or obese, leading to annual expenditure of about $190 billion treating obesity-related health conditions. **(2)** <u>Raising</u> consumption of sugary beverages has been a major contributor to the obesity epidemic. Before the 1950s, standard soft drink bottles were 6.5 ounces **(3)** <u>. Today,</u> 20-ounce plastic bottles are the norm. As a result, more than 10% of US daily calorie intake comes **(4)** <u>purely</u> from sugary drinks. Worse yet, these sugary beverages provide empty calories with no nutritional value, thus contributing to weight increases in people of all ages.

{5} To combat soda's contribution to obesity, some regions have experimented with sugary beverage taxes. A new study of how taxes might be used to curb consumption of sugary drinks suggests that applying a tax based on the amount of calories contained in a serving rather than its size would be more effective. The study found that consumption of calories in drinks would drop 9.3% if a tax of .04 cents **(6)** <u>was</u> added for every calorie. The same study found that consumption would fall by just 8.6% under a tax of .5 cents per ounce.

1. A) NO CHANGE
   B) was
   C) are
   D) were

2. A) NO CHANGE
   B) Rising
   C) Falling
   D) Continuing

3. A) NO CHANGE
   B) .
   C) ; while, today,
   D) ; however, today,

4. A) NO CHANGE
   B) somewhat
   C) innocently
   D) cleanly

5. Which choice most effectively establishes the main topic of the paragraph?

   A) If soda taxes are going to be used, the method that would lead to the biggest decrease in consumption is to tax calories not ounces.
   B) Soda taxes are really more about governments making money than they are about helping people stop drinking sugary beverages.
   C) The researchers hope that their study will convince more governments to implement sugary beverage taxes.
   D) Because the percentage decrease is so similar with both types of taxes, the researchers would favor governments using either type of tax.

6. A) NO CHANGE
   B) were to be
   C) were
   D) was ever

Some researchers suggest that a calorie-based tax **(7)** <u>would create a more fair system for</u> consumers. Such a tax would provide better incentive to switch to lower-calorie drinks, which would be taxed at a lower rate than higher-calorie drinks. At a tax rate of four-hundredths of a penny per calorie, six cents would be added to a 12-ounce can of cola **(8)** <u>; for example,</u> while only four cents would be added to a 16-ounce bottle of flavored water.

Sales of sugary drinks are already falling, even **(9)** <u>in the absence of</u> such taxes. The American Beverage Association, the trade group that represents soda manufacturers, noted that a variety of soda tax proposals have been defeated in various states over the last several years, in large part because people want to make their own health decisions. **(10)** <u>Moreover, the group questions the efficacy of such taxes in the first place, pointing to states like Arkansas and West Virginia, both of which tax soda and suffer from some of the highest obesity rates in the country.</u>

The authors of the new study say that they aren't attempting to encourage sugar taxes **(11)** <u>.</u> "We are not saying you should tax sugar-sweetened beverages," says Dr. Chen Zhen, one of the study's authors. "We're saying that if you're going to tax them, the best way of doing that is on the basis of calories."

7. A) NO CHANGE
    B) would allow a fairer plan for
    C) would create more fairness for
    D) would also be fairer to

8. A) NO CHANGE
    B) , for example,
    C) for example
    D) , for example

9. A) NO CHANGE
    B) without
    C) when there are no
    D) in situations with no

10. Which choice most effectively concludes the paragraph?

    A) NO CHANGE
    B) Delete it. It is unnecessary.
    C) The ABA argues that the taxes actually don't work because the states that have implemented them still have higher obesity rates.
    D) The ABA argues that the taxes are not a wise choice for governments because states like Arkansas and West Virginia that have implemented the taxes have only seen a modest decrease in soda consumption.

11. A) NO CHANGE
    B) .
    C) :
    D) ?

| **Lesson wY3** |
| **Subject-Verb Agreement** |
| **Getting Your Feet Wet** |

1. The principal, as well as the <u>teachers, is participating</u> in the karaoke fundraiser.

   A) NO CHANGE
   B) teachers, are participating
   C) teachers, participating
   D) teachers is

2. Everyone attending the <u>concerts have bought</u> tickets.

   A) NO CHANGE
   B) concerts has boughten
   C) concerts have boughten
   D) concerts has bought

3. The donors who <u>attend the fundraiser receives</u> a generous thank you gift.

   A) NO CHANGE
   B) attend the fundraiser receive
   C) attends the fundraiser receive
   D) attends the fundraiser receives

C2 education
be smarter

Lesson wY3
Subject-Verb Agreement
Wading In

TOPIC OVERVIEW: SUBJECT-VERB AGREEMENT

As we discussed in Lesson 1, a sentence requires both a subject and a verb. For a sentence to be grammatically correct, the subject and the verb must agree.

What does it mean for a subject and a verb to agree? It's all about numbers. The most basic rule of subject-verb agreement is that plural subjects need plural verbs and singular subjects need singular verbs.

Most of the time, a sentence in which the subject and verb disagree will sound wrong, which can make identifying this type of error pretty easy. If it were that simple, we could stop there, but there are many ways that we can miss subject-verb agreement errors.

IDENTIFYING SUBJECTS AND VERBS

In Lesson 1, we learned how to identify subjects and verbs. To determine whether a sentence has an agreement error, we first need to find the subject and the verb.

In each of the following sentences, circle the subject and the verb:

1. The windows in the house are cheap and flimsy.

2. The doctor, as well as the nurses, takes excellent care of the patients.

3. Neither the stove burners nor the oven was working.

These examples show some of the ways that sentences can trick you into misidentifying a subject or verb. Let's go over some important rules for identifying subjects and verbs and addressing subject-verb agreement problems.

FINDING TRICKY SUBJECTS AND VERBS

Let's look at those example sentences.

In the first sentence, there are several nouns that could potentially act as the subject of the sentence. This sentence includes some prepositional phrases we might confuse for the subject. A prepositional phrase modifies another part of the sentence; these phrases begin with a preposition such as "of," "on," "near," "like," "to," or "for."

Step One: Cross out prepositional phrases because a subject can never be part of a prepositional phrase.

Example 1: The windows ~~in the house~~ are cheap and flimsy.

Now that we've gotten rid of that excess noun, it becomes much easier to locate the subject of the sentence – windows.

The second example includes what is known as a nonrestrictive clause. We'll cover those in more detail in Lesson 13. For now, just remember that nonrestrictive clauses are phrases that aren't necessary to the meaning of the sentence and that are usually set apart using commas.

Step Two: Cross out word groups within commas.

Example 2: The doctor, ~~as well as the nurses,~~ takes excellent care ~~of the patients~~.

In this sentence, we have crossed out the prepositional phrase ("of the patients") and the word group within commas ("as well as the nurses"). This leaves us with "doctor" as our subject.

The third example includes a subject broken up by *neither...nor*. But which is the subject – the stove burners, the oven, or both?

Step Three: Cross out word groups from neither to nor and either to or.

Example 3: ~~Neither the stove burners nor~~ the oven was working.

Once we get rid of the beginning of the *neither...nor* phrase, we can easily see that "oven" is the primary subject.

After you eliminate all of the unnecessary words in a sentence, you can more easily locate the subject and the verb.

Step Four: Identify the action taking place – this is the verb. If there is no action verb, look for the helping verbs is/are, was/were, or has/have.

Let's use that first sentence as an example. After we got rid of all of the excess words, we had:

Example 4: The windows are cheap and flimsy.

There is no action taking place, but we do see "are" – so that is our verb.

Step Five: Identify who or what is performing the action – this is the subject.

In this sentence, "the windows" is the subject.

Let's practice with another couple of sentences. First, cross out prepositional phrases, phrases set off by commas, or the beginning of *neither...nor* or *either...or* phrases. Then identify the action to find the verb – circle the verb. Finally, identify who or what is acting to find the subject – circle the subject.

1. One of the students is staying after school to study for a test.

2. Mrs. Sheehan, along with the other teachers, will lead the school assembly.

3. Either my parents or my aunt will attend the conference.

WRAP-UP: IDENTIFYING SUBJECTS AND VERBS

To identify the subject and the verb in a longer or more complex sentence, follow these steps:

1. Cross out prepositional phrases.
2. Cross out phrases set off by commas.
3. Cross out the beginning of *neither...nor* or *either...or* phrases.
4. Identify the action to find the verb, or look for helping verbs.
5. Identify who or what is acting to find the subject.

BASIC RULES FOR SUBJECT-VERB AGREEMENT

Identifying the subject and the verb is just the first step. Next we need to determine whether or not they agree. There are several rules to help determine whether a subject and verb agree.

Rule One: A singular subject takes a singular verb, and a plural subject takes a plural verb.

This is the most basic of all subject-verb agreement rules, and violations of this rule are often easy to spot. For instance, we all know that good academic English does not allow us to say, "He don't mind." *Don't* is plural, but *he* is singular. But what happens when it's hard to identify whether a subject is singular or plural?

Rule Two: Compound subjects connected by "and" generally receive plural verbs.

This rule makes good sense – when we have two subjects that are put together we should treat them as plural. For example:

Example 5: Asia and South America are home to some of the world's fastest growing economies.

Rule Three: In sentences that begin with "here" or "there," the subject follows the verb.

Don't misidentify "here" or "there" as the subject. For example:

Example 6: There are rules about subject-verb agreement.

The word "there" is not the subject. "Rules" is the subject, so we need a plural verb.

Rule Four: Compound subjects connected by "or" or "nor" might get plural or singular verbs. The subject that is closer to the verb determines whether the verb should be singular or plural.

This is similar to getting rid of the beginning of a *neither...nor* or *either...or* phrase. When a sentence is telling you that one of two subjects is acting, you use the subject that is closer to the verb to determine whether the verb should be plural or singular. For example:

Example 7: The dog or the cats have destroyed the rug.

In this sentence, "cats" is closer to the verb, so "cats" determines that the verb should be plural.

The same rule applies when the verb is located someplace else in the sentence. For example:

Example 8: Is the dog or the cats responsible for the destruction of the rug?

Even though this might sound slightly awkward, because "dog" is closer to the verb, we use the singular verb here.

It might not surprise you to learn that there are many more rules that can affect subject-verb agreement. Before we go on to address a few more rules, let's take a moment to review what we've learned so far. In each of the following sentences, circle the subject that determines whether the verb will be plural or singular and then circle the correct form of the verb.

1. There (is / are) many rules about subjects and verbs.

2. Reading and writing (requires / require) familiarity with the rules of

   grammar.

3. (Is / Are) squirrels or a big raccoon living in the attic?

WRAP UP: BASIC RULES

The most basic subject-verb agreement rules include:

1. The biggest rule of all: A singular subject gets a singular verb, and a plural subject gets a plural verb.
2. Compound subjects connected by "and" almost always get a plural verb.
3. In sentences that start with "here" or "there," the subject usually follows the verb.
4. With compound subjects connected by "or" or "nor," the subject that is closer to the verb determines whether the verb should be singular or plural.

INVERTED SUBJECT-VERB ORDER

Most sentences follow a basic structure: Subject + Verb + Object. When a writer flips this order around, it can be difficult to determine subject-verb agreement.

<u>Example 9:</u> In the jungles of Cambodia **hides** an ancient buried **city**.

In this sentence, the subject, "city," appears at the very end of the sentence. This is a situation in which it is important to follow the process for identifying the subject and verb, which we outlined earlier in this lesson:

Step One: Cross out prepositional phrases:

~~In the jungles of Cambodia~~ hides an ancient buried city.

We have no phrases set off by commas and no *neither...nor/either...or* phrases, so we can skip to step three.

Step Three: Identify the action.

In this sentence, we see that "buried" is being used as an adjective to describe "city," which means that "hides" is the only action in the sentence.

Step Four: Who or what is performing the action?

What is hiding? The city is hiding. "City" is the subject.

WRAP UP: INVERTED WORD ORDER

Remember to use the steps we outlined at the beginning of this lesson, *especially* when identifying subjects and verbs in sentences with unusual word order:

1. Cross out any prepositional phrases.
2. Cross out any phrases set off by commas.
3. Cross out the beginning of a *neither...nor/either...or* phrase.
4. Identify the action.
5. Identify who or what is performing the action.

INDEFINITE PRONOUNS

Our final subject-verb agreement issue deals with indefinite pronouns. Indefinite pronouns are pronouns that don't refer to a specific person or thing, and they can be plural or singular depending on the context. We'll list some of the most common indefinite pronouns and whether they are singular or plural here:

singular indefinite pronouns					
somebody	anybody	nobody	everybody	each	much
someone	anyone	no one	everyone	neither	one
something	anything	nothing	everything	either	the number

plural indefinite pronouns		
both	fewer	many
a number	few	several

The following list contains pronouns that can be either plural or singular, depending on what type of noun they are replacing:

variable indefinite pronouns		
any	some	more
all	most	none

If we look at the singular pronouns list and the plural pronouns list, we see that "the number" is singular and "a number" is plural. Let's look at some examples:

Example 10: **The number** of indefinite pronouns **is** daunting.

Example 11: There **are a number** of indefinite pronouns that might be singular or plural.

The pronouns in the final list can be the most confusing. The best rule to address issues with these pronouns is to ask whether the pronoun is referring to individual items or to a group of items. Let's look at some examples:

Example 12: **Some** of the **sentences** on the SAT **include** inverted word order.

Example 13: **Some** of the **confusion** about subject-verb agreement **comes** from the versatility of indefinite pronouns.

In example 12, "some" replaces "sentences," so we treat it as a plural subject because it refers to many things. In example 13, "some" replaces "confusion," so we treat it as singular because "confusion" is one individual thing.

WRAP UP: INDEFINITE PRONOUNS

When the subject of a sentence is an indefinite pronoun, we must determine whether that pronoun is plural or singular:

1. Many indefinite pronouns that might seem to refer to multiple people or things are actually treated as singular subjects. Familiarize yourself with the list of singular indefinite pronouns to help you spot these types of errors.

2. Other indefinite pronouns are always plural. The brief list in this lesson will help you spot such pronouns.

3. A third group of indefinite pronouns can be plural or singular. Use the context of the sentence to determine whether the pronoun is replacing a plural or a singular noun to determine what kind of verb should be used.

Lesson wY3
Subject-verb agreement
Learning to Swim

CONCEPT EXERCISE:

Directions: Find and correct errors in the following sentences. Some sentences may have more than one error, while others will not have any errors.

1. The reforestation campaign consists of the planting of 400 birch trees in Great Falls Park.

2. Deanna asked whether either Mike or his brother were coming to the concert.
   is

3. As soon as you throw that first piece of bread, a huge flock of seagulls are going to start circling you.

4. A touring exhibit of ancient Egyptian relics is at the Art Institute until mid-September.

5. As a result of California's severe drought, the price of almonds in many grocery stores have doubled.
   has

6. A consequence of the increased classroom hours devoted to standardized testing in our schools have been the removal of some topics from the AP History curriculum.
   has

7. The Department of Health and Human Services occupy three office buildings and employ a combined total of more than 2,000 employees.

8. Amid the ancient bristlecone pines of Death Valley National Park flow several gently cascading streams.

9. Much to my irritation, the band my brother and his friends formed last week plans to rehearse in our garage every Tuesday and Thursday night.

10. Candidates with a solid understanding of statistical methods in the biosciences, including regression and significance tests, and knowledge of computer programming is encouraged to apply for the open teaching position.
    are

11. The existence of black holes, a fact which was long doubted by many of the most eminent minds in astrophysics, was confirmed in 1974 when Stephen Hawking proposed a means of detecting them.

12. Along the hunting trails of many Amazonian tribes are found a surprising concentration of fruit trees, as hunters scatter the seeds while coming and going daily.

13. At least once an hour along the tracks behind those new apartments pass a train carrying crude oil from North Dakota to the refinery southeast of St. Paul.
    carries

14. The governor's panel of economic advisors is now saying that the number of newly created jobs is likely to be slightly higher this year than last.

15. In the desolate field three miles outside of town where a plane crashed several years ago stands a makeshift memorial to the victims.

16. Between the airline and its proposed acquisition of the largest of its major rivals stand only the Federal Trade Commission, whose regulators are tasked with preventing a monopoly.

17. Even the support of both the board of directors and several influential groups of shareholders were not enough to pass the resolution that would have put a limit on CEO pay increases.
    is

18. In greatest need of charitable donations this holiday season is the homeless shelter, which saw its budget slashed by nearly half in the latest round of city budget cuts, and our annual food drive.

19. I fear that if Carolyn's analysis of the results compiled from three months' worth of studies proves fruitless, we will have nothing to fall back on to justify our request for continued research funding.

20. The unusual proliferation of cryptic advertisements on buses suggest some sort of stealth marketing campaign, perhaps for an upcoming movie.

Lesson wY3
Subject-verb agreement
Diving into the Deep End

PRACTICE EXERCISE:

Directions: Answer the questions that accompany the following passages.

   (1) Has you ever been at home or in a classroom when all of a sudden, the floor disappears and you are floating in space? This is, of course, no real classroom – you are dreaming. If you are able to determine that this is a dream, rather than reality, you are what scientists **(2)** call a lucid dreamer.

   Lucid dreamers, or people who recognize their dreams as they are happening, may be better at problem-solving while awake. These results, surprising as they may be, **(3)** comes from a recent study published in the U.K. Psychologists from the University of Lincoln divided 68 undergraduate volunteers into three groups. These groups were based on the frequency of the volunteers' lucid dreaming: group 1 never dreamed lucidly, group 2 had lucid dreams occasionally, and group 3 experienced lucid dreaming at least once per month. After these volunteers **(4)** is given word puzzles and logic problems, an interesting fact emerged: those who reported that they frequently had lucid dreams solved 25 percent more of the puzzles than those who did not dream lucidly.

   Study author Hannah Shaw **(5)** are suggesting that lucid dreaming may indicate a greater capacity for insight: "Lucid dreamers can see the more remote connections needed to solve the problems." Their ability to think outside the box, she says, **(6)** is also the process that allows them "to keep themselves from accepting the dream world as reality."

   Lucid dreaming hinges on an ability to think critically: most people who gain self-awareness during sleep **(7)** are doing so either because the dreamer sees something that doesn't seem real —for example, a floor **(8)** that disappear— or because of the overall "dreamlike sense" of their surroundings.

1. A) NO CHANGE
   B) Having
   C) Have
   D) Had

2. A) NO CHANGE
   B) is calling
   C) are calling
   D) calls

3. A) NO CHANGE
   B) are coming
   C) come
   D) coming

4. A) NO CHANGE
   B) were given
   C) was given
   D) give

5. A) NO CHANGE
   B) suggest
   C) suggesting
   D) suggests

6. A) NO CHANGE
   B) were
   C) are
   D) am

7. A) NO CHANGE
   B) doing so
   C) do so
   D) does so

8. A) NO CHANGE.
   B) that disappears
   C) which disappear
   D) that is disappearing

Frequent lucid dreamers have been shown to do better at decision-making, processing out-of-context information, and selective attention. Another study, published in the journal *Sport Psychologist*, **(9)** finds that those who practiced certain motor actions while lucid dreaming were more skilled at performing the same actions while awake.

However, **(10)** caution professor of neurology Patrick McNamara, frequent lucid dreaming may have its downside: "We don't know if you get sleep-deprived when you lucid dream." Your prefrontal cortex, which **(11)** handling such higher cognitive functions as self-awareness, usually takes a break, 'shutting off', during REM sleep - the state during which lucid dreaming occurs. Yet in people experiencing lucidity, the prefrontal cortex remains active. For this reason, some experts believe that lucid dreaming isn't really dreaming at all, but instead a state that exists between sleep and wakefulness—thus, it's still unclear whether lucid dreaming has the same energy-replenishing properties as regular sleep.

9. A) NO CHANGE
   B) are finding
   C) founds
   D) find

10. A) NO CHANGE
    B) cautioning
    C) cautions
    D) is cautioning

11. A) NO CHANGE
    B) is handled
    C) handles
    D) handle

TEST EXERCISE:

Earlier this week, Facebook announced a plan to start testing a "satire" tag, which you may soon find affixed to headlines from sites like the *Onion* and ClickHole. This might sound satirical itself, but the popular social network **(1)** could be starting perhaps yet another new trend.

(2) Although this isn't just about satire; it's also about the problem of purposely false "news" stories. Lesser-known and less obviously joke-y sites like the Daily Currant and the News Nerd will get the "satire" tag, too. This might actually help prevent supposedly intelligent people from believing the many hoaxes spread online through social networks and "news" sites.

[3] The *Washington Post* itself cited a Daily Currant report that Sarah Palin was joining the news network Al-Jazeera America as a contributor. (She wasn't.) **(4)** Palin, given her prominent role in politics, frequently appears in fake headlines that tend to trick real news outlets: In 2011, Rachel Maddow fell for a (fake) Christwire column suggesting Palin lead an invasion of Egypt. About a week later, both *Time* and *US Weekly* based reports on a **(5)** forged article about Palin being angry with Christina Aguilera for botching **(6)** the lyrics at the Superbowl to the National Anthem.

1. A) NO CHANGE
   B) could be starting another new trend again.
   C) could be starting yet another new trend.
   D) could maybe be starting perhaps yet another new trend.

2. A) NO CHANGE
   B) This isn't just about satire; it's also
   C) However, this isn't just about satire, it's also
   D) Even though this isn't about satire; it's also

3. Which of the following should be added to introduce the paragraph?

   A) Sarah Palin usually tricks people with articles like this.
   B) These news sources get in the way of "real" news networks.
   C) Sometimes the "fake" news causes "real" problems.
   D) Individuals on social networks aren't the only people falling for these hoaxes though.

4. A) NO CHANGE
   B) Palin, prominently in politics, frequently
   C) Palin frequently for her prominent role in politics
   D) Palin given her prominent role in politics frequently

5. A) NO CHANGE
   B) mock
   C) simulated
   D) pseudo

6. A) NO CHANGE
   B) at the Superbowl the lyrics to the National Anthem.
   C) the National Anthem and its lyrics at the Superbowl.
   D) the lyrics to the National Anthem at the Superbowl.

So, why do some people—even smart people—choose to believe this fake news? For one, **(7)** <u>it usually happens</u> when people are not giving their full attention to what they're reading, said Dannagal Young, an associate professor of communication at the University of Delaware. "This isn't about 'shortened attention spans,'" **(8)** <u>she said in reply to our question in an email</u>. "This is about an overabundance of decontextualized snippets of info." Facebook headlines and Tweets simply don't give us the cues needed to distinguish weird news from fake news, "unless the [source] is *consistently ironic*," Young said.

"Think about the drama over Colbert's 'ching-chong ding-dong' joke," she continued. "That joke, originally, **(9)** <u>was being</u> ironic satire, comparing the response of the Redskins' owner with an equally offensive and laughably racist gesture made by Colbert. When Comedy Central tweeted it, without context, people were unable to use their past knowledge and cues to process the joke ... and they got angry. At Colbert. For being racist. Ahhhh, the *irony*!"

Processing irony requires some complicated brainwork to use old knowledge housed in your memory to help interpret new stimuli, all of which is filtered through context cues, Young explained. **(10)** "For example, people who tend to dislike thinking too much would tend to favor simple, likely **(11)** <u>physical humor than more complex or text-based humor</u>," she said. "Next, people who are uncomfortable with implicit or unstructured situations—would tend to favor humor that is obvious and clear over that which is more nuanced, like irony."

7. A) NO CHANGE
   B) they usually happen
   C) this usually is happening
   D) it usually happen

8. A) NO CHANGE
   B) she expressed via text in an email responding tour question.
   C) she responded to us in an email.
   D) she wrote in an email.

9. A) NO CHANGE
   B) was
   C) is
   D) had used

10. Which of the following provides the best transition from the previous sentence to the quotation that follows?

    A) And some people are simply unable or unwilling to do that.
    B) Different senses of humor need different clues.
    C) Jokes in different styles only make sense to certain people.
    D) Some people have no tolerance for offensive humor.

11. A) NO CHANGE
    B) physical humor when compared with the more complex or text-based jokes,
    C) physical humor over more complex or text-based humor,
    D) physical jokes to complex jokes,

Lesson wY3
Subject-Verb agreement
Race to the Finish

HOMEWORK EXERCISE 1:

Directions: Find and correct errors in the following sentences. Some sentences may have more than one error, while others will not have any errors.

1. The most famous radio broadcast of all time, *The War of the Worlds* are rightfully hailed by critics as an eternal masterpiece. *is*

2. Orson Welles, a radio and television actor, *was* were instantly propelled into stardom thanks to his masterful direction and acting in this broadcast.

3. The show begins with a normal radio music show that is interrupted by a news bulletin announcing that strange explosions had been sighted on Mars.

4. A famous astronomer and Princeton professor, Richard Pierson, initially scoffs and dismiss *es* any claims of life on Mars.

5. However, the news grows more frightening as another report interrupts the broadcast, announcing that a cylindrical object has landed on a New Jersey farm.

6. Immediate panic ensues when a massive alien with tentacles erupts from the cylinder and incinerates the crowd with heat rays.

7. The normal broadcast is paused, with the radio show now receiving updates that outlines the casualties and destruction caused by more of these aliens.

8. New Jersey announces martial law and sends militia to attack the alien cylinder.

9. The aliens destroy the nearly helpless humans with ease and commences an assault on the surrounding areas.

10. The studio announcers are in a panic and describe the attacks as a Martian invasion.

11. More Martian cylinders land, and from them pours out even more aliens intent on destroying the Earth.

12. As the violence continue, a message of calm is presented on the air by an unnamed Secretary of the Interior.

13. The radio broadcast resumes with accounts from the Army, which are bombarding the invaders with heavy artillery. *is*

14. Even the Air Force sends planes to attack the Martians, but all attacks are futile as the Martians shrugs off each effort.

15. Both of the military branches is *are* defeated by the superior Martian technology, and the Martians release a black smoke that floats toward the cities.

16. Many reporters who announce the dispersion of this smoke soon fall silent and is presumed dead by the radio studio hosts. *are*

17. The broadcast grows increasingly hopeless, as more people are poisoned by the gas that the unstoppable Martians are billowing into the atmosphere.

18. The final broadcast of the show is made by a ham radio operator who asks "Isn't there anyone on the air? Isn't there anyone on the air? Isn't there... anyone?"

19. The story ends with an epilogue in which the Martians are defeated as they get infected by common human germs and succumbs to them.

20. After the broadcast, Orson Welles returns to the air with a message that the previous broadcast had been an elaborate Halloween prank.

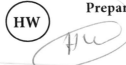
HOMEWORK EXERCISE 2:

Candid Camera

If you watch television tonight, there is a good chance you will **(1)** <u>have watched</u> a reality show. Reality television is everywhere, but despite its modern surge in popularity, **(2)** <u>the concept is nothing new</u>.

[1] One of the first reality shows ever made was *Candid Camera*, which debuted in 1948. [2] *Candid Camera* began as a radio show **(3)** <u>called *The Candid Microphone*, before being moved to television, which ran between 1947 and 1948.</u> [3] Produced and hosted by television personality **(4)** <u>Allen Funt; the show</u> revolved around capturing the reactions of members of the public placed in awkward, often hilarious, situations while **(5)** <u>strategic placed</u> hidden cameras captured every moment. [4] One early episode included a segment in which a sign reading "Walk on White Squares Only" was placed in a black and white tiled hallway. [5] The audience was treated to several minutes of footage of people tip-toeing and hopping their way across the floor in an effort to obey the official-looking sign. [6] Of course, these victims were always informed of the reason for the stunt afterwards and usually reacted good-naturedly to being filmed for television. [7] Other set-ups were simpler, such as cracking eggs into someone's hat under the pretense of performing a magic trick, then just walking away, leaving the confused victim of the prank with a hat full of raw egg. {6}

1. A) NO CHANGE
   B) watch
   C) have been watching
   D) had watched

2. A) NO CHANGE
   B) the concept of using reality in television is nothing out of the ordinary
   C) the reality concept is a anything but a new addition to the world of television.
   D) reality television is nothing new in the television world

3. A) NO CHANGE
   B) before being moved to television, called *The Candid Microphone*, which ran between 1947 and 1948.
   C) , which ran between 1947 and 1948, before being moved to television called *The Candid Microphone*.
   D) called *The Candid Microphone*, which ran between 1947 and 1948 before being moved to television.

4. A) NO CHANGE
   B) Allen Funt, and the show
   C) Allen Funt, the show
   D) Allen Funt, however, the show

5. A) NO CHANGE
   B) strategically placed
   C) strategic placement
   D) strategic, placed

6. To best improve the coherence of the paragraph, sentence 6 should be moved…

   A) NO CHANGE
   B) after sentence 3.
   C) after sentence 4.
   D) after sentence 7.

[1] The subjects for these social experiments were not limited to everyday citizens. [2] Occasionally, celebrities were tricked by the *Candid Camera* team, and sometimes they even agreed to play a role in a segment. [3] For the camera team, hosting famous people on the show must have been exciting. [4] Famous country singer Dolly Parton once pretended to have injured her ankle and begged help from passersby. [5] Each person carried her around a parking lot **(7)** ineffectively looking for her car, which never existed. [6] *Candid Camera* was there to catch the reactions of the men she asked and their growing exhaustion with every trip around the parking lot. **{8}**

The show, whose longest uninterrupted run was from 1960-1967, **(9)** experienced several sporadic stops and starts in production over the many decades and years that it was on the air. Allen Funt, however, stuck with the program until his failing health forced him to step down as host. His son, Peter Funt, who had often served as his father's co-host, took over until 2004, when production was suspended.

{10} In April 2014, the TV Land cable channel announced that it had ordered ten new episodes of *Candid Camera*, with Peter Funt **(11)** planning on returning as host, joined by the actress Mayim Bialik. The nearly seventy-year-old reality show was finally ready for a new audience.

7. Which of the following is the most precise replacement for the underlined word?

A) NO CHANGE
B) fruitlessly
C) uselessly
D) unproductively

8. Which sentence should be removed to most improve the coherence of the paragraph?

A) Sentence 1
B) Sentence 2
C) Sentence 3
D) Sentence 4

9. Which of the following would provide a concise replacement for the underlined portion?

A) NO CHANGE
B) experienced several lulls in production over the many decades on the air.
C) experienced several stops on the air.
D) experienced several lulls in production over the years.

10. Which of the following would provide the most logical connection between this paragraph and the last?

A) Peter Funt went on to host other television shows.
B) But now things are changing for the show.
C) Ten years later, that suspension came to an end.
D) Everyone assumed that *Candid Camera* was gone for good.

11. A) NO CHANGE
B) returned
C) having returned
D) planning to return

C2 education
be smarter

Lesson wY4
Commas, Semicolons, and Colons
Getting Your Feet Wet

1. I have cleaned most of the <u>kitchen, I</u> still need to mop the floors.

     A) NO CHANGE
     B) kitchen, so I
     C) kitchen; I
     D) kitchen: I

2. I have a long list of chores still to <u>do; mop the floors, take out the trash, recycling, and compost, and</u> fold my laundry.

     A) NO CHANGE
     B) do: mop the floors; take out the trash, recycling, and compost; and
     C) do: mop the floors, take out the trash, recycling, and compost, and
     D) do; mop the floors; take out the trash, recycling, and compost; and

3. My mom has this <u>rule: if</u> you don't do your chores, then you don't get to play video games.

     A) NO CHANGE
     B) rule, if
     C) rule; if
     D) rule. If

Lesson wY4
Commas, Semicolons, and Colons
Wading In

TOPIC OVERVIEW: COMMAS, SEMICOLONS, AND COLONS

The most commonly used punctuation marks that we see within sentences are commas, semicolons, and colons. Correct usage of these punctuation marks can be rather confusing because there are so many rules to remember. In this lesson, we will cover some of the various comma, semicolon, and colon errors that you might see on the SAT.

TOPIC OVERVIEW: COMMAS

Commas are very useful punctuation marks. They can be used to set off phrases and clauses, separate adjectives, separate contrasting statements, punctuate dates and places, combine sentences, introduce quotations, and punctuate items in a series. Let's take a look at some of these uses and the errors that can occur.

COMMAS: SETTING OFF PHRASES AND CLAUSES

There are two main types of phrases that commas can be used to set apart from the main sentence: Introductory elements and nonessential elements. Let's look at an example of each:

Example 1: **Although they are home to more than ¾ of the entire U.S. population,** large cities are clustered primarily along the east and west coasts.

Example 2: Large cities, **which are home to more than ¾ of the entire U.S. population,** are clustered primarily along the east and west coasts.

In the first example, we see an introductory phrase. An introductory phrase is a dependent clause (a clause that cannot stand on its own as a sentence) that provides background information or sets the stage for the main part of the sentence. Note that there is a comma at the end of the introductory phrase.

In this particular example, the introductory phrase is a subordinate clause. As we learned in lesson 2, when a subordinate clause appears at the beginning of a sentence, it should always be followed by a comma. The same is true for all other types of introductory phrases.

In the second example, we see a nonessential element. A nonessential element is a clause that isn't important to the overall meaning of a sentence. If you can remove the clause and still have a sentence that makes perfect sense and hasn't lost its meaning, then the clause is nonessential. Nonessential elements always need to be surrounded by commas.

We will discuss the difference between essential and nonessential elements in lesson 13, but let's take a look at an example of an essential element:

<u>Example 3</u>: Large cities that have ocean ports are clustered along the east and west coasts.

In this case, the clause "that have ocean ports" is essential. Why? Because it defines a certain type of large cities. If we took out that clause, we would be talking about *all* large cities instead of only large cities with ocean ports. Essential elements should not be set apart with commas because they are so important to the meaning of the sentence.

WRAP-UP: SETTING OFF PHRASES AND CLAUSES

1. An introductory phrase is a clause that cannot stand on its own as a sentence, that appears at the beginning of a sentence, and that provides background information or sets the stage for the main part of the sentence. They should be followed by a comma.
2. A nonessential element is a clause that is not necessary to the overall meaning of the sentence. Nonessential elements should be set off by commas.
3. An essential element is a clause that is important to the overall meaning of the sentence. Essential elements should not be set apart by commas.

COMMAS: PAIRED ADJECTIVES

Sometimes we use more than one adjective to describe a word. And sometimes, when we use two or more adjectives, we need a comma separating those adjectives. Let's figure out when we should and should not use commas to separate adjectives.

Example 4: He likes **wriggly, adorable** puppies.

Example 5: He built his new puppy an **exquisite custom** doghouse.

In example 4, both "wriggly" and "adorable" describe the puppies. When that happens, we need a comma between the adjectives. A simple test is to switch the order of the adjectives. If it stills sounds correct, then you need a comma between the adjectives. So in example 4, "He likes adorable, wriggly puppies" still makes perfect sense.

In example 5, "custom" describes "doghouse," and "exquisite" describes "custom doghouse." Let's do the simple test: "He built his new puppy a custom exquisite doghouse." This new sentence doesn't make as much sense. When you can't rearrange the adjectives and still maintain the same meaning, you don't need a comma.

WRAP-UP: PAIRED ADJECTIVES

1. If a pair of adjectives can be reversed without altering the meaning of the sentence, put a comma between the adjectives.
2. If a pair of adjectives cannot be reversed without altering the meaning of the sentence, do not put a comma between the adjectives.

COMMAS: CONTRASTING STATEMENTS

Commas should be used to separate contrasting statements and if-then statements. Let's look at a pair of examples:

Example 6: I like vanilla, not chocolate.

Example 7: If you give me chocolate ice cream, then I will not eat it.

Example 6 is an example of contrasting statements. You should place a comma before the "not" in a contrasting statement. A simple test is to ask whether you could use "and" where the comma would go: "I like vanilla **and** not chocolate." If the sentence makes sense with "and," then you need a comma.

As we see in Example 7, in an if-then statement, a comma always has to separate the two clauses.

WRAP-UP: CONTRASTING STATEMENTS

1. If the word "and" could be used instead of a comma in a contrasting statement, then you need a comma.
2. If-then statements always need a comma separating the two clauses.

COMBINING SENTENCES

As we learned in lessons 1 and 2, there are several ways to combine two sentences, and some of them require commas or semicolons. Let's review:

<u>Example 8:</u> I wanted to go to the beach**, but** my sister wanted to go skiing.

<u>Example 9:</u> I wanted to go to the beach**;** my sister wanted to go skiing.

<u>Example 10:</u> My sister said it was too cold for swimming**:** she tends to get cold very easily.

Examples 8 and 9 combine the same two sentences. In example 8, we used a coordinating conjunction, so we needed a comma before the conjunction. Remember that the rules are different when using subordinating conjunctions. If you need to review the rules for combining sentences using conjunctions, review lesson 2.

In example 9, we replaced the comma and conjunction with a semicolon. Semicolons can be used to combine two related sentences. When using a semicolon, do not use a coordinating or subordinating conjunction.

Example 10 is a bit different. In this example, we used a colon to combine two sentences. Colons should be used to connect two sentences when the second sentence summarizes or explains the first sentence. In this case, the second sentence explains why my sister thought it was too cold for swimming.

WRAP-UP: COMBINING SENTENCES

1. Use commas to combine sentences when using a coordinating conjunction or when the first sentence becomes a subordinate clause. To review the rules for using commas and conjunctions to combine sentences, look at lesson 2.
2. Use a semicolon to combine two sentences when the two sentences are clearly related. When using a semicolon, do not use a coordinating or subordinating conjunction.
3. Use a colon to combine two sentences when the second sentence summarizes or explains the first sentence.

Version 1.0
                    Preparation Guide: Redesigned SAT 2016 Yellow Writing
                          Lesson 4: wY4   **65**

PUNCTUATING QUOTATIONS

Commas and colons also play a role in quotations. When introducing a quotation, we usually use either a comma or a colon:

<u>Example 11:</u> I wanted to correct the bad grammar on the sign that said**,** "Keep of the grass."

<u>Example 12:</u> I wanted to correct the bad grammar on the sign that said**:** "Keep of the grass."

Even though we've used two different punctuation marks, both of the examples above are grammatically correct. We can use either a comma or a colon to introduce a quotation. Although either punctuation mark can be used, it is advisable to only use colons when the quotation is longer than 7 words.

<u>Example 13:</u> After seeing the grammatically incorrect sign, the teacher said: "I cannot believe that no one caught that error before printing and placing the sign."

Both example 12 and example 13 are technically correct, but example 13 is a more traditional use of the colon.

WRAP-UP: PUNCTUATING QUOTATIONS

1. Quotations can be introduced using either a comma or a colon.
2. Colons are usually reserved for quotations that are more than 7 words long.

ITEMS IN A SERIES

All three punctuation marks – commas, semicolons, and colons – have a role to play when punctuating items in a series. Let's look at some examples:

Example 14: At the store, I bought apples, peaches, and cherries.

Example 15: At the store, I bought shiny, juicy apples; ripe, fuzzy peaches; and organic cherries.

Example 16: At the store, I bought several things from the produce department: shiny, juicy apples; ripe, fuzzy peaches; and organic cherries.

All three of these examples contain items in a series, which is a fancy way of saying "a list." In the first example, we simply used commas to separate each item. This is the most common way to create a list. In the second example, however, we used semicolons to separate the items. If we didn't use semicolons, the sentence would be awfully confusing:

Example 17: At the store, I bought shiny, juicy apples, ripe, fuzzy peaches, and organic cherries.

As you can see, this version has way too many commas, which makes the sentence somewhat confusing. When the items in a list already contain commas, we use a semicolon to separate the items in order to make the sentence easier to understand.

In example 16, we used all three types of punctuation. We used commas to separate the adjectives; we used semicolons to separate the items in the list because the items in the list already contained commas; and we used a colon to introduce the list. We only use a colon to introduce a list if the list follows an independent clause that could stand on its own as a sentence. In example 16, "At the store, I bought several things from the produce department" could stand on its own as a sentence.

Example 18: At the store, I bought: shiny, juicy apples; ripe, fuzzy peaches; and organic cherries.

Example 18 would be incorrect because "At the store, I bought" cannot stand on its own as a sentence since it doesn't form a complete thought.

WRAP-UP: ITEMS IN A SERIES

1. For a simple list of items, use a comma to separate items in a series.
2. For a list of items in which the items themselves contain commas, use semicolons to separate the items in a series.
3. If the list is introduced by an independent clause that could stand on its own as a sentence, use a colon to introduce the list.

Lesson wY4
Commas, Semicolons, and Colons
Learning to Swim

CONCEPT EXERCISE:

1. Dr. Simon will teach three classes for mathematics majors next semester: Intro to Linear Algebra, Multivariable Calculus, and Intro to Real Analysis.

2. Whereas Jeremiah had always believed in ghosts and spirits, his sister scoffed at him and insisted that there was no such thing.

3. Before the year is up, our goal is to have hired twelve new employees, implemented a new project management system, and completed the marketing plan for January's product launch.

4. New research is revealing that the oceans, once thought to be too vast to be affected by human activity, are in fact heavily polluted, and marine ecosystems such as coral reefs are deeply imperiled.

5. The star running back was recognized as one of the best college football players, but some fans wondered if his distinctive style of play would translate to the NFL or prove less effective at that level.

6. Ireland experienced rapid economic growth during the 1990s and early 2000s. This led some observers to refer to the island country's economy as the "Celtic Tiger."

7. We detected a statistically significant amount of radioactivity in the sample; however, upon repeating the experiment we were unable to reproduce this result.

8. The Caldwell family has three daughters: the eldest, Emilia, is a professor of history; the middle child, Fiona, works as a marine biologist; and the youngest, Clara, is in college studying computer science.

9. Please read the reports I left on your desk, write a summary of the key implications for our global marketing strategy, and be prepared to present it to me on Monday morning.

10. Horatio loves mystery novels in which the good guy ultimately triumphs over the bad guy, but he has little patience for those which choose to obsess over moral shades of gray.

11. One issue, above all others, defined the young mayoral candidate's campaign: the promise of greater transparency in local government, should she be elected.

12. The pet store will open in June and will sell snakes; various lizard species including iguanas, geckos, and bearded dragons; and last but not least, turtles.

13. Combining innovative use of fresh, local, seasonally available ingredients with a unique culinary sensibility rooted in the flavors of the chef's native Lebanon, the restaurant is well worth a visit.

14. It was not until the release of its acclaimed fourth album that the band, whose members had long been veterans of Seattle's grunge music scene, acquired a significant following outside the region.

15. If you can't come on Saturday, I sincerely hope that I still get to see you before you leave town.

16. The researchers, without even intending to do so, had stumbled upon a cure for the deadly disease.

17. Mom needs you to bring the following things when you come meet us: two beach chairs, the cooler, and some sunscreen.

18. The jobs forecast seems to paint a rosy picture of employment growth over the next six months. A closer examination, however, suggests that most of the jobs created will be part-time and lack benefits.

19. Jonas Salk, the creator of the polio vaccine, was hailed for his colossal contribution to public health.

20. Although Seth won't be able to attend his sister's wedding, he insists that knowing that she, after several doomed relationships, has found true love is reward enough.

Lesson wY4
Commas, Semicolons, and Colons
Diving into the Deep End

PRACTICE EXERCISE:

Passwords: The Dodo of the Digital Age

What is your mother's maiden name? The name of your third-grade teacher? The hospital in which you were born? Have you ever had to answer one of these "security questions" to reset a password you'd forgotten? This is an annoying, and increasingly **(1)** common, experience as our digital lives require us to keep track of a greater number of passwords than ever before, and security concerns require that these passwords be **(2)** longer, and more complicated.

Now, some information security experts are arguing that the problem is that passwords themselves are **(3)** obsolete, largely useless. Just ask Heather Adkins, the manager of information security at Google. She **(4)** declared: "passwords are dead" at a presentation in 2013 and says Google will phase out its use of them when possible.

The problem with passwords **(5)** is the fact that: computers have become powerful enough to test trillions of random guesses in short amounts of time. Whereas in the past, an 8-character password might have protected your **(6)** data, now to be truly secure, a password must be much longer and much more random. If it relies on such things as words found in the dictionary; information connected to the **(7)** user, such as a birthdate, patterned strings of numbers, such as *987654321*, or letters, such as *abcxyz*; or anything else a computer algorithm can search through, it may not be secure. But the human brain just isn't very good at remembering very long, obscure passwords.

1. A) NO CHANGE
   B) common experience
   C) common experience,
   D) common experience;

2. A) NO CHANGE
   B) longer and more
   C) longer and, more
   D) longer; and moreover

3. A) NO CHANGE
   B) obsolete and
   C) obsolete; and they are
   D) obsolete:

4. A) NO CHANGE
   B) declared: "passwords are dead,"
   C) declared that "passwords are dead"
   D) declared, "passwords are dead,"

5. A) NO CHANGE
   B) is that computers
   C) is that: computers
   D) is in fact, computers

6. A) NO CHANGE
   B) data now,
   C) data, now,
   D) data; now,

7. A) NO CHANGE
   B) user; such as a birthdate;
   C) user such as a birthdate,
   D) user, such as a birthdate;

Some experts recommend harnessing mnemonic **(8)** <u>devices, these are</u> memory tricks such as acronyms or visual imagery. For example, you could take a favorite song lyric, write down the first letter of each word, and use that as a 20- or 30-character password. Other security gurus recommend generating random, long passwords and storing them all on a protected USB thumb drive. Simply plug in the device, copy, and paste when you need to retrieve a password.

Ultimately, it is likely that passwords will go the way of the dodo. In their place, we may see increased use of biometric **(9)** <u>scanning, a device</u> might read your fingerprint or recognize your eyes to grant you access. Voice-recognition is another **(10)** <u>possibility, although problematic:</u> a person's voice can more easily be imitated than his or her fingerprint! Google's Adkins has suggested yet another possibility: having to touch a protected device, such as a smart phone, to a chip carried on your person. In any case, the recent **(11)** <u>thefts using hacked passwords, of</u> huge amounts of user data such as credit card numbers from national retailers like Target prove that the way we handle cyber security has got to change.

8. A) NO CHANGE
    B) devices,
    C) devices; these are
    D) devices;

9. A) NO CHANGE
    B) scanning: a device
    C) scanning devices, which
    D) scanning devices; which

10. A) NO CHANGE
    B) problematic possibility, although
    C) possibility: although problematic,
    D) possibility; although, problematically,

11. A) NO CHANGE
    B) thefts, using hacked passwords of
    C) thefts, using hacked passwords, of
    D) thefts using hacked passwords:

TEST EXERCISE:

The Mere Exposure Effect

[1]

Many people assume that a song they hear all over the place—on the radio, at the grocery store, in the dentist's waiting room—is played everywhere because it's popular. In fact, many psychologists will tell you, it's more likely the other way **(1)** around, that the song is popular because it's played everywhere! The phenomenon in which people come to like something (in this case, a song) from being exposed to it repeatedly even has a name in psychology. It's called the *mere exposure effect*.

[2]

The effect was first given its name in the 1960s by psychologist Robert Zajonc. Zajonc's experiments **(2)** demonstrating that people have a preference for something familiar to them over something unfamiliar. **(3)** In fact, in one such experiment he split subjects into two groups and had them stare at two different fake Chinese characters. They were told the characters represented adjectives and asked to guess which one had a more positive connotation. Which character they had looked at before **(4)** effected their responses: subjects reacted more positively to the one they had seen than the one they had not, despite the fact that both were actually meaningless!

[3]

The mere exposure effect may arise from evolutionary psychology. When faced with potential dangers in the wild, it is helpful to be comforted by the familiar and wary of the unfamiliar. Your brain, for instance, **(5)** inclined you to prefer the berries you've eaten dozens of times and to dislike or reject a different kind of berry that you've never had before and that might be poisonous. **(6)** People know where to find shelter and food in places they have been before, another reason it's wise to stick to the familiar.

1. A) NO CHANGE
    B) around,
    C) around:
    D) around and

2. A) NO CHANGE
    B) demonstrated
    C) would have demonstrated
    D) were demonstrating

3. A) NO CHANGE
    B) Therefore
    C) In actuality
    D) For example

4. A) NO CHANGE
    B) affected
    C) effecting
    D) had an affect on

5. A) NO CHANGE
    B) has inclined
    C) will have inclined
    D) inclines

6. Which replacement for the underlined sentence most logically and cohesively develops this paragraph's main idea?

    A) NO CHANGE
    B) In such a situation, sticking to the familiar might have greatly improved an early human's odds of survival.
    C) Given the sheer number of poisonous berry species that exist, this was a useful trait for early humans.
    D) The mere exposure effect most likely exists in other animals as well, although conclusive studies have not been done.

[4]

The mere exposure effect may also explain the process of acquired tastes. For example, most people do not initially like strong flavors like those of coffee or **(7)** beer, upon repeated exposure, they learn to. The mere exposure effect might even help explain racial prejudice among people who have spent little time with members of other racial groups. In any case, there is no doubt that advertisers understand the effect well. That annoying commercial jingle you can't get out of your head? They want it to be stuck there. **(8)** Even if you hate the ad; its creators know that the more often you've thought about their product, the more likely you are to buy it over a competing brand.

[5]

(9) Back to where we started, labels used to engage in *payola*, the practice of paying radio stations to play certain songs. Those songs, unsurprisingly given the mere exposure effect, often became popular hits. **(10)** Now illegal, the industry no longer uses payola, but it still has plenty of ways to make sure you hear the songs they want to you to hear—over, and over, and over again. {11}

7. A) NO CHANGE
   B) beer, but upon repeated exposure,
   C) beer upon repeated exposure;
   D) beer: upon repeated exposure

8. A) NO CHANGE
   B) Since you hate the ad, its
   C) Since you hate the ad; its
   D) Even if you hate the ad, its

9. A) NO CHANGE
   B) Rewinding to the beginning
   C) As for our original example of popular music
   D) With regard to the application of the mere exposure effect to music preferences

10. A) NO CHANGE
    B) Having been banned,
    C) Now that this kind of direct bribery is illegal,
    D) It being illegal now,

11. Which of the following would most effectively conclude the passage?

    A) Thanks to the mere exposure effect, the top hits of today may be due more to the strategies of record labels than to the real tastes of listeners.
    B) For example, they often pay to have songs featured in television commercials.
    C) Now you know why you hear the same songs repeatedly.
    D) After all, that's how the mere exposure effect works.

Lesson wY4
Commas, Semicolons, and Colons
Race to the Finish

HOMEWORK EXERCISE 1:

1. It was widely anticipated that the governor, an opponent of tax increases would veto the bill.

2. Sarah and her friends had expected the weather to be cold for their camping trip but they had not prepared for snow.

3. At night, the jaguar stalks its prey silently and can ambush and kill a small animal in mere seconds.

4. The latest uptick in housing prices is unlike that of ten years ago, this time, far more buyers are paying with cash instead of taking out mortgages.

5. With his tenth birthday coming up, Evan couldn't decide where, or when, he wanted to have the party.

6. We have three main advantages over our nearest competitors, our more efficient supply chain, our location in a rapidly growing metropolitan area, and a greater range of premium products at higher price points.

7. Although not callous toward her subordinates, the executive director was able to make hard-nosed and impersonal decisions when she found it necessary for the greater good of the organization.

8. Anna, beset by worries that she would not find a job after graduation, began to save every penny she could, this habit of frugality that she cultivated would persist for many years.

9. In order to maximize his play time, Brett pretended not to hear his parents the first time they called him to come downstairs for dinner.

10. Would you believe me, if I told you that I was considering leaving school and joining the circus?

11. In recent years, a broad consensus had developed among economists that the stimulus program had been effective; however, opinions among the general public were more varied.

12. The report concluded that California's stringent emissions standards had, on account of the desire of automakers to keep their production processes uniform, led to gains in fuel efficiency even outside of California.

13. I have decided to accept the post of Secretary of Defense; therefore, I shall be resigning my senate seat as of the end of this month.

14. Crime rates have steadily dropped over the decade, and, furthermore, our detectives are solving a greater percentage of cases than they did in the past.

15. Your son or daughter is asked to bring to school two spiral notebooks, a set of colored pencils, which will be used in art class, and a calculator.

16. However you may decide to get there, I recommend bringing your phone in case you get lost.

17. Upon leaving, please do the following things: take out the trash, turn off the water heater, and set the thermostat to 80 degrees.

18. Throughout your life, wherever it may lead you, may you always remember to be humble, be conscientious, and never lose your sense of wonder.

19. A series of electric barriers is all that currently prevents Asian carp, an invasive fish that has wreaked havoc on the ecosystem of the lower Mississippi River from swimming into the Great Lakes.

20. Inspired by the pioneering research of Werner Heisenberg, a German theoretical physicist, into the underpinnings of quantum mechanics; playwright Michael Frayn wrote the play *Copenhagen*.

HOMEWORK EXERCISE 2:

The Evolution of Animation

Only a generation ago, animating a feature film consisted of painstakingly drawing, by hand, thousands upon thousands of individual frames. Since then, animation, with the help of computers, **(1)** have evolved into a much more varied and specialized range of jobs. Nearly every movie released today, and certainly every movie involving special effects, has animated elements.

One technique that blurs the boundary between animation and live-action **(2)** footage: *rotoscoping*. A rotoscope artist literally traces over the silhouettes of characters or objects, one frame at a time. This can be used to create animation based on a real actor's movements, to remove an object or person from a scene, or even to place them in front of an entirely different **(3)** background, this is useful for special-effects-laden action movies. Rotoscoping is **(4)** tedious, and it is very painstaking work, but it is often an early career step for an artist looking to break into the movie industry.

[1] *Motion capture,* or mo-cap, is a computer-aided technique rapidly gaining in popularity that has inspired vigorous debate about what is animation and what is live-action. [2] Motion-capture data is used by CG artists to animate a 3D character based on the actor's real movements and facial expressions. [3] A mo-cap actor wears a skintight suit fitted with sensors that record every detail of his or her movements. {5}

(6) Andy Serkis is an actor who does motion-capture work. You wouldn't recognize him on the street, but he has played such iconic characters as Gollum in *The Lord of the Rings* and Caesar in the recent *Planet of the Apes* films. Because the characters are animated, motion-capture actors have traditionally not been considered for acting awards such as the Oscars. This may be **(7)** changing, however thanks to Serkis's popularity. Many feel his incredibly expressive performances give a sense of life and realism to his

1. A) NO CHANGE
   B) evolved
   C) evolves
   D) has evolved

2. A) NO CHANGE
   B) footage is
   C) footage: this is called
   D) footage;

3. A) NO CHANGE
   B) background is
   C) background, which is
   D) background:

4. A) NO CHANGE
   B) tediously
   C) tedious,
   D) tedious, not to mention it is

5. In which order should the sentences of this paragraph be placed in order to improve its cohesion?

   A) NO CHANGE
   B) 1, 3, 2
   C) 2, 3, 1
   D) 3, 2, 1

6. Which version of the underlined sentence provides the most cohesive transition from the previous paragraph?

   A) NO CHANGE
   B) Acclaimed actor Andy Serkis illustrates the process of motion-capture animation.
   C) One such actor is Andy Serkis, who has been praised for his exceptional motion-capture work.
   D) Have you heard of Andy Serkis, the motion-capture actor?

7. A) NO CHANGE
   B) changing, however,
   C) changing; however,
   D) changing; however

characters that animators alone could not achieve. **{8}**

[1] *Photorealistic* animation—scenery and characters **(9)** <u>that are like photos</u>—has become a more achievable goal than ever, and the lengths studios will go to in pursuit of it are incredible. [2] Rhythm & Hues, the company responsible for the award-winning special effects in *Life of Pi*, spent an entire year doing research on Bengal tigers in order to create a convincing one for the film! [3] Much of the film takes place on a raft at **(10)** <u>sea, and these scenes were</u> shot in a large indoor wave pool which required visual effects artists to make it look like an ocean. [4] In the end, the film had two stars: a real actor and an animated, but fully lifelike, tiger. **{11}**

8. Which of the following sentences, if added here, would most enhance the focus of the passage as a whole?

   A) Still, bringing these characters to life is ultimately a joint effort between an actor and many talented animators working behind the scenes.
   B) In the end, though, Serkis's performances are not live-action and should not be considered as such.
   C) Others believe that actors like Serkis contribute little to the development of characters like Gollum.
   D) Perhaps one day, all animated characters will be played by actors like Serkis.

9. A) NO CHANGE
   B) that might as well be photographs
   C) that resemble photography
   D) so lifelike they appear to be photographed

10. A) NO CHANGE
    B) sea: these scenes,
    C) sea; these scenes were
    D) sea, scenes which were

11. Which sentence should be removed from the final paragraph to enhance its cohesion and focus?

    A) Sentence 1
    B) Sentence 2
    C) Sentence 3
    D) Sentence 4

Lesson wY5
Effective Language Use – Concision and Precision
Getting Your Feet Wet

Directions: Use the paragraphs below to answer the questions.

A Roget-style thesaurus doesn't organize entries alphabetically, as a dictionary does, but taxonomically, under eight broad classes that branch into smaller categories. To many users, **(1)** it might be preferable to have an alphabetical listing, but to a lover of language, traveling a thesaurus's branching lines of categories and subcategories to explore subtle shifts in meaning provides its own adventure. I've found few things as gratifying as consulting my dear friend and reaping the reward of encountering an elusive word.

Finding the precise word matters. Take that last sentence: I first wrote, "Finding the right word matters." Although right wouldn't have been wrong, precise is more, well, precise. Several words might **(2)** transport the same general meaning in a particular sentence, but using a word that does more than simply state meaning is what makes prose memorable.

A good thesaurus is among a writer's most powerful tools, but it can be easily **(3)** wasted. With the unwitting assistance of a thesaurus, **(4)** the arcane can be substituted for the commonplace by a writer in a misguided attempt to make the final product seem more scholarly; the end result, sadly, is often laughable rather than intellectual.

1. Which of the following is the most concise replacement for the underlined portion of the sentence?

   A) NO CHANGE
   B) preferential treatment is given to alphabetical listings
   C) an alphabetical listing might be preferable
   D) they might prefer an alphabetical listing

2. Which of the following is the most precise replacement for the underlined word?

   A) NO CHANGE
   B) convey
   C) carry
   D) transmit

3. A) NO CHANGE
   B) wronged
   C) exploited
   D) misused

4. A) NO CHANGE
   B) a writer can substitute the arcane for the commonplace
   C) the arcane can replace the commonplace
   D) the commonplace can be replaced by the writer

Lesson wY5
Effective Language Use – Concision and Precision
Wading In

TOPIC OVERVIEW: CONCISION AND PRECISION

Every SAT writing section will contain at least one precision or concision question. Precision questions test your ability to choose the most appropriate word for a particular context. Concision questions test your ability to recognize and correct wordiness and redundancy. Taken together, these questions are similar to the Words in Context questions that you will see in the reading section of the SAT.

RECOGNIZING PRECISION QUESTIONS

Precision questions can be presented in one of two ways. The first is easy to recognize: There will be a question that asks, "Which of the following is the most precise replacement for the underlined word?" The key word "precise" is your clue that this is a precision question. Alternatively, precision questions may be slightly hidden. You may see just one word underlined and accompanied by answer choices containing only one (or rarely two) word. No matter which way the question is presented, it is asking the same thing: Choose the answer choice that is most precise.

TOPIC OVERVIEW: PRECISION

Precision questions require you to know the nuance of vocabulary, the slight difference in the meanings of words. The SAT will not test you on high-level "SAT words" anymore. Instead, the test will focus on common words with multiple meanings. There are two general concepts to keep in mind when faced with a precision question.

General vs. Specific

Oftentimes, a precision question will include answer choices that are technically correct within the sentence, but that are still not the correct answer to the question. That's because there is a difference between accurate word choice and precise word choice. Let's look at an example:

Example 1: As the captain of the debate team, she was responsible for ensuring adequate funds for tournaments, so she **participated in** the fundraisers.

Example 2: As the captain of the debate team, she was responsible for ensuring adequate funds for tournaments, so she **oversaw** the fundraisers.

The first example is accurate: Clearly, as captain of the debate team, she would have participated in fundraisers. But since she was responsible for ensuring funds, we can also assume that she did more than merely *participate*, so the

second example is more precise. She not only participated, but also *oversaw* the fundraisers.

Connotations

The second concept to consider when answering precision questions deals with the connotations of different words. A connotation is an implied meaning of a word. For example, all of these words mean "skinny": bony, gaunt, lanky, scrawny, slender, lean, thin. If you were a skinny person, though, you would probably prefer to be called "slender" or "lean" than "scrawny" or "gaunt." This is because some of these words have more positive connotations than others.

But how do we know which word to choose when dealing with connotations? Let's look at another pair of examples.

Example 3: During the graduation ceremony, Mr. and Mrs. Smith looked on with **arrogance** as their son took the stage.

Example 4: During the graduation ceremony, Mr. and Mrs. Smith looked on with **pride** as their son took the stage.

Although both arrogance and pride have similar meanings, they have different connotations. Arrogance suggests a negative connotation, while pride suggests a positive connotation. Since the sentence provides context that would suggest that a positive word is more appropriate, pride is a better word choice for the sentence.

ANSWERING PRECISION QUESTIONS

To answer precision questions, draw on your own knowledge of vocabulary. Follow these steps to arrive at the best answer:

1. Cover up the answer choices and cross out the underlined word in the passage. You should now have a sentence with a blank in it.
2. Re-read the sentence. Using the context of the sentence and the surrounding paragraph, come up with a word that you think would work well in the sentence.
3. Uncover the answer choices and eliminate any words that would not work based on the word that you selected to fill the blank.
4. Use the context of the passage to eliminate any additional answer choices that are either too general or have the wrong connotation.
5. If there is more than one answer choice remaining, and if there is a preposition in the sentence that has not been underlined, choose the answer choice that best fits the sentence based on standard English conventions for prepositions.

Let's go through these steps using an example.

Example 5:

Many students <u>mistake</u> the vital role of a college education in an individual's career, believing that college is unnecessary for success.

    A) NO CHANGE
    B) undervalue
    C) overestimate
    D) misunderstand

Step one requires that we replace the underlined word with a blank: Many students _____ the vital role that a college education plays in an individual's career.

In step two, we look at the sentence as a whole to come up with a word choice that might fit in the blank. In this sentence, the phrase "vital role" suggests that the writer believes that a college education is very important. The final phrase of the sentence, "believing that college is unnecessary for success," suggests that many students underestimate the important role of college. So we know that we need to find a word that means "underestimate."

When we look at the answer choices, we know we can eliminate choice C because "overestimate" is the opposite of "underestimate."

Although both "mistake" (choice A) and "misunderstand" (choice D) could work in the sentence because they both suggest that students don't see the value of a college education, both of these words are too general. Neither "mistake" nor "misunderstand" clarifies that the student's lack of understanding causes them to underestimate the value of a college education.

This leaves us with choice B, "undervalue," as the correct answer.

RECOGNIZING CONCISION QUESTIONS

Concision questions can be a little harder to identify. As with precision questions, the test will sometimes give you a big clue by asking, "Which of the following is the most concise replacement for the underlined portion?" The key word "concise" tells you that this is a concision question. Other times, concision questions may be harder to spot. As with precision questions, some concision questions will simply provide you with answer choices without giving you a specific question. The answer choices will generally be synonymous or superfluous alternatives to the underlined portion of the sentence.

TOPIC OVERVIEW: CONCISION

There are two primary concepts to keep in mind when confronted with concision questions.

Wordiness

The first is wordiness. Good writers never use five words when one will do. When faced with a concision question, we always look for the answer that provides the same meaning in fewer words, which helps to eliminate wordiness. Let's look at some of the most common mistakes that lead to wordiness:

PASSIVE VOICE

There are times when passive voice is acceptable in writing, but as a general rule, it's best to use active voice. One reason for this is wordiness: Passive voice is more likely to result in unnecessarily long sentences. Let's look at some examples:

Example 6: The award was given to Susan by the coach.

Example 7: The coach gave Susan the award.

Example 6, which is written in passive voice, takes up 9 words. Example 7, which says the same thing using active voice, takes only 6 words. On the SAT, if you have a choice between active voice and passive voice, active voice will almost always be the more correct choice, especially when dealing with wordiness.

UNNECESSARY THIS AND THAT

Sentences can often be combined or shortened by eliminating words like "this," "that," or "which." Let's look at some examples:

Example 8: Good writers always begin by planning. This is because planning makes writing easier.

Example 9: Good writers always begin by planning, making writing easier.

Both of these examples say the same thing, but by combining the sentences and eliminating "this is because…" we can trim the word count from 13 words to 9 words.

"THERE IS," "IT IS," AND "THERE ARE"

By eliminating these phrases from the beginnings of sentences, we can reduce wordiness and make sentences more interesting. Let's look at some examples:

Example 10: There are too many students in this class.

Example 11: This class has too many students.

When a sentence begins with a phrase like "There are," we can often make the sentence more concise by altering the sentence structure to eliminate the phrase.

Example 10, for instance, contains 8 words. By changing the sentence structure in Example 11, we were able to reduce the word count to 6 words.

Redundancy

The second concept to keep in mind with concision questions is redundancy. Redundancy occurs when there is needless repetition of words, phrases, or ideas within a given sentence or paragraph. Let's look at some examples:

Example 12: During the Great Depression, millions of people who were once employed lost their jobs.

Example 13: During the Great Depression, millions of people lost their jobs.

In Example 12, the phrase "who were once employed" is redundant. If the people lost their jobs, then they had to have had jobs in the first place; the fact that they were once employed is already implied in the sentence. Eliminating the redundant phrase, as we've done in Example 13, makes the sentence much shorter without sacrificing clarity or meaning.

ANSWERING CONCISION QUESTIONS

Concision questions are best answered by selecting the answer that expresses the same idea as the original in the fewest number of words. To arrive at the correct answer, follow these steps:

1. Read the entire sentence containing the underlined portion. Identify any redundancies in the sentence.
2. Read the sentences immediately before and after the sentence containing the underlined portion. Identify any redundancies.
3. Choose the answer choice that maintains the same clarity and meaning.
4. Re-read the sentence with the answer choice you've selected. Ensure that the answer choice does not create any new redundancies.

Let's practice these steps with an example.

Example 14:

Experts recommend that people <u>create emergency plans ahead of time in order to be prepared for natural disasters</u> such as tornadoes, hurricanes, or blizzards.

> A) NO CHANGE
> B) plan ahead of time to prepare for natural disasters
> C) create emergency plans for natural disasters
> D) be prepared for natural disasters

There are some redundancies in this sentence. First, a plan is generally prepared in advance, so the phrase "ahead of time" is redundant. Second, the phrase "in

order to be prepared" is redundant because being prepared is the purpose of an emergency plan.

We can skip step 2 for this example because it has been removed from the surrounding paragraph.

Based on the redundancies within the sentence, we know that we can eliminate choices A and B, so we must decide between C and D. Although choice D is shorter, which might make it seem more concise, choice D loses clarify and meaning. Experts are not merely recommending that people be prepared for disasters; they are recommending that people prepare by creating emergency plans. Because choice C is both concise and specific, choice C is the correct answer.

Lesson wY5
Effective Language Use – Concision and Precision
Learning to Swim

CONCEPT EXERCISE:

Directions: Re-write the underlined portion of each sentence to correct errors in concision and precision. Some sentences may have no errors.

1. The area of Texas known as the Big Bend <u>has often been talked about ~~and described~~ as a scientist's paradise.</u>

2. Geologists find the region to be a trove of information because the area's sparse vegetation allows the various layers of rock and soil to be easily <u>contemplated</u>.

3. The intense scientific interest in the Big Bend <u>is also a ~~fact that is due in part to the~~ complex geologic history of the area, which presents a unique challenge to students and researchers.</u>

4. The abundance, diversity, <u>and ~~also~~ complexity of visible rock outcrops ~~that can be easily seen~~</u> are staggering, particularly to first-time observers.

5. The region is sparsely populated, arid, and rugged, making it <u>~~a place where not many people would want~~ to visit or stay.</u> *an undesirable place*

6. <u>~~When viewed~~ from space</u>, the Big Bend appears to be as desolate and empty as the moon.

7. *Despite* <u>~~Although~~ the region's apparent emptiness ~~may sometimes make it seem barren~~</u>, it is home to more than 1,200 species of plants, 450 species of birds, 56 species of reptiles, and 75 species of mammals.

8. This exceptional diversity of animal- and plant-life results from a wide <u>~~alteration~~ in</u> climate across the region, which ranges in altitude from 1,800 feet to nearly 8,000 feet. *variation*

9. Interestingly, the region's emptiness makes the Big Bend National Park <u>one of ~~just only~~ ten places ~~on the planet Earth~~</u> certified for dark sky stargazing, which may be why the region is home to the McDonald Observatory. *the only*

10. Researchers who visit the Big Bend often do so to study either astronomy or geology, and the region is perfect for studying either <u>field</u>.

11. Although researchers believe the earth to be approximately 4.6 billion years old, the oldest rocks that have been found in the Big Bend region are <u>only about 500 million years old, ~~which, according to many researchers, is much younger than the earth itself~~</u>.

12. Initial commentary on the geology of the Big Bend <u>was provided by early-day daring and adventurous explorers and discoverers ~~in the 1800s~~.</u>

13. Subsequent studies by <u>~~numerous~~ 20th century researchers</u> have helped to reconstruct the complex geologic history of the Big Bend.

14. Until about 300 million years ago, a deep-ocean trough had extended from present-day Arkansas and Oklahoma into the Big Bend region of Texas; <u>this trough existed for an approximate period of about 200 million years ~~or more~~.</u>

15. Sediment from higher altitudes to the north accumulated in that trough, <u>gathering, layering, ~~and building~~ to form layers</u> of gravel, sand, and clay.

16. With the passing of time, these layers formed sandstone and shale beds.

17. About 300 million years ago, these layers were squeezed upward as two land masses met, a geologic event that formed the ancestral Ouachita Mountains.

18. Subsequent erosion over an interval of 160 million years left only the roots of those mountains visible; the tops of the mountains have worn away.

19. Today, these mountain remnants can be observed in southeastern Oklahoma, in the immediate vicinity of Marathon, Texas. and

20. Together with the Ozark Mountains, the Ouachita Mountains form the U.S. Interior Highlands, one of the few major mountainous regions with high altitudes between the Rocky Mountains and the Appalachian Mountains.

Lesson wY5
Effective Language Use – Concision and Precision
Diving into the Deep End

PRACTICE EXERCISE:

Directions: Answer the questions that accompany the following passages.

A Day in the Life

Putting yourself in other people's shoes is a **(1)** great, fantastic way to really learn what they do every day and how we can make their lives better. This week, I joined the President's "Day in the Life" effort. Throughout the summer, senior administrators are **(2)** touring the country speaking with—and learning from—the people we work for every day.

While in Los Angeles this past week, I had such fun spending time with two extraordinary individuals—Matthew Gonzales, **(3)** an employee who works at the U.S. Air Force Space and Missile Systems Center, and Megan Rodriguez, an Air Force veteran who works for the state of California as an employment assistant helping other veterans find jobs. Both are young Latinos driven by a **(4)** passion for public service.

Matthew entered the federal government as an intern for Pathways, a program that brings the best young talent into government and **(5)** sets them on the path to the beginning of a federal career. Matthew is now a civilian program manager at the space and missile center. He also co-led the first chapter of Young Government Leaders in Los Angeles.

1. A) NO CHANGE
   B) great way to really, truly learn
   C) great way to learn and find out
   D) great way to learn

2. Which version of the underlined word fits best in the context of the passage?

   A) NO CHANGE
   B) moving around
   C) migrating
   D) sightseeing

3. A) NO CHANGE
   B) a working employee
   C) an employee
   D) who is

4. Based on the context of the passage, which word is most appropriate?

   A) NO CHANGE
   B) fury
   C) warmth
   D) craving

5. A) NO CHANGE
   B) sets them up to begin the path of a federal career
   C) sets them on the path to a federal career
   D) sets their federal career to begin

Matthew shared an extraordinary **(6)** <u>thing</u> with me. At his job, he is exposed to a wide variety of tasks, **(7)** <u>and he is experiencing and doing many of these tasks for the first time</u>. While he is not always expected to know everything right away, he *is* always expected to learn. Matthew takes pride in learning, and he knows he has the support and tools that he needs to keep growing. That is part of the reason why he believes the federal government is a great place to start his career. That spirit of service is exactly what our nation needs. I know that Matthew is one of hundreds of thousands of federal employees with that same enthusiasm.

Megan has a passion for helping **(8)** <u>coexistent</u> veterans find jobs. While attending Mount St. Mary's College, she founded its Veterans Outreach Association, **(9)** <u>and she has continued that work now that she has graduated from college</u>. We discussed our shared passion for helping women veterans get federal jobs. She would be a great fit in the federal government.

In Matthew and Megan, I saw so many positive qualities: passion, dedication, an overwhelming desire to help people, and a truly hopeful vision **(10)** <u>for what will happen in the future</u>. Their insights helped me understand firsthand what young Latinos are thinking and what we need to do to attract them to federal service. I know there are obstacles they face each day, but their commitment to public service makes me confident that we will continue to have a **(11)** <u>different,</u> talented, caring, and devoted federal workforce.

6. Which word provides the most precise replacement for the underlined word, based on the context of the passage?

   A) object
   B) joke
   C) task
   D) fact

7. A) NO CHANGE
   B) and he is doing these tasks, many of them for the first time
   C) and many of them are being experienced for the first time
   D) many of which are first-time experiences

8. Based on the context of the passage, which word is most appropriate?

   A) NO CHANGE
   B) equivalent
   C) fellow
   D) matching

9. A) NO CHANGE
   B) work that she has continued since graduating
   C) and that work has been something she has continued since graduating
   D) which is work that she has continued after graduating from college

10. A) NO CHANGE
    B) for the future
    C) for the events that will happen in the future
    D) for the events that will happen

11. Which version of the underlined word fits best in the context of the passage?

    A) NO CHANGE
    B) contrasting
    C) diverse
    D) mismatched

TEST EXERCISE:

Phthalates

[1]

(1) Phthalates might be the world's latest underappreciated public health threat. Phthalates (pronounced "THAY-lates") are ubiquitous in many types of commercial products, and nearly all people have detectable quantities of **(2)** it in their bloodstreams. An increasing body of research suggests that these chemicals may be harmful.

[2]

Phthalates, or phthalate esters, are synthetic chemicals added to plastics to increase their flexibility and durability. Phthalates are used in a large variety of **(3)** products, including adhesives and glues, electronics, building materials such as PVC pipe, medical devices, packaging, and even cosmetics.

[3]

Phthalates are easily released into the environment—for example, exposure to heat or strong solvents can cause them to leach out of plastic. They may enter food products prepared or stored in plastic; diet is **(4)** what is believed by people to be the main source of some phthalates in humans. A 2012 Swedish study found that phthalates from PVC flooring were found in the bodies of children, showing that phthalates can also be absorbed through the skin.

1. Which of the following revisions to this sentence would result in the clearest, most logical introduction of the essay's topic?

   A) NO CHANGE
   B) Replace "Phthalates" with "A class of chemicals found in many plastics"
   C) Replace "might be" with "are without a doubt"
   D) Replace "public health threat" with "pollutant"

2. A) NO CHANGE
   B) it in one's bloodstream
   C) phthalates in their bloodstreams
   D) them in one's bloodstream

3. A) NO CHANGE
   B) products: including
   C) products; including
   D) products including:

4. A) NO CHANGE
   B) what people believe may be
   C) believed to be
   D) believed, according to some,

[4]

[1] The biggest concern about phthalates is **(5)** how they could be endocrine disruptors. [2] The body's endocrine system produces hormones, chemical messengers that tell cells what to do by "binding" to receptors on the cells' surfaces, like a key fits into a lock. [3] An endocrine disruptor is a substance that either blocks a hormone from working or **(6)** imitating a hormone and binding to receptors itself. [4] One famous endocrine disruptor is DDT, an insecticide that was banned in the U.S. in 1972. [5] Because hormones work in very small doses, even a tiny amount of an endocrine disruptor can disrupt proper cell function. {7}

[5]

[1] Endocrine disruptors have been linked to effects ranging from learning disabilities to reproductive problems. [2] Studies have found that phthalates **(8)** can cause birth defects in rats. [3] A British study showed that the phthalate DBP suppresses steroidogenesis in fetal Leydig cells in both primates and rodents. [4] In 2009, South Korean scientists reported findings tentatively linking phthalate exposure to ADHD (attention deficit hyperactivity disorder). [5] More research is needed on phthalate effects on humans, as our current knowledge is based on relatively few studies. {9}

5. A) NO CHANGE
   B) they could be
   C) being possibly
   D) that they may act as

6. A) NO CHANGE
   B) imitates a hormone and binds
   C) else it imitates a hormone and binds
   D) it can imitate a hormone and bind

7. In this paragraph, Sentence 5 would most logically and cohesively be placed

   A) where it is now.
   B) after Sentence 1.
   C) after Sentence 2.
   D) after Sentence 3.

8. A) NO CHANGE
   B) would cause
   C) were causing
   D) had caused

9. Which sentence in Paragraph 5 is inconsistent with the tone and style of the essay and should be removed or altered?

   A) Sentence 2
   B) Sentence 3
   C) Sentence 4
   D) Sentence 5

[6]

The existing research prompted Congress to ban the use of phthalates in children's toys in 2008, but **(10)** <u>a more far-reaching ban may well be warranted</u>. Industry spokespeople claim there is no conclusive evidence that phthalate exposure occurs at harmful levels in adults, but a lack of information does not justify inaction. There was a time when the science was inconclusive about DDT, lead and asbestos. {11} In such cases, <u>you better walk on the safe side!</u>

10. Which choice for the underlined portion is most consistent with the tone and overall thesis of the essay?

A) NO CHANGE
B) the looming danger of phthalates from other sources continues to menace us all
C) it caved in to corporate demands by refusing to pass a total ban
D) the time for a broader ban may not yet have come

11. Which choice for the underlined portion is most consistent with the tone of the essay as a whole?

A) NO CHANGE
B) it is better to be safe than sorry.
C) there is a case to be made that the precautionary principle should be applied.
D) can't be too careful!

Lesson wY5
Effective Language Use – Concision and Precision
Race to the Finish

HOMEWORK EXERCISE 1:

Directions: Re-write the underlined portion of each sentence to correct errors in concision and precision.

1. Because he had a note from his doctor, Ramiro was excused from ~~having to participate in~~ gym class.

2. Marlena won ~~something in~~ the lottery, so now she can buy a big house.

3. The Tibetan people use yak's milk to make butter, and ~~they~~ make sculptures out of yak butter.

4. The fuels that power plants ~~can be~~ run on include many types of fuel, including coal, natural gas, and nuclear material.

5. When writing a story, it is good to always use ~~good~~ words that help your readers imagine the story's events.

6. In geometry, it is said that the shortest path between any two points forms a line segment.

7. American fans of the Japanese video game *Translated* ~~made~~ *Play* it into English so that more people could ~~do~~ it.

8. Captain James Cook was one of the prior European explorers to exchange ~~things~~ *goods* with many Polynesian cultures.

9. Because of the way that the singer used her voice, her words were sung in a high-pitched tone.

10. His implausible story led many to think that he was a liar, but ~~the reality was that~~ the story was actually true.

11. In recent years, the majority of college graduates have ~~lately proven to be~~ *been* women.

12. The *Spirit of St. Louis* is the machine that Charles Lindbergh flew across the water from New York to France on his record-breaking 1927 voyage.

13. The herbal sleep aid can be accepted as the reason that I was finally able to sleep in a peaceful manner.

14. My birthday, like most people's, only lasted for a while, but I ~~managed to have~~ *had* three parties, so I received many ~~things~~ *gifts*.

15. Though Kate's worldview is largely optimistic and hopeful, she has slowly acquired the negative opinions about government ~~that she has gradually grown to have.~~

16. ~~I experienced the passing of a large amount of time as~~ *passed as* I painstakingly assembled this collection of photographs.

17. The lawyer presented her words ~~to the people~~ and hoped that they would deliver a "not guilty" statement to the judge.

18. As Rudy struggled to ride a bicycle without falling over, he had difficulty keeping his balance.

19. If I were not so full of pizza, I would agree with ~~you that~~ *yess* your suggestion of ording dessert ~~is a good idea.~~ *yess*

20. Carter would have had the spelling bee if he had not left out one ~~thing~~ *letter* when he did "insouciant."

HOMEWORK EXERCISE 2:

The Death of Vacation

Americans are too scared to go on vacation. According to the U.S. Travel Association and GfK, a market research firm, about 40 percent of American workers don't plan on using all of **(1)** their paid time off this year.

[1] The two most common reasons workers give for not taking a break are the dread of returning to a pile of incomplete tasks and the fear that no one else is capable of filling in for them. [2] Researchers have come to call this "the martyr complex." [3] Many employees claim that they enjoy working. [4] More than twenty percent of workers say they aren't taking all of their vacation days because they don't want to appear replaceable. [5] Insecurity seems to be crippling Americans into staying at work. {2}

"Fundamentally what's going on there is fear," said Michael **(3)** Leiter – a psychology professor at Acadia University who studies people's relationship with their work. "People are afraid if they're not present and they're not continually churning stuff out that bad things are going to happen."

{4} This number proves to be a historic low. In the 1970s, about eighty percent of American workers took a week-long vacation every year, according to a recent analysis by Vox. Today, that number has **(5)** lapsed to barely above fifty percent.

Compounding this fear of taking time off is the "perception…that being away from work means we're bad employees," according to Chris Moessner, vice president of public affairs at GfK. The modern work culture in the U.S. **(6)** has became almost an enslaving force for many Americans.

1. A) NO CHANGE
   B) its
   C) his
   D) our

2. Which of the following sentences should be removed in order to improve the focus of the paragraph?

   A) Sentence 1
   B) Sentence 2
   C) Sentence 3
   D) Sentence 4

3. A) NO CHANGE
   B) Leiter; a
   C) Leiter. A
   D) Leiter, a

4. For the sake of the logical flow of the passage, this paragraph should be

   A) left where it is
   B) before the first paragraph
   C) between the first and second paragraphs
   D) between the second and third paragraphs

5. Which of the following is the most precise replacement for the underlined word?

   A) NO CHANGE
   B) fallen
   C) lowered
   D) failed

6. A) NO CHANGE
   B) became
   C) has becoming
   D) has become

HW 7/2

{7} The declining popularity of vacations **(8)** <u>have</u> broad effects not only on workers but also **(9)** <u>on employers and the overall economy are affected</u>. Studies have found that taking fewer vacations is correlated with increased risk of heart disease in both men and women. Other research has shown that workers who take vacations–or even smaller breaks like naps or walks–are more productive when they return. This proves to be a serious issue for companies looking to get as much as possible out of their employees, particularly because many jobs require workers to show up with the capacity to contribute intellectually and creatively.

However, employers do little to encourage workers to take time off. Two-thirds of surveyed employees report that their bosses **(10)** <u>mix and confuse messages</u> or actually discourage vacations. According to the Center for Economic and Policy Research, The United States is the only "advanced" economy that doesn't require companies to give paid vacation days. **(11)** One way to push workers to take all of their time off is to implement a "use it or lose it" policy, which means that vacation days don't roll over from year to year.

7. Which of the following creates the best transition from the previous paragraph?

   A) This decreased vacation time correlates to declining health.
   B) As a result of decreased vacation time, employers need to hire smarter and more artistic people.
   C) Although this would seem to greatly benefit employers, the decline of vacations has wide-ranging negative effects.
   D) Naps are crucial to employee productivity.

8. A) NO CHANGE
   B) has
   C) having
   D) had

9. A) NO CHANGE
   B) on employers and the overall economy as well
   C) on employers, and also on the overall economy
   D) on employers and the overall economy

10. A) NO CHANGE
    B) send confusing messages that are mixed
    C) confusingly send mixed messages
    D) send mixed messages

11. Which of the following sentences, if added here, would best improve the flow of the paragraph?

    A) The CEPR recommends several ways in which employers can encourage their workers to take a break.
    B) Multiple economies have arisen in the past decade.
    C) Some workers take twenty vacation days per year.
    D) The CEPR was begun to monitor changing job trends in the U.S.

Lesson wY6
Pronoun Errors
Getting Your Feet Wet

Directions: The questions below are intended as a short diagnostic exam:

1. For members of the admissions board, no personal feelings affect their <u>decision; it considers</u> each application objectively, based on merit.

    A) NO CHANGE
    B) decision, it considers
    C) decision; they consider
    D) decision, they consider

2. When considering which colleges one wishes to <u>attend, we must</u> take into account not only the prestige of the college in question but also the cost of tuition and availability of scholarships.

    A) NO CHANGE
    B) attend; we must
    C) attend, we should
    D) attend, one must

Lesson wY6
Pronoun Errors
Wading In

TOPIC OVERVIEW: PRONOUN ERRORS

Pronouns take the place of nouns to make writing less repetitive. In this lesson, we'll discuss some of the pronoun errors that appear on the SAT.

TOPIC OVERVIEW: PRONOUN AGREEMENT

The noun that a pronoun replaces is called an antecedent. Just as subjects must agree with verbs, so must pronouns agree with antecedents.

Agreement in Number

When a pronoun replaces a singular noun, the pronoun must also be singular; when it takes the place of a plural noun, the pronoun must be plural. This is called number agreement. Although it seems like a simple enough concept, number agreement can be confusing in certain sentences.

Example 1: Each of the dancers follows a strict diet and exercise regimen; he or she must maintain the same weight in order to participate in the upcoming show.

In this example, the pronoun *he or she* in the second clause is referring back to the subject *Each of the dancers*. Each is singular, so the pronoun must be singular.

Many writers use the pronoun *they* as a pronoun that doesn't specify gender, but because *they* is considered to be a plural pronoun, it should not be used to refer to singular nouns in formal writing.

Agreement in Person

The "person" of a pronoun refers to first, second, and third person. Here is a chart showing the different pronouns for each person:

First Person	I, we, me, us
Second Person	you
Third Person	he, she, it, one, they, him, her, them

Writers must use the same person, or point of view, throughout a sentence. Let's look at some examples:

Example 2: *I* am looking forward to next month's book club meeting because *they* are reading my favorite book.

In this example, the writer has switched from the first person to the third person. To correct the error, we need to make both pronouns first person pronouns:

Example 3: *I* am looking forward to next month's book club meeting because *we* are reading my favorite book.

Another common error when dealing with pronoun person is to change from third person to second person.

Example 4: When *one* is applying to college, *you* should proofread the application before submitting.

To correct the error in this sentence, we must either make both pronouns second person pronouns or third person pronouns – we can't mix and match.

Example 5: When *one* is applying to college, *one* should proofread the application before submitting.

Example 6: When *you* are applying to college, *you* should proofread the application before submitting.

TOPIC OVERVIEW: PRONOUN CASE

When we discuss the "case" of a pronoun, we are referring to whether it is being used as the subject or the object in a sentence. The table below summarizes the information about pronoun case:

Subject Case

	singular	plural
1st person	I	we
2nd person	you	you
3rd person	he/she/it/one	they

Object Case

	singular	plural
1st person	me	us
2nd person	you	you
3rd person	him/her/it/one	them

When solving a question involving pronouns, we need to figure out whether the pronoun is being used as a subject or as an object. Then we need to make sure that the correct version of the pronoun is used in the sentence. Remember that the subject of a sentence performs the action, and the object of a sentence has the action performed on it.

Example 7: When we were much younger, *my brother and I* got into trouble frequently.

We use the pronoun *I* (and not *me*) in the sentence because the phrase *my brother and I* acts as the subject of the sentence.

<u>Example 8:</u> My mother often sent *my brother and me* to time out.
Because the phrase *my brother and me* is the object of the verb *sent,* we need to use the object pronoun *me* and not *I*.

This topic tends to confuse people because well-intentioned teachers or relatives may have insisted that correct grammar requires *my brother and I* all the time, without taking case into account. One simple test is to take apart the compound sentence or object and use the pronoun by itself—you wouldn't say *my mother sent I to time out,* so it would be inappropriate to use *I* in this example.

TOPIC OVERVIEW: AMBIGUOUS REFERENCE

An ambiguous pronoun is a pronoun for which the antecedent is unclear. Let's look at an example:

<u>Example 9:</u> Hannah and Grace loved *her* new puppy.

In this sentence, *her* is an unclear pronoun – whose puppy did Hannah and Grace love? To correct the error, we have to specify who the puppy belonged to:

<u>Example 10:</u> Hannah and Grace loved *Grace's* new puppy.

This sentence is relatively simple to fix because the sentence itself gives us two potential antecedents. Sometimes an unclear pronoun will refer to an antecedent that is not actually identified in the sentence:

<u>Example 11:</u> When Grace adopted the puppy, *they* told her that he was already housetrained.

Although we can probably figure out that *they* refers to the people from whom Grace adopted the puppy, the sentence fails to make this clear, which means that the pronoun has no antecedent. To correct the problem, we must clarify who *they* are:

<u>Example 12:</u> When Grace adopted the puppy, *the staff at the shelter* told her that he was already housetrained.

This same problem is very common with the pronoun *it*. Let's look at another example:

<u>Example 13:</u> Although the puppy was usually very obedient, *it* did not seem to apply to his housetraining.

In this sentence, *it* is an unclear pronoun. *It* does not refer to *puppy*; *it* refers to obedience. Because the sentence fails to make this clear, we have to fix the pronoun reference:

<u>Example 14:</u> Although the puppy was usually very obedient, *his obedience* did not seem to apply to his housetraining.

TOPIC OVERVIEW: RELATIVE PRONOUNS

Relative pronouns introduce relative clauses, which are dependent clauses that modify something within the sentence. They are called *relative* pronouns because they *relate* to the word that the relative clause modifies. Like all pronouns, relative pronouns must agree with their antecedent.

The two types of relative clause are **essential** (defining the antecedent and giving necessary information) and **nonessential** (giving extra, unnecessary information). To review the concept of essential and nonessential clauses, look back at lesson 4, where we talked about nonessential elements. We will also discuss this concept in lesson 13.

First, let's talk about relative pronouns in essential clauses. Here is a table that shows the relative pronouns we might use in an essential relative clause:

Type of pronoun...	*Used in reference to...*				
	<u>People</u>	<u>Things or Concepts</u>	<u>Place</u>	<u>Time</u>	<u>Explanation</u>
<u>Subject</u>	who, that	that			
<u>Object</u>	that, who, whom	that	where	when	what/why
<u>Possessive</u>	whose	whose, of which			

As you can see in the chart, we only use the pronoun *who* to refer to people. We can use *that* for either people or non-people. Of course there are exceptions to this rule. We can also use *who* to refer to non-humans that either are personified or possess human-like traits. So, for example, we could use *who* to refer to Watson (the computer who won *Jeopardy*), Wall-E (the robot from the film of the same name), Yoda (an intelligent alien), or Goofy (a fictional character).

Let's look at some examples of pronoun use in essential relative clauses:

<u>Example 15</u>: The house *that* had those horrible holiday decorations is now for sale.
<u>Example 16</u>: The real estate agent *that* is selling the house is my neighbor.
<u>Example 17</u>: The real estate agent *who* is selling the house is my neighbor.

In Example 15, we use *that* because we are referring to an object (the house). In Examples 16 and 17, we can use either *that* or *who* because we are referring to a person (the real estate agent).

The rules for using pronouns in nonessential relative clauses are similar, except that we usually use *which* instead of *that* to refer to a thing. Though there are exceptions to the rule, if a relative clause is set off by commas, we should use *which* instead of *that*. Let's look at some examples:

Example 18: The house, *that* was not well cared for, needs a lot of work.

Example 19: The house, *which* was not well cared for, needs a lot of work.

Because the relative clause is not very important to the overall meaning of the sentence, it is a nonessential clause and should be set off with commas. In this case, it is incorrect to use *that,* so we use *which* instead.

One final concern regarding relative pronouns is the issue of *who* and *whom*. If we look at the table of relative pronouns, we see that *whom* is only used to refer to people who are the object of the sentence or the object of a preposition. Let's look at some examples:

Example 20: *Who* will be your lab partner?

Example 21: *Whom* have you chosen as a lab partner?

Example 22: I am not sure with *whom* I will be lab partners.

In Example 20, *who* refers to the subject; in Example 21, *whom* refers to the object; and in Example 22, *whom* refers to the object of the preposition *with*. If all of this seems confusing, follow this simple process: If *who/whom* could refer to *him*, use *whom*; if *who/whom* could refer to *he*, use *who*. So in Example 21, we would say *he will be my lab partner*, so we use *who*. In Example 22, we would say *I have chosen him as my lab partner*, so we use *whom*.

ANSWERING PRONOUN QUESTIONS

Answering pronoun questions requires identifying the type of error. To identify the pronoun error, follow these steps:

1. Identify the pronoun in the sentence.
2. Identify the antecedent to which the pronoun refers. If the antecedent is not made clear in the sentence, then the error in question is an ambiguous pronoun reference.
3. If the antecedent is clear, check to be sure that the pronoun agrees with the antecedent in number and in person. If not, the error is a lack of pronoun-antecedent agreement.
4. If there is more than one pronoun in the sentence, and if the pronouns refer to the same antecedent, make sure that the pronouns are in the same person. If not, error is a lack of agreement in person.
5. Identify whether the pronoun is the subject or the object of a verb. Ensure that the pronoun is in the correct case. If not, the error is a pronoun case error.
6. If the pronoun is a relative pronoun, ensure that the correct relative pronoun is used. Remember that *that* can refer to people or things, but *who* can only refer to people (or things that are very similar to people).

Lesson wY6
Pronoun Errors
Learning to Swim

CONCEPT EXERCISE:

Directions: Find and correct errors in the following sentences. Some sentences will not have any errors.

1. When one has lost something, ~~you~~ *one* should always retrace your steps to try and find it.

2. When Felicia bumped into Mrs. Brinton, ~~her~~ *Felicia's* glasses slipped from her face and fell to the ground.

3. Although our mother generally tried very hard to be patient with us, she would still sometimes scold ~~my sisters and I~~ *me and my sisters* on long car trips.

4. Teachers and parents may try to instill good values into children, but ultimately each child must decide for ~~themselves~~ *himself or herself* what they think is right or wrong.

5. The ballerina, which practically stole the show, totally amazed the audience with her grace and beauty.

6. The rambunctious piglet ran into the billy goat at full speed, which caused ~~it~~ *the piglet* to lose its balance and topple over.

7. While the principal always felt the music teacher was difficult and too demanding, ~~he in~~ the band always appreciated his passion and dynamic *had* leadership.

8. When it seemed that everything that could go wrong on our date had gone wrong, my boyfriend and I couldn't help but laugh about it.

9. I screeched on the brakes to avoid hitting the little fawn in the road, who in turn only looked at me with a quizzical expression.

10. Mr. Cadorna was an insufferable know-it-all, always going around telling everybody how ignorant or mistaken they were. *he or she*

11. The regiment got lost several times after its commander was injured; without ~~his~~ *the commander's* leadership, they seemed lost.

12. Dennis pitched a fit after Dale accidentally broke his new toy; ~~he~~ *Dale* was always doing things like this.

13. Erica and ~~me~~ *I* got a good hearty laugh out of the ridiculously ornate decorative umbrella in my smoothie.

14. In addition to cooking more traditionally American fare, the celebrity chef also dabbled in Chinese and Japanese cuisine, and had even written several books on ~~it~~ *them*.

15. The City Assembly was so tired and frustrated with everyone blaming ~~them~~ *it* for everything that went wrong.

16. Snow White saw the dwarves off to work every morning, making certain to give each of them a kiss on ~~their~~ *his* head before they walked out the door.

17. Acrobats must have nerves of steel, as well as bodies in peak physical condition; if they make one faltering movement, ~~you~~ *they* might very well endanger ~~yourself~~ *themselves* or ~~your~~ *their* partner.

18. Many Italians feel a special reverence for Byron, Shelley, and Keats, all of ~~which~~ *whom* lived extensively in Italy.

19. Pooh and Christopher Robin wandered through the wood, talking about the weather, but the whole time all ~~he~~ *Pooh* could really think about was honey.

20. My heart swelled when I read my girlfriend's love-letter; the letter was so passionate yet eloquent.

Lesson wY6
Pronoun Errors
Diving Into the Deep End

PRACTICE EXERCISE:

Directions: Answer the questions that accompany the following passages.

Orangutan Research

Virtually every animal behavior study begins with finding an animal and recording its behavior at a given interval to produce what's called an *ethogram*. As a researcher specializing in orangutan behavior, I have been able to experience **(1)** this process first-hand.

Before one can track an orangutan, **(2)** you must find one. Orangutans are exceptionally difficult to study because they live in low densities and are widely dispersed in thick jungle habitats.

While searching, ~~each~~ person in our group creeps along the path while **(3)** they look for any new nests or discarded fruit, stopping regularly to listen for the telltale signs of an orangutan: the crunch of fruit being eaten, a branch breaking in the distance, or a long-call, a vocalization meant to attract mates.

Until **(4)** us researchers got our "jungle legs," this was all much easier said than done. At first, most of our time was spent watching **(5)** one's feet, crashing through the undergrowth, falling into streams and missing any signs of an orangutan. Despite the difficulties inherent in finding orangutans, however, it is possible.

Once **(6)** we have found an orangutan, we will spend our next several days following it. A "follow day" starts at 4 or 5 a.m. The goal is to follow the animal from the time it wakes up until the time it builds its nest for the evening. Every two minutes, we note down a dizzying amount of information, including a shorthand code for the animal's behavior, **(7)** their height in the jungle canopy, and myriad other observations related to social activities and travel. It sounds complicated, but these observation methods are actually standardized. **(8)** They are able to share their data, helping us make valuable comparisons.

1. A) NO CHANGE
   B) them
   C) these
   D) it

2. A) NO CHANGE
   B) we
   C) one
   D) they

3. A) NO CHANGE
   B) it looks
   C) you look
   D) he or she looks

4. A) NO CHANGE
   B) my fellow researchers and I
   C) me and my fellow researchers
   D) the researchers

5. A) NO CHANGE
   B) our
   C) your
   D) the

6. A) NO CHANGE
   B) one has
   C) he has
   D) they have

7. A) NO CHANGE
   B) its
   C) it's
   D) they're

8. A) NO CHANGE
   B) These methods
   C) The standards
   D) Researchers

Often the animal is out of sight, resting, or asleep. I'm sure every orangutan researcher has a favorite story of a day **(9)** he or she spent watching an individual who woke up, moved 6 meters to a fig tree, and proceeded to eat at an invisible height for 14 long and boring hours.

Other times, **(10)** it's flying through the jungle, forcing **(11)** the field assistants and I to keep up. Once we've been following an individual for ten hours or more, we're thankful when it makes its nest, signaling that it's time to head back to camp. Typically, we repeat this process with each orangutan for five days to ten days within a given month.

Orangutan research requires long, occasionally boring days and careful concentration, and some days I wonder why I chose to study orangutans. But the honest truth is: the good days – when the orangutans are behaving in the most astoundingly intelligent way, making us gasp and laugh as we follow them – make up for everything else.

9. A) NO CHANGE
   B) they
   C) we
   D) him or her

10. A) NO CHANGE
    B) we are
    C) the orangutan is
    D) the search is

11. A) NO CHANGE
    B) I and the field assistants
    C) the field assistants and myself
    D) the field assistants and me

TEST EXERCISE:

A Short-Sighted Speech?

The latest buzzword in the ever-shifting politics of American education is STEM. For the uninitiated, STEM is an acronym for Science, Technology, Engineering, and Math. **(1)** More relatedly, to hear many elected officials and well-meaning school reformers tell it, it's the only thing a young graduate can hope to get a decent job in anymore. An English major, you say? **(2)** You might as well get in line to apply at Burger King.

When it comes to STEM, Florida Governor Rick Scott is a true believer. In a 2011 interview published in the Sarasota Herald-Tribune, **(3)** it sparked controversy as Scott not only said Florida's public universities should devote more money to STEM programs and less to the humanities, but seemingly suggested that experts in less technical fields were not needed in Florida.

"We don't need a lot more anthropologists in the state," said Scott. "It's a great degree if people want to get it, but we don't need them here."

1. A) NO CHANGE
   B) The relevant part being
   C) More to the point
   D) To clarify what is truly meant

2. Which choice for the underlined sentence supports the author's characterization of the views of "many elected officials and… reformers"?
   A) NO CHANGE
   B) That would not qualify as a STEM field.
   C) You will probably need more years of schooling.
   D) Why would anyone want to study something so useless?

3. A) NO CHANGE
   B) Scott sparked controversy as he
   C) sparking controversy, it
   D) he sparked controversy as it

The governor's comments, to no one's surprise, didn't sit well with one group of **(4)** <u>people in particular:</u> anthropologists. Many quickly leapt to their profession's defense, accusing the governor of ignorance of **(5)** <u>their many</u> practical, and profitable, applications. Brent Weisman, chair of the Department of Anthropology at the University of South Florida (USF), retorted, "Anthropologists at USF work side by side with civil and industrial engineers, cancer researchers, specialists in public health and medicine, chemists, biologists, and others in the science, technology, and engineering fields that the governor so eagerly applauds." {6}

Students in Weisman's department prepared an online **(7)** <u>presentation, in it</u> various anthropologists describe their jobs. One helps doctors understand the cultural issues that complicate improving health care for migrant farm workers. Another advises businesses on cultural differences that affect international negotiations. Yet another, a forensic anthropologist, helps detectives reconstruct the events that led to a crime scene.

4. A) NO CHANGE
   B) people, in particular
   C) people, in particular,
   D) people in particular,

5. A) NO CHANGE
   B) one's many
   C) many of their
   D) its many

6. Which addition to this paragraph would best support the claim that anthropology is a relevant and practical field of study?

   A) A criticism of low salaries for anthropologists
   B) An explanation of how anthropologists use math
   C) A statistic indicating an increasing number of jobs and professions requiring anthropological training
   D) A defense of the idea that anthropology is a valid science

7. A) NO CHANGE
   B) presentation; in which,
   C) presentation where
   D) presentation in which

[1] **(8)** Accordingly, even within the field not everybody is sold on the virtues of an anthropology degree. [2] And although there are jobs for anthropologists outside of academia, most are available to other social scientists as well. [3] As a practicing anthropologist, **(9)** Governor Scott might have a point, says Janice Harper. [4] She observes that the median age of an anthropology Ph.D. graduate is 36, higher than for any other field of study. [5] For these grads, finding a tenure-track job as a college professor can be a bit like finding a unicorn. {**10**}

Perhaps the governor's decision to single out the field for criticism above all other less-lucrative majors **(11)** was a personal issue. Critics of Governor Scott's remarks soon noted that his own daughter had recently graduated from a small liberal arts college. Her degree was in—what else?—anthropology.

8. Which choice for the underlined portion provides the most logical transition from the previous paragraph?

A) NO CHANGE
B) Still,
C) In fact,
D) In contrast,

9. A) NO CHANGE
B) Janice Harper says Governor Scott might have a point
C) says, Governor Scott might have a point, according to Janice Harper.
D) Governor Scott, according to Janice Harper, might have a point.

10. In this paragraph, Sentence 2 would most logically and cohesively be placed

A) where it is now.
B) after Sentence 3.
C) after Sentence 4.
D) after Sentence 5.

11. Which choice for the underlined portion is clearest and most precise?

A) NO CHANGE
B) was his personal opinion.
C) ultimately had a more personal origin.
D) was a personal one.

Lesson wY6
Pronoun Errors
Race to the Finish

HOMEWORK EXERCISE 1:

Directions: Find and correct errors in the following sentences. Some sentences will not have any errors.

1. During our last period class, our teacher informed us that every student had to bring ~~their~~ own lunch on the field trip tomorrow. *his or her*

2. In the courtroom, the witness identified the defendant after ~~he~~ put on his glasses. *the witness*

3. In Jennifer's book report on *The Giver*, it states that she greatly enjoyed the story and characters.

4. Not a single one of us boys likes to get up early in the morning for ~~their~~ first period class. *our*

5. My sister Gloria, along with her best friend Sam, went to Hawaii to celebrate their college graduation.

6. Luckily, unlike last week, this week the committee arrived with ~~their~~ presentation ready for the meeting. *its*

7. On the day of the soccer championship, all the team members, including the captain, forgot to bring ~~her~~ cleats to the game. *their*

8. It was evident that everyone accepted the principal's rules because ~~they~~ were applied fairly. *the rules*

9. Are you certain that these homework assignments are for him and ~~I?~~ *me*

10. In my opinion, if you want to get good grades, *you* ~~one~~ must make sure to study regularly and to attend class consistently.

11. After the boxing match between David and John, ~~he~~ was declared the winner. *David*

12. Do you think that the board of directors will give my partner and ~~I~~ a chance to work on the proposal? *me*

13. All of the members of the debate team have ~~his or her~~ schedule for the weekend *their* tournament.

14. After your birthday party, please make sure to send thank you notes to ~~her and he.~~ *the guests*

15. Each teacher declared that ~~they~~ would make sure every student was prepared before the SAT. *he/she*

16. When I asked both my aunt and my mother for a loan to buy a car, ~~she~~ said no. *my aunt & mom*

17. When one gets ready to start freshman year of college, ~~you~~ must make sure to be neat and organized. *one*

18. In the letter from Jessica and Sophia, ~~she~~ *they* states that the two week vacation in New Zealand was an amazing adventure.

19. Despite our fundamental ideological differences, ~~him~~ *us* and I agreed to work on the class project together.

20. Since everyone here is an adult, each person is responsible for her or his actions.

HOMEWORK EXERCISE 2:

Achieving the Right to Vote: Tactics of the National Women's Party

The National Woman's Party (NWP), founded in 1913, was instrumental in raising public awareness of the women's suffrage movement. Many members of the NWP faced imprisonment for their actions, but they turned this experience into a strategy that helped successfully pressure President Woodrow Wilson, members of Congress, and **(1)** assisted in convincing state legislators to support passage of the 19th Amendment, guaranteeing women the right to vote. {2}

The NWP effectively commanded the attention of politicians and the public through aggressive agitation, relentless lobbying, clever publicity stunts, and creative civil disobedience. **(3)** Traditional lobbying and petitioning were mainstays of the NWP, these activities were supplemented by more public actions, including parades, pageants, street speaking, and demonstrations. Most important among these was picketing the White House over many months, leading to the arrest and imprisonment of many suffragists.

1. A) NO CHANGE
   B) convince state legislators
   C) state legislators
   D) convincing state legislators

2. Which of the following would most effectively introduce the passage?

   A) Until the ratification of the 19th Amendment to the U.S. Constitution in 1920, American women struggled for the right to vote.
   B) The National Women's Party was originally known as the Congressional Union for Woman Suffrage.
   C) The original draft of the Constitution granted only white, land-owning men the right to vote.
   D) Throughout American history, marginalized groups have had to struggle for their basic human rights.

3. A) NO CHANGE
   B) While traditional lobbying and petitioning were mainstays of the NWP, these
   C) Traditional lobbying and petitioning were mainstays of the NWP, and these
   D) Because traditional lobbying and petitioning were mainstays of the NWP, these

[1] Upon facing imprisonment, suffragists **(4)** <u>had striven</u> to be recognized as political prisoners instead of criminals. [2] Participating in hunger strikes became one of the most powerful tactics used by the NWP to gain public awareness of the issue. [3] Beginning in fall 1917, imprisoned suffragists engaged in nonviolent, passive resistance, refusing to do assigned sweatshop sewing and manual labor, or even to eat until their political status was acknowledged. {**5**}

As the process of picketing, arrest, sentencing, and imprisonment continued from June into late fall 1917, former government leniency gave way to harsher treatment. Not only were suffragists' prison sentences **(6)** <u>postponed</u> from days to months, but prison guards began to subject **(7)** <u>it</u> to brutal tactics, including beatings, harmful force-feeding techniques, and psychological intimidation.

The campaign of civil disobedience and the public outcry over the prisoners' treatment led to the release of prominent suffragette prisoners by December of 1917. The NWP subsequently staged a mass meeting in Washington, D.C. to honor those **(8)** <u>that had served</u> time in jail or prison. Picketing proceeded at the White House, in front of the U.S. Capitol, and at the Congressional office buildings. More NWP protesters were imprisoned and participated in hunger strikes in 1918. The Watchfire demonstrations of 1919, which involved burning President Wilson's speeches in front of the White House, **(9)** <u>resulted in even more arrests.</u>

4. A) NO CHANGE
   B) strove
   C) striven
   D) would strive

    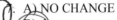

5. Which of the following would create the most logical and coherent paragraph?

   A) Eliminate sentence 2
   B) Add a sentence to the beginning of the paragraph about the state of the prisons
   C) Add a sentence explaining what hunger strikes are after sentence 2
   D) Switch sentences 2 and 3

6. A) NO CHANGE
   B) deferred
   C) delayed
   D) extended

7. A) NO CHANGE
   B) the women
   C) the prison sentences
   D) punishments

8. A) NO CHANGE
   B) which had served
   C) who had served
   D) that served

9. Which of the following would best suit the style and tone of the passage?

   A) NO CHANGE
   B) landed way more women in the slammer.
   C) resulted in an adequate number of women finding themselves in prison.
   D) led the corrupt government to unjustly imprison the brave female protesters.

Nevertheless, **(10)** the NWP utilized the experience of imprisonment in order to use it to help spread the call for a federal suffrage amendment. In February 1919, ex-prisoners traveled around the country in a campaign called the "Prison Special" tour. Mass meetings in which prominent suffragettes spoke to large audiences, often times donning their prison uniforms, were held in major cities. The "Prison Special" tour helped create a groundswell of local support for the ratification effort that began in the states months later, following the approval of the 19th Amendment by Congress in June 1919. **{11}**

10. A) NO CHANGE
    B) the NWP utilized the experience of imprisonment, used it to help spread the call for a federal suffrage amendment.
    C) the experience of imprisonment was used to promote a federal suffrage amendment.
    D) the NWP used the experience of imprisonment to push for a federal suffrage amendment.

11. Which of the following would best conclude the passage?

    A) The Prison Special was an incredibly popular campaign that won the suffragists many additional allies.
    B) Other women's rights issues, such as equal pay and educational opportunities, remained to be addressed.
    C) Thus, suffragists strategically utilized the hardships and obstacles they faced as tools to achieve their goals.
    D) By the time suffrage was won in 1920, 168 NWP activists had served time in prison or jail.

| **Lesson wY7** |
| **Misplaced Modifiers** |
| **Getting Your Feet Wet** |

Directions: Choose the answer that best corrects the misplaced modifier error.

1. <u>Mike wore his best tie to the job interview</u>, which was unfortunately stained with salad dressing.

    A) NO CHANGE
    B) For the job interview, Mike wore his best tie
    C) Mike's best tie was worn to the job interview
    D) To the job interview, his best tie was worn by Mike

2. Running late for school, <u>the bus left without me anyway and I put on</u> <u>two different shoes because I was in such a hurry.</u>

    A) NO CHANGE
    B) two different shoes wound up on my feet and the bus left without me anyway because I was in such a hurry.
    C) the bus left without me because I was in such a hurry and I put on two different shoes anyway.
    D) I was in such a hurry that I put on two different shoes and the bus left without me anyway.

3. When I tried it on, <u>the jacket was just too small in the store.</u>

    A) NO CHANGE
    B) the store was just too small for the jacket.
    C) in the store the jacket was just too small.
    D) the jacket in the store was just too small.

4. On his way home from work, <u>Jeff found a gold man's watch.</u>

    A) NO CHANGE
    B) a man's gold watch was found by Jeff.
    C) Jeff found a man's gold watch.
    D) Jeff found a man's watch that was gold.

Lesson wY7
Misplaced Modifiers
Wading In

TOPIC OVERVIEW: MISPLACED MODIFIERS

A modifier in a sentence can be either a single word (usually an adjective) or a phrase. The SAT will test your ability to notice when a modifying phrase is out of place. The way this usually occurs is when the object being modified does not appear directly before or after the modifier.

RECOGNIZING MISPLACE MODIFIERS

For a question to involve a misplaced modifier error, the sentence must contain a modifying word or phrase. The underlined portion of the sentence will either be the modifying phrase itself or the object being modified.

Modifying phrases are often – but not always – set apart by commas and usually provide information about the noun (or pronoun) immediately before or after the phrase. For example:

Example 1: Floating on the lake, the boat bobbed up and down.

Example 2: The boat, which was floating on the lake, bobbed up and down.

Example 3: The boat bobbed up and down floating on the lake.

Examples 1 and 2 do not contain misplaced modifiers. In both of these examples, the modifying phrase (*floating on the lake*) is clearly modifying *boat*. In Example 3, however, the modifying phrase is too far away from *boat*, so the sentence contains a misplaced modifier.

Often, misplaced modifiers will be slightly harder to spot because there will be several nouns that the phrase might be modifying.

Example 4: *Waving in the strong wind*, we watched the trees bend to and fro as the hurricane approached.

This sentence contains several nouns (or pronouns) that the modifying phrase could refer to: we, trees, and hurricane. As currently written, the phrase *waving in the strong wind* is modifying *we*. We probably aren't waving in the strong wind, so this is a misplaced modifier. Instead, the phrase should be modifying *the trees*. To correct the error, *the trees* need to be closer to *waving in the strong wind*:

Example 5: We watched the trees, *which were waving in the strong wind*, bend to and fro as the hurricane approached.

Example 6: *Waving in the strong wind*, the trees bent to and fro as the hurricane approached.

ANSWERING MODIFIER QUESTIONS

Once you've identified the question as a Misplaced Modifier question, you can follow the steps below to answer it:

1. Identify the modifying phrase.
2. Find the noun being modified as the sentence is written.
3. Determine which noun *should* be modified by the phrase.
4. Choose the answer that rearranges the sentence correctly and does not create any new errors.

Example 7:

Churning in the Gulf of Mexico, <u>we anxiously watched the weather report about Hurricane Eileen.</u>

    A) NO CHANGE
    B) the weather report about Hurricane Eileen was anxiously watched.
    C) we watched Hurricane Eileen on the weather report anxiously.
    D) Hurricane Eileen was on the weather report that we anxiously watched.

1. The modifying phrase here is *Churning in the Gulf of Mexico*, which gives additional information about the noun/pronoun that follows.
2. The thing being modified in the sentence as it is written is *we*.
3. In this sentence, the thing that is churning in the Gulf of Mexico has to be Hurricane Eileen.
4. The correct answer will place *Hurricane Eileen* directly after the modifying phrase, which is done only by Choice D.

Example 8:

Although the hurricane was moving slowly, <u>it was gaining strength as it approached the coast quickly.</u>

    A) NO CHANGE
    B) it approached the coast quickly gaining strength.
    C) it was quickly gaining strength as it approached the coast.
    D) it was gaining quickly strength as it approached the coast.

1. This question demonstrates how a single modifying word can be misplaced. In this sentence, the misplaced modifier is *quickly*.
2. In this sentence, the word *quickly* is modifying *approached*. Because the first phrase of the sentence states that the hurricane was moving slowly, we know that it can't be approaching quickly.
3. The word that *quickly* needs to be modifying is *gaining*.
4. Choose the answer that moves the modifier so that it is clearly modifying the word *gaining*. Both choices C and D accomplish this goal, but choice D creates a new error.

WRAP-UP

Misplaced Modifiers questions can be answered using the following steps:

1. Identify the modifying phrase.
2. Find the noun being modified as the sentence is written.
3. Determine which noun *should* be modified by the phrase.
4. Choose the answer which rearranges the sentence correctly and does not create any new errors.

Lesson wY7
Misplaced Modifiers
Learning to Swim

CONCEPT EXERCISE:

Directions: Find and correct errors in the following sentences. Some sentences will not have any errors.

1. Hidden deep under the dresser, Rachel finally found her missing keys.

2. At the age of 7, Slavoj's family left Slovenia and emigrated to the United States.

3. Beneath a thick crust of salt, the chef unveiled a perfectly baked sea bass.

4. The car near that house with the flat tire is mine.

5. Abandoned by the former owner, the foreclosed home was purchased by an investor for a song.

6. Always the fashion victim, Monty was wearing a bright yellow fedora on his head that he had found at an exclusive Soho boutique.

7. She was told she had been hired by the last person who interviewed her.

8. In describing the dire poverty of Victorian London, not the smallest detail escaped the pen of Charles Dickens.

9. The neighbors handed out Halloween candy to trick-or-treaters wrapped in colorful Mylar sheets.

10. Leaping behind the steering wheel, the engines roared to life.

11. The cat crossing the street is the one that belongs to the neighbor living on the second floor.

12. Walking into the expensive antique store, the human skeleton was a complete surprise.

13. This morning, I saw a garbage truck peeking through the window.

14. It's always bliss to be greeted by the smell of a roasting chicken coming home from work.

15. After arguing with her date, she left the restaurant fuming.

16. Without knowing the rules of cricket, it was difficult for Kevin to follow the game.

17. The distressed homeowner finally cornered the mouse wielding a broom and dustpan.

18. Having checked the original transcript, the newspaper report is definitely incorrect.

19. Knowing only English, Robert was flustered by the menu given to him by the waitress that was written in French.

20. Megan's host served hand-made sushi wearing a vintage kimono.

Lesson wY7
Misplaced Modifiers
Diving into the Deep End

PRACTICE EXERCISE:

Directions: Answer the questions that accompany the following passages.

James Baldwin

[1]

In the 1960s, James Baldwin's *The Fire Next Time* sold a million

copies, and its stated goal of explaining the African-American view of

U.S. race relations in a way the white majority **(1)** <u>could understand</u>

turned Baldwin into a household name. He was frequently

interviewed on television **(2)** <u>and was a personal friend of Martin</u>

<u>Luther King, Jr.</u> However, in the 1970s he was harshly criticized by

leaders of the Black Power Movement. By the 2010s, Baldwin was

posthumously decorated by cultural critics with such titles as

"America's greatest essayist." Rarely taught in schools, **(3)** <u>few</u>

<u>Americans can quote any of his writings.</u> This is the contradictory

legacy of a unique and complex voice in American literature.

[2]

The Fire Next Time, published in **(4)** <u>1963 draws it's title</u> from an

old spiritual: "God gave Noah the rainbow sign; no more water but

fire next time." The book pleads for nonviolence and racial

reconciliation, yet the title reads as an ominous warning of the

(5) <u>turmoil and unrest to come</u> if white America **(6)** <u>refuse</u> to see the

depth of black suffering and oppression—if it refuses to change. {**7**}

1. A) NO CHANGE
    B) could understand that
    C) could understand;
    D) could understand, and

2. Which choice would best
    support the idea that Baldwin
    was a widely acclaimed writer?

    A) NO CHANGE
    B) and seen as a candidate for
       the Nobel Prize.
    C) and viewed by many
       Americans as a leading
       advocate for civil rights.
    D) about his book.

3. A) NO CHANGE
    B) he is hardly quoted in
       modern discussions.
    C) his writings are not widely
       known.
    D) even "experts" do not
       recognize his work.

4. A) NO CHANGE
    B) 1963 draws its title
    C) 1963, draws it's title
    D) 1963, draws its title

5. A) NO CHANGE
    B) turmoil to come
    C) turmoil and unrest that
       would come in the future
    D) impending unrest to come

6. A) NO CHANGE
    B) would refuse
    C) refuses
    D) refused

7. Paragraph 2 would most
    logically be placed

    A) where it is now.
    B) before Paragraph 1.
    C) after Paragraph 3.
    D) after Paragraph 4.

[3]

Born in Harlem in 1924, Baldwin moved to France in 1948 to escape American prejudice. It was there that he would live out most of his life. Baldwin was uncomfortable with the thought that he would be seen as "merely a Negro; or, even, merely a Negro writer." **(8)** <u>Wanting to escape</u> such a characterization, his 1956 novel, the deeply controversial *Giovanni's Room*, has mostly white characters and deals with themes of social alienation and alternative life styles. Baldwin's work explores a range of complex psychological and social issues, but the turbulence of the civil rights movement in the 1960s brought his focus back to race relations.

[4]

After the massive success of *The Fire Next Time,* Baldwin found himself criticized by the more radical leaders of the black nationalist movement, who did not believe his call for love and understanding would **(9)** <u>impact</u> white readers. **(10)** <u>Yet like</u> those leaders, Baldwin's rhetoric could be fiery and uncompromising. In 1979, he rejected the label "civil rights movement," choosing to call it "the latest slave rebellion." In *The Fire Next Time*, Baldwin combines black pride and nationalism with a message of integration: "Why I should want to marry your sister is a great mystery to me. But your sister and I have every right to marry if we wish to, and no one has the right to stop us. If she cannot raise me to her level, perhaps I can raise her to mine." Too unique and complex a voice to have remained the spokesperson of a movement, **(11)** <u>many have nonetheless been inspired by</u> the beauty and moral clarity of his words.

8. A) NO CHANGE
   B) Perhaps written to avoid
   C) Careful to deny
   D) Arguing against

9. Which choice for the underlined portion is clearest and most precise?

   A) NO CHANGE
   B) get through to
   C) speak to
   D) change the attitudes of

10. A) NO CHANGE
    B) Yet like the impassioned speeches of
    C) Yet, comparable to
    D) Still like

11. A) NO CHANGE
    B) it nonetheless inspired
    C) the inspiring thing about Baldwin has been
    D) Baldwin has nonetheless inspired many with

TEST EXERCISE:

Drought and the Dust Bowl

Drought is a natural phenomenon in which rainfall is lower than average for an extended period, resulting in water shortage. **(1)** Drought has affected the United States, and cycles of drought throughout history have affected North America for the last 10,000 years. During recent history, serious drought events have regularly occurred in the U.S. In 2012, 60 percent of the contiguous U.S. suffered the worst drought in 60 years. A decade earlier, a **(2)** difficult 2002 drought across the Midwest greatly increased the danger of that year's fire season. In 1999, extensive heat waves and drought conditions affected the Northeast. **(3)** And the North American Drought of 1988 is one of the worst on record, which killed thousands of people and livestock across the country.

1. A) NO CHANGE
   B) Drought has affected the United States throughout history, and cycles of drought have affected North America for the last 10,000 years
   C) Throughout history, drought has affected the United States and North America, as well as for the last 10,000 years
   D) For the last 10,000 years, drought has affected both the United States and North America throughout history

2. Given the context of the passage, which of the following represents the most precise replacement for the underlined word?

   A) NO CHANGE
   B) Disrespectful
   C) Exhausting
   D) Devastating

3. A) NO CHANGE
   B) And one of the worst on record, the North American drought of 1988, which killed thousands of people and livestock across the country.
   C) And the North American Drought of 1988, which killed thousands of people and livestock across the country, is one of the worst on record.
   D) And one of the worst droughts on record, killing thousands of people and livestock across the country, the North American Drought of 1988.

{4} One of the most severe droughts in American history, the Dust Bowl affected 65% of the U.S and was characterized by substantial clouds of dust and sand that often blocked out the sun for days at a time. A number of adverse health effects and conditions were attributed either directly or indirectly to the drought. For example, people exposed to dust clouds were at increased risk for acquiring "dust pneumonia," an often fatal type of pneumonia caused when dust fills the lungs and inflames them, resulting in high fever, chest pain, and difficulty breathing.

During droughts, dry soils—and often wildfires—increase the amount of airborne particles, such as pollen and smoke. These particles can irritate the airways and worsen chronic respiratory illnesses such as asthma. Poor air quality can also increase the risk of respiratory infections, such as bacterial pneumonia and valley fever, a common cause of pneumonia in many areas of the southwestern United States. (5)

[handwritten annotations: reason for bad problems caused by... You may start sentences + paras with "but" "and," any of the FANBOYS]

4. Which of the following best introduces the paragraph?

A) Compared to these recent drought events, the Dust Bowl of the 1930s is even better known
B) And along with these drought events, there is the Dust Bowl of the 1930s, perhaps the most well-known of them all.
C) The Dust Bowl of the 1930s may be more well-known than any other drought event
D) But perhaps the most well-known drought event is the Dust Bowl of the 1930s

5. Which of the following facts, if added here, would best support the previous sentence?

A) Poor air quality is directly or indirectly responsible for approximately seven million deaths every year worldwide
B) Poor air quality is directly or indirectly responsible for approximately seven million deaths every year worldwide
C) Poor air quality also increases the likelihood of numerous other diseases besides infections
D) Given the increased likelihood of drought during the 21st century, poor air quality may soon become an even bigger public health problem

[handwritten: no real connection]

In addition to reduced air quality, drought poses many far-reaching health implications. Some drought-related health effects occur in the short-term and can be directly observed and measured. But drought also can result in lasting, indirect health implications that are not always easy to anticipate or monitor, such as more severe sanitation problems and increased rates of chronic disease. Drought also affects the quantity as well as the quality of America's crops and produce. **(6)** Drought, resulting in increased food prices and therefore decreased nutrition, can lower crop yields and kill livestock. Mental stress and its deadly effects are another result of drought. {7}

6. A) NO CHANGE
   B) Lowering crop yields and killing livestock, drought resulting in increased food prices and therefore decreased nutrition
   C) Resulting in increased food prices and therefore decreased nutrition, drought can lower crop yields and kill livestock.
   D) Drought can lower crop yields and kill livestock, resulting in increased food prices and therefore decreased nutrition

7. Which of the following best supports the ideas in the paragraph?

   A) Food prices can also increase due to other environmental events (like hurricanes and earthquakes)
   B) During and after the North American Drought of 1988, rates of depression, diabetes, and heart disease all increased significantly
   C) Simply worrying about the possibility of severe drought can have significant health effects
   D) Improved technology has allowed U.S. farmers to increase overall crop yields in the last fifty years even as droughts have become more common

(8) Because drought is a recurring event, it is important for government agencies to prepare for this particular public health challenge in order to stay safe and healthy when it happens. Advances in science and technology have allowed researchers from federal agencies to use rainfall patterns, climate models, and other indicators to predict the amount and distribution of precipitation in the U.S. in the twenty-first century. **(9)** These researchers, particularly in mid-latitude areas like the U.S., concur that severe droughts are likely to occur within the next century.

A) NO CHANGE

B) It is important for government agencies to prepare for this particular public health challenge, because drought is a recurrent event, and in order to stay safe and healthy when it happens

C) Because drought is a recurring event, it is important for government agencies to prepare for this particular public health challenge in order to help people stay safe and healthy when it happens

D) In order to stay safe and healthy when it happens, it is important for government agencies to prepare for this type of public health challenge, because drought is a recurring event

9. A) NO CHANGE

B) Particularly in mid-latitude areas like the U.S., these researchers concur that severe droughts are likely to occur within the next century

C) Concurring that severe droughts are likely to occur within the next century, these researchers, particularly in mid-latitude areas like the U.S.

D) These researchers concur that severe droughts are likely to occur within the next century, particularly in mid-latitude areas like the U.S.

{10} In response to these developments, in 2008 the National Center for Environmental Health (a division of the Centers for Disease Control) created a working group composed of experts representing **(11)** different fields from environmental protection to water-related sciences. This action marks a first step toward creating public health guidance focused on drought. The group's efforts have assisted numerous public health officials, practitioners, and other stakeholders, but more work is needed to ensure that citizens and governments are prepared for the challenges of surviving a severe drought.

10. Which of the following best expresses the main idea of the paragraph?

A) It may be impossible to fully protect citizens from all of the possible dangers associated with drought
B) The government, not individual citizens, should be primarily responsible for preparing for severe droughts
C) Recent efforts have helped address public health problems related to drought, and such efforts should be expanded in the future.
D) If public health officials had worked harder to prepare for drought, there would be no need for further efforts now

11. Given the context of the passage, which of following represents the most precise replacement for the underlined word?

A) NO CHANGE
B) Diverse
C) Peculiar
D) Special

100%

	Lesson wY7
	placed Modifiers
	ce to the Finish

HOMEWORK

Directions: Find and correct errors in the following sentences. Some sentences will not have any errors.

1. *While* Walking to school with her brother, Martha's backpack broke.

2. Shelly missed the bus ^running down the street.

3. In a fit of rage, *I broke my ~~my~~ computer ~~broke~~ while* when I threw it out the window.

4. Speeding down the highway, a car accident seemed likely.

5. ~~Known for being strict,~~ I was scared to tell my mom about the broken lamp, *since she's known for being strict.*

6. After searching for days, I finally found my keys ~~looking~~ in my sister's room.

7. I realized that I forgot my homework walking to school. *while*

8. *After* Painting a picture for his mother, Jordan's hands were dirty.

9. *After* Participating in the impromptu snowball fight, Elise's favorite sweater was ruined.

10. To be prepared for the concert, a strict practice schedule was made.

11. Drumming his fingers nervously, the aspiring writer's anxiety was apparent.

12. After working on the assignment for a month, the teacher told us that it would not count.

13. A horror writer like no other, Stephen King's ~~books~~ often feature gruesome plots. *in his books.*

14. Running a million dollar industry, the businessman's stress levels ~~were very high.~~ *had high*

15. *when* Attempting to run for president, good people skills are necessary.

16. Simmering on the stove, ~~I smelled~~ the chicken noodle soup. *smelled great*

17. *In order* To fall asleep quickly, doctors recommend not watching TV before bed.

18. We picked up apples, oranges, and other fruit *while* walking down the aisle.

19. *while* Describing a meteor shower, the professor's students were in awe.

20. On the run from the cops, ~~a car was stolen by the robbers~~ *stole a car.*

HOMEWORK EXERCISE 2:

A Home for Cicadas

Hidden away in the woods of Connecticut is a private preserve dedicated to a rather unusual insect: *Magicicada septendecim*, the 17-year periodical cicada. These insects are well known for filling the summer air with their deafening mating calls and covering every visible surface with **(1)** its discarded exoskeletons. **(2)** But scientists are concerned that increasing land development is destroying many of these creatures before they ever have a chance to emerge from the ground and serenade us with their song.

{3} The *Magicicada septendecim* has the longest developmental cycle of any **(4)** insect. It spends seventeen years underground before coming up to molt. The insects in a given population, or **(5)** "brood," is developmentally synchronized: they all emerge in the same year, even within a few weeks of each other. This creates the astounding—and earsplitting—effect of an insect invasion.

1. A) NO CHANGE
   B) it's discarded exoskeletons
   C) their discarded exoskeleton
   D) their discarded exoskeletons

2. A) NO CHANGE
   B) Likewise,
   C) Finally,
   D) As a result,

3. Which choice most effectively establishes the main topic of the paragraph?

   A) The cicada can be very invasive and destructive.
   B) The cicada has an intriguing, unique life cycle.
   C) The cicada is becoming endangered.
   D) The cicada produces the loudest sound of any insect.

4. Which choice most effectively combines the sentences at the underlined portion?

   A) insect, and it then spends
   B) insect that spends
   C) insect but spends
   D) insect, spending

5. A) NO CHANGE
   B) "broods," is
   C) "brood," are
   D) "brood," was

(6) A longtime professor at Yale and the Peabody Museum's first curator of entomology, the Magicicada Preserve was established by Dr. Charles Remington a year prior to the cicadas' 1996 appearance. The preserve is located on 90 acres owned by the South Central Connecticut Regional Water Authority, just north of Sleeping Giant State Park, a popular hiking spot. Dr. Remington would visit his forest **(7)** frequently and take notes and write down his observations of the insects. In one note from June 1996, he observed "very many actively climbing (virtually all on tree trunks, some high up)." In creating the preserve, Dr. Remington wanted to draw attention to cicadas and their unique biology in an untouched environment, said the University of Connecticut lab's founder, Chris Simon, a professor of ecology and evolutionary biology. "He could see that their territory was being taken away," she said.

6. A) NO CHANGE
   B) The Magicicada Preserve was established by Dr. Charles Remington, being a longtime professor at Yale and the Peabody Museum's first curator of entomology
   C) Dr. Charles Remington, a longtime professor at Yale and the Peabody Museum's first curator of entomology, established the Magicicada Preserve
   D) Established by a longtime professor at Yale and the Peabody Museum's first curator of entomology, Dr. Charles Remington opened the Magicicada Preserve

7. A) NO CHANGE
   B) frequently and take notes and write down his observations of what he saw
   C) frequently and take notes on his observations
   D) frequently, taking notes and observing what he saw

Although anyone who has experienced a mass cicada emergence may find it hard to believe, periodical cicada populations have been **(8)** <u>shriveling</u> and even disappearing. Scientists believe this is largely due to climate change and land development. Chris T. Maier, an entomologist with the Connecticut Agricultural Experiment **(9)** <u>Station, said</u> that from 1945 to 1979, the state lost roughly 5 percent of its cicada population, much of it as a result of Interstate System highway development. **{10}**

Those who grew up in suburban **(11)** <u>Chicago may recall,</u> the emergence of Brood XIII in 1969, four years early, blanketing summer lawns with exoskeletons that made a satisfying crunch when walked upon, like spilled popcorn at a movie theater. Let's hope that, with the aid of people like Dr. Remington, this unique experience is one that people can enjoy every seventeen years for generations to come.

8. Which of the following is the most precise replacement for the underlined word?
   A) NO CHANGE
   B) shrinking
   C) condensing
   D) withdrawing

9. A) NO CHANGE
   B) Station; he says
   C) Station, saying
   D) Station. He said

10. Which choice best supports the main idea of the paragraph?
    A) Cicadas have been increasing in some areas outside of Connecticut.
    B) Climate change is a complex problem with many unforeseeable consequences.
    C) Scientists are now able to use GIS-GPS technology to map cicada populations with remarkable accuracy.
    D) A big discount store on Long Island was built on top of a large cicada population.

11. A) NO CHANGE
    B) Chicago may recall
    C) Chicago may recall;
    D) Chicago, may recall,

Lesson wY8
Main Ideas and Topic Sentences
Getting Your Feet Wet

Directions: The following questions are intended as a short diagnostic exam.

{1} The work of Shakespeare, whose written vocabulary consists of 17,245 words, includes hundreds of authorisms. Some of them never went further than their appearance in his plays. But others, like "bump," "hurry," "critical," and "bedazzled," are essential parts of the standard vocabulary today. Extraordinary claims have been made for the Bard's ability to coin words. A number of recent books claim the count to be as high as 1,700. These numbers work only if, and here's the rub, you count phrases like "brave new world," "all's well that ends well," "setting your teeth on edge," "being cruel only to be kind," and so on. These numbers also hint at another authorism, the term George Bernard Shaw created for excessive worship of Shakespeare: bardolatry.

[1] In fact, though few dispute Shakespeare's literary genius, many believe that he is given too much credit for his contributions to the English language. [2] Other authors, many of whom published their greatest works long before Shakespeare's time, have arguably had a greater impact on the evolution of the English language. [3] John Milton coined the most new words in the English language, with Geoffrey Chaucer, Ben Jonson, John Donne, Sir Thomas Moore, and Shakespeare not far behind. [4] Milton is credited with 630 authorisms, from "ensanguined," "emblazonry" and "horrent" to the more commonly used "earthshaking," "lovelorn," "fragrance," and "by hook or crook," as well as "pandemonium." [5] Chaucer's immense contribution of thousands of written words, with many originals, gave us "bagpipe" and "universe," while Moore contributed "anticipate" and "fact." [6] Ben Johnson invented 558 words; and John Donne minted 342. **{2}**

Though such authors should certainly be admired for the depth and quality of their published works, perhaps their most lasting legacy is their contribution to the development of the ever-changing English language.

1. Which of the following sentences, if added here, would best establish the main idea of the passage?

    A) English is an ever-evolving language that adapts to each new era.
    B) Authors often make up words in order to add color and depth to their works.
    C) The English language has long evolved with the help of authorisms, words or phrases created by authors.
    D) Too many people credit Shakespeare with broadening the English vocabulary, choosing to overlook the contributions of other authors.

2. Which choice most effectively functions as the topic sentence of the paragraph?

    A) Sentence 1
    B) Sentence 2
    C) Sentence 3
    D) Sentence 4

Lesson wY8
Main Ideas and Topic Sentences
Wading In

TOPIC OVERVIEW: MAIN IDEAS AND TOPIC SENTENCES

The SAT Writing section is intended to test how well we write, not simply how many grammar rules we know. To do that, the test includes several types of questions that focus on how well we can evaluate and improve the development of ideas within a passage. Some of these questions will ask us to identify the main idea of a passage or paragraph or to create a topic sentence for a paragraph.

TOPIC OVERVIEW: MAIN IDEA

It may seem pretty simple to identify the main idea of a passage or paragraph – after all, it's the *main* idea, so it should be fairly clear – but the details can often hide the main idea. On the SAT, the answer choices will often include items that are valid based on the passage, but that express a detail of the text rather than the overarching ideas.

Many passages will include a thesis statement that defines the purpose (and thus the main idea) of the passage; this statement is usually found in the first paragraph and is often the very first sentence. Identifying the passage's thesis statement can help to determine the passage's main idea.

Additionally, most paragraphs include topic sentences that identify the primary purpose or idea of the paragraph; this sentence is often the first sentence of the paragraph. Just as identifying the thesis statement can help pinpoint the main idea of a passage, identifying the topic sentence can help pinpoint the main idea of a paragraph.

ANSWERING MAIN IDEA QUESTIONS

Main idea questions will include the key phrases "main idea" or "main topic." Since we know that there will usually be a thesis statement or topic sentence to help us determine the main idea, we can use this information to create a strategy for answering these types of questions.

For questions that ask for the main idea of the passage:

1. Read the first paragraph of the passage.
2. If possible, identify and summarize the thesis statement. If you cannot locate the thesis statement, summarize the information in the first paragraph.
3. Read the last paragraph of the passage. Summarize the information in that paragraph.
4. Compare your summaries to the answer choices.
5. Select the answer choice that most nearly matches your summary.

6. If none of the answers seem reasonable, read the first sentence of each paragraph.
7. Review the answer choices again.

For questions that ask for the main idea of a paragraph:

1. Read the paragraph carefully.
2. If possible, identify and summarize the topic sentence. If you cannot locate the topic sentence, summarize the information in the paragraph.
3. Compare your summary to the answer choices.
4. Select the answer choice that most nearly matches your summary.

TOPIC OVERVIEW: TOPIC SENTENCES

Topic sentences typically identify the main idea of a paragraph, so topic sentence questions are fairly similar to main idea questions. The biggest difference between the two question types is that topic sentence questions may ask you to either identify or add a topic sentence.

ANSWERING TOPIC SENTENCE QUESTIONS

Topic sentence questions will usually include the key phrase "topic sentence," but sometimes they might be phrased more like a main idea question. For example a topic sentence question might ask, "Which of the following sentences, if added here, would best establish the main idea of the paragraph?" It's important to recognize that topic sentences state the main idea, so a sentence establishing the main idea of a paragraph is a topic sentence.

Follow these steps to answer topic sentence questions:

1. Carefully read the paragraph.
2. Without looking at the answer choices, summarize the main idea of the paragraph.
3. Choose the answer choice that most closely matches your summary of the main idea.
4. If none of the choices seem reasonable, read the paragraph again. Be careful not to be distracted by details. Rephrase your summary.
5. Examine the answer choices again. Eliminate any answer choices that do not relate to your summary.
6. Choose from the remaining answer choices.

Let's look at some examples to make these strategies a bit clearer.

[1] The Murray River failed to reach the sea for the first time ever in 2002. [2] Australia experienced the worst and most consistent dry period in its recorded history over much of the past decade. [3] Fires swept much of the country, and dust storms blanketed major cities for days. [4] Australia's sheep population dropped by 50 percent, and rice and cotton production collapsed in some years. [5] Tens of thousands of farm families gave up their livelihoods. [6] The Australian drought ended in 2010 with torrential rains and flooding. {1}

{2} What happened in Australia could happen in the U.S., with devastating consequences to the region and to the nation. We can avoid the worst, however, if we pay attention to Australia's experience and learn the right lessons.

{3} As was the case in Australia before the drought, the southwestern U.S. contains arid regions where thirsty cities and irrigated agriculture are straining water supplies and damaging ecosystems. As a result, the Colorado River no longer flows to the sea in most years. The water level in many major reservoirs has steadily declined over the past decade; some analysts project that the largest may never refill. The U.S. and Australia also share a changing global climate that is increasing the risk of drought.

1. Which choice most effectively functions as the topic sentence of the paragraph?

   A) Sentence 2
   B) Sentence 3
   C) Sentence 5
   D) Sentence 6

2. Which of the following sentences, if added here, would best establish the main idea of the paragraph?

   A) Australia could have prevented such a severe drought if it had taken measures similar to those taken by the U.S.
   B) Australia's sheep population would have increased if the drought had not occurred.
   C) It is likely that American sheep populations and rice and cotton production will also collapse.
   D) Australia's drought is a wake-up call for residents of drought-plagued regions of the U.S.

3. Which of the following best reflects the main idea of the paragraph?

   A) Several countries in the world suffer from droughts.
   B) Australia's climate is become increasingly similar to that of the U.S.
   C) The southwestern U.S. bears some resemblance to parts of Australia before the drought.
   D) The increased risk of drought is the result of climate change.

Since the first question specifically asks for a topic sentence, we'll use the topic sentence strategies.

1.   Carefully read the first paragraph.

2.   Summarize the main idea of the paragraph. Most of the paragraph describes the terrible effects of a long drought in Australia, so we now that the main idea will be that Australia had a terrible drought.

3.   Look at the answer choices and match them to the summary you just made. Sentences 3 and 5 describe detailed effects of the drought. Since they focus only on details without encompassing the main idea, we can eliminate choices B and C. Sentence 6 tells us when the drought ended, but still doesn't address the main idea of the paragraph, so we can eliminate choice D. Sentence 2 clearly identifies the main idea of the paragraph – Australia's long drought – so choice A is the correct answer.

We didn't have to use the remaining steps to answer this question.

For Question 2, we can use the topic sentence strategies again. Note that although the question doesn't specifically say "topic sentence," it is looking for a sentence that establishes the main idea.

1.   Carefully read the second paragraph.

2.   Summarize the main idea of the paragraph. The paragraph talks about similarities between Australia and the U.S., specifying that the U.S. should learn from Australia's drought experience.

3.   Now look at the answer choices. Choice A suggests similarities between the U.S. and Australia, but since it says that Australia could learn from the U.S., it has the relationship backwards; we can eliminate A. Choice B relates to a detail from the first paragraph, but has no relation to anything in the second paragraph, so we can eliminate B. Choice C draws a similarity between the U.S. and Australia, but fails to say anything about the U.S. learning from Australia's experience, so we can eliminate C. Choice D not only implies a relationship between the situations in the U.S. and Australia, but also specifies that the U.S. should learn from Australia's experience. Choice D is the correct answer.

We didn't have to use the remaining steps to answer this question.

For Question 3, we will use the main idea strategies because the question asks for the main idea of the paragraph.

1. Read the paragraph carefully.

2. Identify the topic sentence. In this paragraph, the first sentence works as a topic sentence because it encompasses all of the details in the paragraph. We can summarize this sentence as, "The southwestern U.S. is similar to Australia before the drought."

3. Now we look at the answer choices. We can eliminate both A and D because they are not similar to our summary.

4. This leaves us with choices B and C. Choice B shows similarities between Australia and the U.S., but seems to have the relationship backwards. Since the southwest is similar to Australia before Australia's drought, it wouldn't make sense for the main idea to be that Australia's climate is becoming more similar to that of the southwest. Choice C, on the other hand, is very close to our original summary. Choice C is the right answer.

Lesson wY8
Main Ideas and Topic Sentences
Learning to Swim

minimum

CONCEPT EXERCISE:

Directions: For each paragraph, write a topic sentence on the lines provided. Remember that a topic sentence should identify the main idea or main claim of the paragraph, a task that you will be asked to perform on many SAT writing passages.

1. U.S. Lacrosse has seen the number of youth members (that is, members younger than 16) triple since 1999, with membership levels soaring to over 120,000. These numbers don't include the more than 160,000 high school students nationwide who play lacrosse, a huge increase in just the last ten years. They also do not tell the story of the staggering growth of the sport at the collegiate level. More than 400 colleges and universities in the United States sponsor club and varsity lacrosse teams, and the number keeps growing every year. In addition, NCAA conferences continue to add lacrosse to their lists of championship sports, with the Big Ten becoming one of the most recent to do so.

   Lacrosse in the U.S. has recently experienced a large increase in players.

2. The roots of lacrosse can be traced to Native American combat-style games which were being played long before the first Europeans came to North America. Indeed, some of the earliest French explorers saw the game being played, and they were the ones who named it *la crosse*, most likely referring to the sticks that the players used. Several centuries later, in the mid-1800s, North Americans of European descent began to establish competitive teams and write official rulebooks. Women were not part of this development for many decades; the first organized women's lacrosse team was not created until 1926.

   Seeing the Native Americans play, the Europeans adopted lacrosse and made it their own.

   The sport of lacrosse has a long history

3. In boys' and men's lacrosse, players are allowed to body check each other, using their sticks to hit each other in an attempt to get the ball away from the player who is carrying it. Girls and women, on the other hand, cannot attack in this fashion, and even rules about the sticks themselves are stricter. It is probably no surprise, therefore, that male players wear a lot more protective equipment than female players. Most high school boys, for example, are required to wear helmets, shoulder and elbow pads, gloves, and mouth guards. By contrast, girls wear virtually no protective covering other than eye goggles and occasionally soft helmets and mouth guards, except for the goalie, who wears full-body pads and a hard helmet.

   The rules of lacrosse vary based on genders; boys play much more violently and physical while girls play with stricter rules.

4. The statistics are clear. The American Journal of Sports Medicine found that, between 2008 and 2010, concussions happened among girls' lacrosse players at a rate of .035% of all exposures, while the concussion rate for boys was .04%. These might seem like a small numbers, but they were noticeably higher than the overall concussion rate (.025%) across all 20 sports studied. In fact, the only sports with higher rates of concussions were boys' football and boys' ice hockey. In girls' lacrosse, the majority of concussions were caused by contact with equipment, while over 25% occurred due to body-to-body contact with other players.

   The concussion rate for lacrosse players is a dangerous 0.01–0.015% higher than the overall rate across 20 other sports.

5. Running across a field that is 110 yards l[...]
    and 60 yards wide is a high-impact aerob[...]
    activity, burning hundreds of calories per [...]
    and building up cardiovascular endurance [...]
    The variety of other actions that a lacrosse
    player performs in a given game or practice—
    swinging, throwing, catching, cradling—work
    nearly every major muscle in the body. Like
    other forms of intense physical activity,
    lacrosse can also improve a player's mental
    state, such as helping to release tension or
    relieve symptoms of mild depression.

    _____
    _____
    _____
    _____

6. Some high school lacrosse players can do very
    well based solely on their natural athletic
    abilities. They may not have a deep
    understanding of game strategy or even very
    good technique, but since there is such a huge
    range of strength and physical development
    among players in high school, especially boys,
    those who are bigger and faster can sometimes
    succeed on those characteristics alone. Players
    in college, on the other hand, tend to be much
    more physically similar to each other, and
    they are as a group bigger, faster, and stronger
    than high school lacrosse players. Successful
    college players nearly always need to have
    accurate shooting ability, excellent footwork,
    awareness and understanding of what is
    happening on the field around them, and most
    importantly, a superb work ethic.

    _____
    _____
    _____
    _____

7. When training, many lacrosse players just
    assume that, like football players, they should
    try to bench press as much as possible. In fact,
    lacrosse players mostly need to strengthen
    their core, which helps increase shot speed
    and makes scoring easier, and to make their
    legs quick and flexible. Good arms are also
    important, but it's not the biceps that matter
    most; instead, the key is to have strong
    forearms, which make it possible to grip the
    stick firmly and snap through when passing
    and shooting.

    _____
    _____
    _____
    _____

[...]lligent and consistent physical
[...] layers must also watch better
players [...] closely, and figure out the
[...] how they play the game. Asking
questions and applying the answers
thoughtfully is crucial. Good players also
develop an understanding of how the best
teams work together. Lacrosse is not an
individual sport; even a very good player
won't win many games if he doesn't think
about how he fits as a part of the whole team.

_____
_____
_____
_____

9. In lacrosse, attackers need to be able to put on
    quick bursts of speed, be able to send and
    receive passes at a moment's notice, and
    identify gaps in the defense that they can
    exploit. Midfielders especially need to be able
    to move the ball forward quickly to avoid
    being blocked by defensive slides.
    Defensemen, for their part, need to be able to
    slide effectively to shut down incoming
    attacks and to clear the ball quickly after
    forcing turnovers. Goalies need to be able to
    read the entire field of play and direct the
    defense in keeping the other team from getting
    into good scoring position.

    _____
    _____
    _____
    _____

10. The world lacrosse championship was first
    held in 1967, with four countries competing.
    In the final, the United States defeated
    Australia 25-11. The next world
    championship, also won by the United States,
    took place in 1974. Championships have been
    awarded every four years since then, and
    although the number of teams has increased
    greatly (reaching 38 at the 2014
    championship), the United States has
    continued to dominate the list of winners. It
    currently has nine victories under its belt. The
    only other country to win a world
    championship, Canada, has but three trophies
    to its name.

    _____
    _____
    _____
    _____

Lesson wY8
Main Ideas and Topic Sentences
Diving Into the Deep End

PRACTICE EXERCISE:

Directions: Answer the questions that follow the accompanying passage.

A Prescription for Fake Cures

(1) <u>Imagine trying to find a particular medicine 100 years ago, when medications were still poorly regulated.</u> Once found, you pop the lid and tap out a few pills into your palm. Living in a country that strictly regulates pharmaceutical production and distribution, (2) <u>the pills must be safe, so you take</u> them without a second thought.

What if these protections were not provided, though? What if (3) <u>you're</u> illness that required medication that you couldn't be sure was safe or effective? What if you learned too late that this medication contained no active ingredient or was mixed with toxic components?

1. Which version of this sentence most clearly introduces the topic of the paragraph?

   A) NO CHANGE
   B) Imagine having to fight with hundreds of other sick people for a limited supply of medication.
   C) Imagine walking into a drug store and immediately being handed the medication you need.
   D) Imagine rummaging through your medicine cabinet for a vital medication.

2. A) NO CHANGE
   B) the government vouches for the pills' safety, so you take
   C) you assume the pills are safe, and you take
   D) the safety of the pills is assumed, and you take

3. A) NO CHANGE
   B) they're
   C) their
   D) your

(4) <u>For millions of people in developing countries, these</u> <u>questions are all too real.</u> In 1995, a meningitis epidemic hit Niger, in West Africa. Although the Government of Niger **(5)** <u>carried</u> out an efficient vaccine program, more than 50,000 people were administered fake vaccines that contained no active ingredient, resulting in 2,500 deaths.

{6} Counterfeit drugs are estimated to be as high as 30 percent of all drug sales in the developing world. Globally, more than 100,000 people die every year as a result of these dangerous **(7)** <u>drugs, this likely represents</u> a significant underestimation. High profit margins and minimal risk, along with lack of political commitment and weak regulation, drive the counterfeit market.

4. Which of the following is the best version of the paragraph's topic sentence?

    A) NO CHANGE
    B) These questions, fortunately, do not apply to those of us in the United States.
    C) Many believe that these questions are no longer relevant to global health.
    D) These questions are just as important today as they were fifty years ago.

5. A) NO CHANGE
    B) carries
    C) will carry
    D) carrying

6. Which sentence, if added here, would best state the paragraph's main idea?

    A) Similar incidents continue to occur worldwide.
    B) Most pharmacists in developing nations have inadequate training.
    C) New medical technology may hold the key to solving this problem.
    D) Profits from the sale of counterfeit drugs often are used to fund other criminal enterprises.

7. A) NO CHANGE
    B) drugs, and this likely represents
    C) drugs; likely representing
    D) drugs and likely represents

(8) This problem seems to only be growing more severe, despite authorities' best efforts. PharmaChk, a fast, easy, and inexpensive screening technology for counterfeit and substandard medications, is being developed at Boston University to help combat the perils of poor quality drugs in the developing world.

(9) The PharmaChk device is quite expensive, but most units will be donated by foreign aid agencies. The device mixes the drug sample with a molecular probe specific to the drug. The reaction between the probe and the drug sample is then quantified by a light receiver embedded within the device to determine the exact amount of the active ingredient present in the sample. The strength of the light indicates the concentration of the drug. This process is fast and automated, with low power requirements and minimal user training required.

8. Which sentence most clearly states the paragraph's main idea?

A) NO CHANGE
B) The country that donated the counterfeit vaccines to Niger believed they were real.
C) Many in the United States are campaigning for greater regulation of medication quality.
D) This is the dire scenario that a promising new device called PharmaChk is hoping to prevent.

9. Which version of the underlined sentence best introduces the paragraph's topic?

A) NO CHANGE
B) To test a medication, a user simply places a drug sample into the briefcase-sized PharmaChk device.
C) Scientists are also using advanced printing techniques to mark drug packages as authentic.
D) Early tests have proven the efficacy of the PharmaChk's unique testing system.

{10} The intention is for PharmaChk to be used at multiple levels of a health system—within local pharmacies, **(11)** <u>medicine warehouses</u>, and at customs border crossings. A 2014 field test in Ghana showed the PharmaChk device to be 99.6 percent accurate in quantitatively identifying the amount of the drug in an injectable antimalarial medication. As a result, the device is now recommended by the World Health Organization as part of the first-line treatment for severe malaria.

10. Which sentence, if added here, would most clearly state the main idea of the paragraph?

A) Several other devices claim to analyze medication quality, but they are less precise.
B) Malaria is largely confined to tropical nations with poor sanitation systems.
C) The new device could soon be implemented on a wide scale.
D) Doctors do not expect the device to have a large or immediate impact.

11. A) NO CHANGE
B) warehousing medicine
C) they warehouse medicine
D) in medicine warehouses

TEST EXERCISE:

Directions: Answer the questions that follow the accompanying passages.

Climate Change in the Great Plains

Stretching from Canada to Mexico across the midsection of the country, the Great Plains region has a climate that varies greatly from north to south and east to west. **(1)** <u>Since</u> some southern portions of the region typically experience 70 to 100 days each year over 90°F, the northern portions typically see only 10 to 20 days above 90°F.

{2}

Although all of the region can experience sweltering summers and cold winters, northern portions are known for their bitterly cold and snowy winters. Nevertheless, during the last 30 years, northern portions of the region have seen average winter temperatures rise to 7°F above historical averages. Average year-round temperatures are also increasing. During this century, temperatures are projected to continue **(3)** <u>increasing especially</u> in the southern and central Great Plains during the summers. Projections for future precipitation patterns vary within the region. Northern areas may become wetter while southern areas may become drier, especially during the summer.

{4} [1] Although the population in most Great Plains counties has declined in the last 50 years, the population of the entire Great Plains region has increased by 102% since 1950. [2] Currently, more than two-thirds of the region's population lives in urban areas. [3] Major cities in the Great Plains regions include Tulsa, Oklahoma City, Kansas City, and Omaha. [4] Additionally, about 25% of the country's most rapidly growing cities are located in the Great Plains. [5] Ninety-six percent of this growth has occurred in and around the metropolitan areas of Texas and Colorado.

1. A) NO CHANGE
   B) While
   C) Moreover,
   D) Therefore,

2. Which of the following sentences should be added here in order to further support the ideas presented in the first sentence of the passage?

   A) The southern portion of this region is much hotter on average than the northern portion.
   B) Climate change threatens these temperatures, and will have a devastating impact on cities.
   C) Meanwhile, the western Great Plains is semi-arid, while the eastern portion is considerably wetter.
   D) The average temperature in the Great Plains is far higher than that of the Northeast.

3. A) NO CHANGE
   B) increasing: especially
   C) increasing; especially
   D) increasing, especially

4. Which of the following sentences should be eliminated in order to improve the focus of the paragraph?

   A) Sentence 1
   B) Sentence 2
   C) Sentence 3
   D) Sentence 4

This urban migration and rapid growth increase the region's vulnerability to the impacts **(5)** of climate change. For example, as populations decline in rural areas, health services may become concentrated primarily in cities. Moreover, in some cases, the growing cities are already struggling to manage their water resources, because demand for these resources **(6)** are greater than supply. {7}

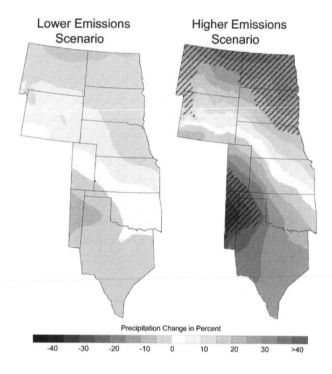

Most of the region's water is supplied by the Ogallala aquifer (also known as the High Plains aquifer), which provides drinking water for more than 80% of the population and **(8)** provides water that is used for irrigation for 13 million acres of land. This underground reservoir is fed by precipitation and ancient stores of water that have been trapped in layers of sediment dating back to the last ice age.

5. A) NO CHANGE
   B) from
   C) through
   D) in

6.  A) NO CHANGE
   B) was
   C) have been
   D) is

7. Based on the information in the graphic, which of the following sentences should be added here in order to further develop the ideas presented in this paragraph?

   A) Increased emissions threaten to worsen this struggle by leading to decreased precipitation, especially in the southwestern portion.
   B) Higher emissions will mean an end to many of these concerns in northern Great Plains cities.
   C) Emission standards must be tightened to prevent a drought throughout the region.
   D) Still, cities in the middle portion of the Great Plains region have little to worry about in regards to increased emissions.

8. A) NO CHANGE
   B) irrigates
   C) provides irrigation and water for
   D) irrigates by providing water for

C2 education
be smarter

Population, agricultural, and **(9)** growth by the economy have increased the demand for water in the region, even as the area's aquifer recharge rate, the rate at which water is replaced, declines. Water use now **(10)** keeps going up. As a result, since 1950, the average level of the aquifer has dropped by about 13 feet, approximately a 9% decrease in stored water. In areas with heavy irrigation, the level has dropped by as much as 100 to 250 feet. Without alternative resources and better water management practices, projected temperature increases, more frequent droughts, and higher rates of evaporation are likely to further stress the water supply. **{11}**

9. A) NO CHANGE
   B) economical growth
   C) economic growing
   D) economic growth

10. A) NO CHANGE
    B) exceeds the recharge rate
    C) is completely out of control
    D) continues on more than before

11. Which of the following sentences, if inserted here, would best conclude the passage?

    A) Unless much of the population of the Great Plains region moves to the country, the region is in serious trouble.
    B) These water concerns, when coupled with population growth and concentration, forecast a bleak future for the Great Plains region.
    C) Unfortunately, it is now too late to solve the problems posed by a combination of population growth and climate change.
    D) The government must take steps to find more water so that this stress does not become a threat in the future.

Lesson wY8
Main Ideas and Topic Sentences
Race to the Finish

HOMEWORK EXERCISE 1:

Directions: For each paragraph, write a topic sentence on the lines provided.

1. _____
   _____
   _____
   _____
   _____.

   Personal genomics refers to the sequencing of part or all of an individual's genome from his or her DNA. In the past few years, this has become dramatically more affordable, and soon it promises to revolutionize medicine as we know it. By having your genome sequenced, you can learn whether you are at risk for any of a huge range of inherited diseases. Genomic information can also inform what drug to prescribe a patient, and it may soon be possible to identify and target specific genes associated with cancer. This technology will let doctors customize medical treatment for each individual in a way that was never possible before.

2. _____
   _____
   _____
   _____
   _____.

   GDP stands for *Gross Domestic Product*, a measure of the total economic output of a country or region in one year. Its inventor, Simon Kuznets, warned in 1934 that it was a measure of economic size and should not be treated as a measure of human well-being. Unfortunately, GDP has been consistently misused in exactly the way Kuznets warned against. Many governments base their economic policy on maximizing GDP—growth at any cost, even if it increases inequality, pollutes the environment, or otherwise leaves many citizens worse off.

3. It is a common theme in political writing to bemoan the loss of manufacturing jobs in the United States. Automation has reduced the need for assembly-line workers, many of whose jobs can now be done by robots or machines.

   _____
   _____
   _____
   _____.

   After all, someone has to operate the machines. Manufacturing jobs aren't gone at all; rather, there are many available to those with the math, engineering, and computer skills to operate the complex machinery found in modern factories.

4. _____
   _____
   _____
   _____.

   Jupiter's fourth-largest moon, Europa has a thick ice sheet covering its entire surface. The ice sheet's smoothness and lack of craters suggest that it is relatively young. This in turn makes for an exciting prospect: underneath the ice may be a massive liquid ocean! Could there even be extraterrestrial life deep in Europa's seas? We are sure to continue uncovering this moon's mysteries in the decades to come.

5. _____
_____
_____
_____
_____ .

For one thing, despite being English, the Rolling Stones played music rooted in the most American of genres—the blues—and did it more convincingly than most Americans. Furthermore, out of frontman Mick Jagger, a white English boy from Kent, came a voice and stage presence indebted more to African-American bluesmen such as Muddy Waters than it was to anyone else. The final apparent contradiction that helped catapult the Stones to fame was that their music was extraordinarily technically accomplished, and yet it felt raw, almost amateurish: a sort of perfect imperfection.

6. _____
_____
_____
_____ .

For one thing, cigarettes carry with them the dangers of second-hand smoke, a compelling reason for government to regulate them. The consumer of a sugary soft drink, on the other hand, is harming no one but his or herself. Cigarette smoke is a direct cause of cancer. The link between refined sugar and conditions such as obesity and diabetes is not so direct; many individual lifestyle choices, such as exercise habits, also come into play. Finally, cigarettes are physically addictive in a way that can hardly be said of Coca-Cola.

7. Today, the phrase "Crossing the Rubicon" refers to a point of no return; that is, a decision that cannot be undone.

_____
_____
_____
_____ .

The Rubicon River is a shallow river in northern Italy that once marked the boundary between the Roman Republic and the province of Cisalpine Gaul. Julius Caesar, a popular Roman general, had been ordered to disband his army and return to Rome to face criminal charges. Instead, Caesar made a fateful decision, one from which there was no going back. He marched his army across the Rubicon, which was considered an act of treason. This provoked a civil war which led to Caesar's victory and ascension as dictator of Rome.

8. _____
_____
_____
_____ .

One way to misuse statistics is called *data dredging*. This consists of testing an enormous set of data for apparent relationships between any two seemingly unrelated variables. Did you know that for the last ten years, the divorce rate in Maine has decreased at almost exactly the same rate as the average U.S. consumption of margarine? Of course, this doesn't mean that divorces in Maine are caused by eating margarine—or vice versa! It simply illustrates that if you test enough random things, pure coincidence suggests eventually some of them will appear to be related.

9. In 2014, an online-only magazine called *Vice* sent a reporter into Syria in the midst of its civil war, where he conducted exclusive video interviews with Islamist militants. In the past, such daring, dangerous reporting would have been the province of the New York Times or CNN. But today, such traditional news organizations are struggling while the free-for-all world of online journalism continues to surprise. Even *Buzzfeed*, a website often ridiculed for its mindless, repetitive content, now occasionally produces serious original reporting.

_____

_____

_____

_____

_____ .

10. A common lament of those critical of modern pop culture is that, from films to books to music, we don't seem to produce anything classic or timeless anymore. When was there last a musical artist to rival Frank Sinatra, the Beatles, or Elvis Presley? What was the last book that had a serious claim to the title of "Great American Novel"?

_____

_____

_____

_____

_____ . Perhaps the new classics are among us already, and we just don't recognize them as classics yet. After all, not every creative genius from prior generations was fully appreciated in his or her time. Who can predict what from our era our grandchildren will still be reading, watching, or listening to half a century from now?

HOMEWORK EXERCISE 2:

Directions: Answer the questions that follow the accompanying passages.

[1]

David Christian wants to change how you study history. He wants to do this using a movement called Big History that aims to replace **(1)** normal high school history with a broad and interdisciplinary "history of everything," drawing connections all the way from the Big Bang to this morning's news. **(2)** With the help of a famous billionaire, Christian's innovative Big History may soon be coming to a school near you.

[2]

[1] As a young professor at Australia's Macquarie University, Christian found that he had a persistent urge to examine his subjects from unusual angles and seek out interconnections **(3)** between many subject areas. [2] At the time, he was teaching a course on Russia in the 19th century. [3] Christian's idea is to start at the Big Bang **(4)** and divides all of history into eight eras, covering the formation of stars and galaxies, the beginnings of life on Earth, the evolution of humankind, and the rise of civilizations. [4] A lesson on the early use of iron to make tools might begin with a discussion of how elemental iron forms in stars and why it is so plentiful in Earth's crust. [5] A lecture on the Spanish conquest of Peru might include a look at the biology of the potato plant, native to the Peruvian Andes; the reasons the potato became the staple food of Europe's **(5)** poor and the devastating consequences three centuries later, when Ireland suffered a massive famine after its potato crop was ravaged by disease. {6}

1. A) NO CHANGE
   B) the old version of history
   C) the traditional high school history curriculum
   D) the regular study of history

2. Suppose the author's intent in writing this essay is to inform readers about the growth of a new movement in education. Which of the following choices for the underlined sentence most logically and cohesively accomplishes this goal?

   A) NO CHANGE
   B) Christian has been developing this curriculum for over 25 years.
   C) Christian's plan is a daring reinvention of a time-tested subject, but may in fact be a good idea.
   D) Big History encompasses far more than just history.

3. A) NO CHANGE
   B) among many
   C) of many
   D) with various

4. A) NO CHANGE
   B) and divide
   C) and dividing
   D) and divided

5. A) NO CHANGE
   B) poor, and
   C) poor; and
   D) poor, and finally,

6. The cohesion and focus of Paragraph 2 would be most enhanced by removing which sentence?

   A) Sentence 1
   B) Sentence 2
   C) Sentence 3
   D) Sentence 4

[3]

Christian and a number of other experts hope that this format will be more engaging for **(7)** <u>students and prompts</u> a deeper level of critical thinking, than the traditional approach to world history—a chronological survey of major events. "We didn't know what we were doing, but the really magical thing, and I think it's what still drives me today, was the reaction of the students," he says. "What this course can do, however it's taught, is validate big questions that are impossible to even ask within a more silo-ized education."

[4]

[1] In Christian's hands, Big History might have been a quirky approach confined to a few Australian colleges, but a video he put online recently got the attention of Bill Gates, the Microsoft multibillionaire who has made it his mission to promote **(8)** <u>the next best thing for teachers</u>. [2] Within a week, Gates was in San Diego asking **(9)** <u>him how he</u> could help to get Big History into classrooms. [3] **(10)** Gates is disliked by many educators, who perceive him as throwing his money around to promote his pet ideas without soliciting the input of education experts. [4] Still, at last count, with the help of funding from Gates, the Big History program was offered to over 15,000 students at 1,200 schools across America. This number is growing every year. {11}

7. A) NO CHANGE
   B) students, and prompting
   C) students and prompt
   D) students, and prompt

8. A) NO CHANGE
   B) pet projects he can pressure schools to implement
   C) innovative ideas in education
   D) a novel pedagogical praxis

9. A) NO CHANGE
   B) him how one
   C) asking Christian how he
   D) asking Christian how Gates

10. Assuming all of the following sentences are true, which one, if added before Sentence 3, would most logically and cohesively connect Sentence 3 to the rest of the paragraph?

    A) Christian was eager to spread Big History.
    B) Gates was adamant about the idea.
    C) Gates's involvement was by no means guaranteed to be a boon to the movement.
    D) Changes to the history curriculum tend to draw the scrutiny of politicians.

11. Suppose the author wants to add a quote from a professor of psychology on how students retain information better when they can relate it to multiple areas of knowledge. To which paragraph would this addition most logically be made?

    A) Paragraph 1
    B) Paragraph 2
    C) Paragraph 3
    D) Paragraph 4

Lesson wY9
Logical Sequence
Getting Your Feet Wet

Directions: Use the paragraphs below to answer the questions.

[1]

[1] In the 1870s, Iowa farmer Jesse Hiatt discovered a mutant seedling in his apple orchard. [2] Hiatt named the apple the Hawkeye and entered it in a contest, which it handily won. [3] No matter how many times he cut the tree down, it grew back, and a decade later, the tree bore its first fruit. [4] Stark Brothers, the company that held the contest, bought the rights to the Hawkeye, changed its name to Stark Delicious, and began an ambitious marketing campaign. {2}

[2]

The Red Delicious apple can be found everywhere, but its omnipresence is hardly due to its taste – beautiful they may be, but Red Delicious apples are generally considered to be inferior in terms of texture and flavor. So how did such an unlikeable apple come to dominate the produce markets of America?

[3]

[1] Eventually, the Stark Delicious became the Red Delicious of today. [2] Careful breeding focused on the apple's bright red color and storage ability, without giving any attention to taste. [3] Consumers failed to notice the shortcomings of the Red Delicious, seeming to believe that apples are supposed to be bland and mealy – that is, until the introduction of new varieties in the late 1990s awakened taste buds across the nation. [4] Perhaps one day soon, the Red Delicious will fade away, replaced by apples with flavor and taste. {3}

1. In which order should the paragraphs be arranged in order to improve the logic of the passage?

   A) NO CHANGE
   B) 3, 1, 2
   C) 2, 3, 1
   D) 2, 1, 3

2. The author of the passage is considering adding the following sentence to the third paragraph:

   "Today, producers still grow millions upon millions of Red Delicious, but they are being shipped overseas in ever larger amounts."

   Where should it be placed to most improve the logical flow of the paragraph?

   A) Before sentence 1
   B) Between sentences 1 and 2
   C) Between sentences 2 and 3
   D) Between sentences 3 and 4

3. Which of the following would most improve the logical flow of the paragraph?

   A) NO CHANGE
   B) Switch sentences 2 and 3
   C) Remove sentence 2
   D) Switch sentences 3 and 4

Lesson wY9
Logical Sequence
Wading In

TOPIC OVERVIEW: LOGICAL SEQUENCE

The SAT writing section is intended to test how well we can recognize and solve various problems in writing, which means that the test goes beyond grammar, usage, and mechanics. We've already seen some of the non-grammar questions in Lesson 5 and Lesson 8. Today we'll look at another type of non-grammar question, Logical Sequence.

Logical Sequence questions look at whether we can recognize and address problems in organization. These questions ask us to put ideas in logical order, whether that means rearranging sentences within a paragraph, adding sentences in appropriate places, or rearranging paragraphs within a passage.

TOPIC OVERVIEW: SENTENCE LOGICAL SEQUENCE

Sentence Logical Sequence questions ask us to rearrange the sentences within a paragraph, eliminate a sentence from a paragraph, or add a sentence to a paragraph. Either way, our task is to ensure that the final paragraph is presented in the most logical sequence possible.

The best order can usually be determined by the content of the sentences. Concepts that relate to each other should appear close to each other in the paragraph, and if there is a cause and effect relationship within the paragraph, the cause should usually come before the effect. Often, transitional words or phrases can provide clues to help us arrange the sentences.

TOPIC OVERVIEW: PARAGRAPH LOGICAL SEQUENCE

Paragraph Logical Sequence questions ask us to arrange the paragraphs within the passage in the most logical order. These questions will often ask where a certain paragraph should be placed.

As with Sentence Logical Sequence questions, we must look at the content of the paragraphs to determine the most logical order. Again, transition words and phrases can provide us with clues to help arrange the paragraphs.

Understanding the basic structure of a well-written passage will help when answering Paragraph Logical Sequence questions. In any given passage, the first paragraph will typically serve as an introduction that offers a brief overview of the main topic. The middle paragraphs, or body paragraphs, provide supporting information and should flow logically from one idea to the next. As you read the passage, look for any awkward or sudden shifts from one paragraph to the next; this is often a clue that one of the paragraphs is misplaced. The final paragraph usually serves as a conclusion that wraps up the main ideas of the passage.

ANSWERING SENTENCE LOGICAL SEQUENCE QUESTIONS

Once we have identified a question as a Sentence Logical Sequence question, we need to examine the part of the passage being referenced. It is usually pretty easy to locate the correct part of the passage because the sentences in the paragraph being referenced will be numbered.

Closely examine the specific paragraph, looking for any transitional words or phrases that might suggest the most logical order of the sentences. If there are transitions that don't make sense in the original paragraph, that is a clue that a sentence is out of place.

Look for sentences that contain related ideas but that are not placed close together. This is another red flag that may indicate that a sentence is out of place.

Look for a sentence that seems to relate to the paragraph immediately before or after the paragraph in question. If a sentence relates to the preceding paragraph, that sentence may best be placed at the beginning of the paragraph to act as a transitional sentence. If a sentence relates to the following paragraph, that sentence might be intended as a transition to the next paragraph, in which case it should appear at the end of the paragraph in question.

After you have looked for clues to indicate where a sentence is out of place, look at the answer choices. Select the answer choice that puts the sentence in the most logical order. Once you have chosen an answer, reread the paragraph using the answer choice. If the paragraph makes logical sense, move on to the next question.

Here is a summary of the strategy for Sentence Logical Sequence questions:

1. Locate the part of the passage referenced in the question.
2. Closely examine the paragraph to look for signs that one or more sentences are out of place. Signs include:
    a. Transitional words or phrases that don't seem to make sense.
    b. Sentences that contain related ideas but that are not placed close together in the paragraph.
    c. Sentences that relate to other paragraphs, which might suggest that the sentence is intended to transition between paragraphs.
3. Based on these signs, select the answer that seems to place the sentences in the most logical order.
4. Reread the paragraph as it should be given the answer choice you selected. If the paragraph now makes logical sense, move on to the next question.

ANSWERING PARAGRAPH LOGICAL SEQUENCE QUESTIONS

Once we identify a question as a Paragraph Logical Sequence question, we should quickly skim through the passage. As we skim, we need to look for the relationships between the ideas of each paragraph. It's a good idea to jot down notes identifying the main ideas in each paragraph.

As with Sentence Logical Sequence questions, we should look for paragraphs that contain related ideas but that are not placed near each other. This is a sign that one of these paragraphs is out of order.

We can also look for transitional words, phrases, or sentences that seem out of place. Transitions can provide clues to indicate the order in which the paragraphs are *supposed* to be arranged, so if a transition doesn't seem to make sense, it may be because the paragraphs are out of order.

Once we've looked for clues suggesting the order in which the paragraphs should be placed, we can look at the answer choices. Select the answer choice that seems to place the paragraphs in the most logical order. Finally, skim through the passage using that answer choice to be sure that the revised version makes more sense.

Here is a summary of the strategy for answering Paragraph Logical Sequence questions:

1. Skim the passage and jot down notes identifying the main ideas of each paragraph.
2. Look for clues that suggest that the paragraphs are out of order, including:
   a. Paragraphs containing related ideas that are not placed near each other.
   b. Transitional words, phrases, or sentences that don't seem to fit.
3. Select the answer choice that seems to place the paragraphs in the most logical order.
4. Quickly skim through the passage again, this time with the paragraphs in the order indicated by the answer you've chosen. If the revised version of the passage makes more sense, move on to the next question.

Lesson wY9
Logical Sequence
Learning to Swim

CONCEPT EXERCISE:

Directions: For each paragraph below, list the order of the sentences that would create the most logical and coherent flow of ideas.

1. [1] Avoidance of corruption is an essential organizing principle of our representative democracy. [2] Madison and other Founding Fathers also understood that rooting out corruption on a case-by-case basis would be extraordinarily difficult, so they sought to prevent the emergence of this problem through the structure of the Constitution and the new nation's laws. [3] Benjamin Franklin was so alarmed at the prospect of corruption that he wanted public officials to receive no salary because he worried they might seek office for selfish reasons. [4] These measures were designed to encourage public virtue and reduce the temptation to put one's private interests before those of the general public.

    __1__ __3__ __2__ __4__   1 2 4 3

2. [1] The jets are thought to be no more than 300 kilometers wide, and when they reach the surface, they produce hot spots which create huge lava flows. [2] The jets act as pipes that transfer heat from the core but how they are created isn't clear. [3] They have been assumed to originate near the boundary between the Earth's core and the mantle, almost 3,000 kilometers underground, nearly halfway to the planet's center. [4] According to current mantle-plume theory, heat from Earth's core somehow generates narrow jets of hot magma that gush through the mantle to the surface.

    __4__ __2__ __3__ __1__

3. [1] First, one must put the bait in an area where fish are likely to be lurking. [2] Learning the behaviors and preferred habitats of various fish will help the careful sportsperson aim the bait at the right spot, thus increasing the chances of success. [3] Fishing is a rewarding activity that can be done at any age and can provide a robust and enjoyable challenge for the mind and body. [4] It's not difficult to learn how to fish, but one must plan and organize his or her efforts to ensure fun and success.

    3 4 1 2

    __3__ __2__ __1__ __4__

4. [1] Adding these figures together yields a figure of $1.2 trillion in student debt—about 7% of the 2014 U.S. Gross Domestic Product. [2] Despite receiving grants, tax incentives, and scholarships, students may accumulate an astounding $30,000 in debt for a four-year university degree. [3] Many have loans in excess of $100,000, and shoulder other financial liabilities such as lost savings. [4] These figures are only for an undergraduate degree; additionally, attending graduate school—an often necessary step in a student's career path—can burden him or her with a lifetime of mountainous debt. [5] Unfortunately, that is just the average.

    __2__ __3__ __5__ __1__ __4__

    2 5 3 4 1

5. [1] Historian Frederick Jackson Turner presented his "Frontier Thesis" in an address at Chicago's 1893 World's Columbian Exposition. [2] He claimed that "the existence of an area of free land, its continuous recession, and the advance of American settlement westward explain American development." [3] Turner asserted that expansion was the most important factor in shaping American history. [4] "Now, four centuries from the discovery of America, at the end of a hundred years of life under the Constitution, the frontier has gone, and with its going has closed the first period of American history," Turner concluded. [5] In 1890, however, the Census Bureau stated that all the land within the United States was claimed, and there was no longer a frontier.

1 2 4 3 5

Lesson wY9
Logical Sequence
Diving Into the Deep End

PRACTICE EXERCISE:

Directions: Read the passage to answer the questions provided.

[1] Most of us never actually bother to read text labeled "terms and conditions," "privacy policy," or "financial prospectus." [2] We usually just check the "accept" box, assume all is well, and move on. [3] Still, wouldn't it be better to have a computer program that could read these documents for us and alert us to any problems? **{1}**

[4] This field, which dates back to the 1950s, works at the intersection of computers and language. [5] The goal of natural language processing is to enable computers to glean meaning from ordinary human ("natural") language. [6] This ultimately could be among the potential benefits of natural language processing. [7] To accomplish this goal, computer scientists use automated algorithms that process linguistic data from text. **{2}**

[8] These tools could also be applicable "wherever text serves as data," he says, for example in sociolinguistics, political science, or economics. [9] Smith designs algorithms with the goal of creating such reading software, but the algorithms aren't limited to just reading. [10] His research also produces valuable software tools for translation, text mining, question answering, and information extraction. [11] For instance, a sociolinguist could use Smith's software to analyze web posts to track the spread of new slang terms. **{3}**

[12] Smith specifically is studying computational models for natural language parsing and semantic analysis. [13] That is, he designs computer programs to "take a sentence and try to figure out what it means," Smith says. [14] Most people would rather delegate these tasks to a computer that will perform consistently and without getting tired. **{4}**

1. Where in the preceding paragraph should the author add the following sentence?

   In such a scenario, we'd certainly be more likely to catch companies who want to misuse our personal information.

   A) Before Sentence 1
   B) Before Sentence 2
   C) Before Sentence 3
   D) After Sentence 3

2. In context, where in the paragraph would Sentence 6 be most logically placed?

   A) Where it is now
   B) Before Sentence 4
   C) Before Sentence 5
   D) After Sentence 7

3. In context, Sentence 8 would best be placed

   A) where it is now.
   B) after Sentence 9.
   C) after Sentence 10.
   D) after Sentence 11.

4. Where in the preceding paragraph should the author add the following sentence?

   Doing this could help with certain tasks that people cannot do easily, such as extracting information out of very large collections.

   A) Before Sentence 12
   B) Before Sentence 13
   C) Before Sentence 14
   D) After Sentence 14

"Imagine a computer program that reads text and interprets it to do something useful, but not the way you and I would do," says Noah Smith, a professor at Carnegie Mellon University. "This program could read to people who don't like to read, or who don't have time to read." {5}

[15] The process is the automated equivalent of the sentence diagramming that many of today's adults engaged in during elementary school. [16] "Our programs analyze sentences into deeper linguistic structures," Smith says. [17] Focusing on these structures helps the computers understand fine but crucial distinctions of meaning, such as those found in legal contracts. {6}

[18] Fortunately, these areas are precisely where computer programs have their greatest strengths. [19] To be sure, these programs have a long way to go before attaining human-like reading and comprehension skills. [20] However, "humans are rarely perfect at these tasks, either" Smith says. [21] People do have cognitive limitations, such as flawed memories and susceptibility to distractions. {7}

"The public perception of this artificial intelligence branch of computer science is often colored by fears that robots might replace us," he adds. "We are, in fact, trying to make tools that will make life easier and less tedious for people." {8}

[22] Smith also has applied his methods to other problems. [23] The latter could benefit economists who study how companies interact with government or with each other. [24] For instance, he has measured public opinion as expressed in social media messages and compared companies by scrutinizing their press releases. {9}

5. Where in the passage would the preceding paragraph be most logically placed?

    A) Where it is now
    B) Before the 1st paragraph
    C) Before the 3rd paragraph
    D) Before the 4th paragraph

6. In which order should the sentences in the paragraph be arranged in order to improve the logic and cohesion of the paragraph?

    A) NO CHANGE
    B) 15, 17, 16
    C) 17, 15, 16
    D) 17, 16, 15

7. Where in the paragraph would Sentence 18 be most logically placed?

    A) Where it is now
    B) Before Sentence 20
    C) Before Sentence 21
    D) After Sentence 21

8. Where in the passage would the preceding paragraph be most logically placed?

    A) Where it is now
    B) Before the 7th paragraph
    C) Before the 10th paragraph
    D) After the 11th paragraph

9. In which order should the sentences in the paragraph be arranged in order to improve the logic and cohesion of the paragraph?

    A) NO CHANGE
    B) 22, 24, 23
    C) 23, 24, 22
    D) 24, 23, 22

[25] As for social media, "text exists in a larger social context," Smith says. [26] People don't create language purely because they enjoy creating language. [27] The advent of these platforms allows researchers like Smith to observe many more interactions than they could have previously. [28] This wealth of textual data could lead to statistical methods that help us better understand what people mean when they write or talk. {**10**}

[29] Finally, Smith's research group makes its software publicly available. [30] The goal is to for as many people as possible to experiment with the new algorithms. [31] They are not meant just for students in the classroom, but for other researchers, startup companies, and even regular people who want to try their hands at natural language processing. [32] If you're sick of skipping past all the "terms and conditions" pages without reading them, now you can learn how to make your computer read them for you. {**11**}

10. Where in the preceding paragraph should the following sentence be added?

Social media, like Twitter and Facebook, are intended to be read by people we know, but often there is a much larger conversation that goes on.

A) Before Sentence 25
B) Before Sentence 27
C) Before Sentence 28
D) After Sentence 28

11. Where in the paragraph would Sentence 30 be most logically placed?

A) Where it is now
B) Before Sentence 29
C) Before Sentence 32
D) After Sentence 32

TEST EXERCISE:

Ancient Origins of the Modern Population Explosion

[1] A revolution is afoot in the science of human population growth. [2] A new study of demographic and archeological data **(1)** suggest that the human population explosion, commonly attributed to industrialization and better public health during the 18th and 19th centuries, arose from events occurring 2,000 years ago. [3] According to Aaron Stutz, the study's author, modern developments did lead to longer life spans, but new evidence shows that a **(2)** vital threshold of political and economic change occurred 1,500 to 2,000 years ago which set the stage for the later population boom. [4] This new reality created opportunities for more people to get resources, form successful families, and generate capital that could be handed down to the next generation.{**3**}

Population dynamics has been a controversial topic since English scholar Thomas Malthus argued that disease and famine inevitably **(4)** obstruct population growth. He formulated the "Malthusian Catastrophe" theory just prior to the global population reaching one billion. While it took over 200,000 years for humans to achieve this population milestone, it took only another 120 years for world population to double. Huge population growth in the last two centuries seemed to confirm Malthus's grim predictions.

1. A) NO CHANGE
    B) is suggestive
    C) suggests
    D) suggested

2. Within the context of the passage, which of the following is the best replacement for the underlined word?

    A) NO CHANGE
    B) critical
    C) essential
    D) important

3. Which sentence most effectively establishes the main topic of the first paragraph?

    A) Sentence 1
    B) Sentence 2
    C) Sentence 3
    D) Sentence 4

4. What would be the best replacement for the underlined word?

    A) NO CHANGE
    B) suppress
    C) stifle
    D) check

{5}The new evidence indicates that human population can grow despite environmental degradation, conflict, **(6)** <u>and suffering disease</u> because of a subtle interaction between competition and organization. At a certain tipping point, this interaction created opportunities for individuals to gain more control over their lives and prosper, opening the door to beneficial economies of scale.

5. Which of the following sentences would improve the logical flow from the second to the third paragraph?

A) Unlike Malthus, Stutz argues that population growth destroys personal freedom.

B) Consequently, Stutz argues population growth leads to a number of harmful results.

C) In contrast to Malthus's work, Stutz's study points out the potential benefits of explosive population growth.

D) Stutz's study, however, has demonstrated that explosive population growth is, in reality, an entirely positive phenomenon.

6. A) NO CHANGE
   B) and disease
   C) and to suffer disease
   D) and suffer disease

Stutz cites the Roman Empire, which spanned 500 years, from just before the Common Era to 476 CE, as a classic example of passing through this threshold. The Roman Empire was one of the largest and most prosperous in history **(7)** , however, the lifespan of its citizens was often short and full of suffering. Farm laborers and miners were reduced to misery while producing surplus goods for trading and empire building. Large numbers of young males had to serve in the military to ward off rebellions. Life expectancy was only twenty to thirty years. **{8}** Paradoxically, amid all this suffering, the dynamic labor force increased the potential for providing more democracy and competition. Stutz argues this process, in turn, led to a more complex, inter-generational dynamic. Parents could better care for **(9)** their children and even provide them with resources well after infancy.

7. A) NO CHANGE
   B) ; however,
   C) , however,
   D) –however–

8. Based on the information in the graph provided, which of the following facts could be added here to support the ideas presented in this paragraph?

   A) Over a third of Roman newborns did not survive their first year.
   B) Romans who reached their twentieth year had a good chance of living into their forties.
   C) Five year olds only made up a tenth of the total population of the Roman Empire.
   D) Adolescence was a time of increased risk in Ancient Rome.

9. A) NO CHANGE
   B) his or her
   C) it's
   D) one's

(10) <u>The tipping point having been reached,</u> Stutz argues, and the trend continued despite the collapse of the Roman Empire; consequently, the complex political reality that emerged at the beginning of the Common Era created opportunities for individuals, states, and massive powers like England, France, and China to benefit from large-scale economic development.{11}

Life Expectancy of Young People in the Roman Empire			
Age	Projected Life Expectancy	Percent of Total Population	Approximate Chance of Being Dead by the End of the Year
0	21	4%	36%
1	33	10%	24%
5	42	11%	6%
10	42	11%	5%
15	46	10%	7%
20	48	9%	8%
Adapted from Bruce Frier's *Landlords and Tenants in Imperial Rome*, 1980			

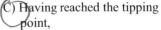

10. A) NO CHANGE,
   B) The tipping point had been reached,
   C) Having reached the tipping point,
   D) Reaching the tipping point,

11. Which of the following sentences would best conclude the passage?

   A) Additionally, Stutz believes this revised understanding of human population growth could help scientists analyze the societal effects of modern and future population growth.
   B) In fact, these new insights could help countries bring population growth under control.
   C) Stutz believes his research could help scientists accurately predict the total world population in 2100.
   D) Unfortunately, these new findings indicate that Malthus's dire predictions are increasingly likely to occur.

Finish 8/6 START

Lesson wY9
Logical Sequence
Race to the Finish

HOMEWORK EXERCISE 1:

Directions: For each paragraph below, list the order of the sentences that would create the most logical and coherent flow of ideas.

1. [1] It may be hard to believe it today, but at one time recorded rap music was considered a novelty. [2] Wonder Mike, Big Bank Hank, and Master Gee may not have performed on the very first rap recording, but their infectious "Rapper's Delight" became the first rap hit and, incidentally, changed popular music forever. [3] That is, until 1979, when Sylvia Robinson, co-owner of Sugar Hill Records, gathered three young rappers from Englewood, New Jersey, dubbed them the Sugarhill Gang, and brought them into a recording studio in order to cash in on the "rap fad." [4] Back in the 1970s, when hip-hop was being born at Bronx street parties, rap was an art form created and performed live.

   1 4 2 3

2. [1] Unfortunately, the amount of vegetables children ate did not change from 2003 to 2010. [2] The amount of whole fruit – that is, fruit in all forms except juice – that children two to eighteen years old ate increased by 67% from 2003 to 2010 and replaced fruit juice as the main contributor of fruit to children's diets. [3] Moreover, in 2007- 2010, children did not meet recommendations for the amount of fruit and vegetables they should eat. [4] This increase in the consumption of whole fruit is a positive development, since nutrition experts recommend that most fruit come from whole fruit, rather than from juice.

   2 3 4 1

3. [1] When a host brushes the spot where a tick is waiting, it quickly climbs aboard and then finds a suitable place to bite its host. [2] Ticks can't fly or jump. [3] While questing, ticks hold onto leaves and grass by their lower legs. [4] Instead, they wait for a host, resting on the tips of grasses and shrubs in a position known as "questing." [5] They hold their upper pair of legs outstretched, waiting to climb onto a passing host.

   2 4 3 5 1

4. [1] In 1959 he recorded the album *Mingus Ah Um*. [2] *Mingus Ah Um* has stood the test of time and remains one of the finest recordings in a career full of fine recordings. [3] The album features such classic Mingus compositions as "Goodbye Pork Pie Hat" (an elegy to Lester Young) and "Fables of Faubus" (a wordless protest against segregationist Arkansas governor Orval E. Faubus). [4] Jazz composer and performer Charles Mingus ended the 1950s in top form. [5] Even in that year – 1959, the year of such masterpieces as Dave Brubeck's *Time Out*, Miles Davis's *Kind of Blue*, and Ornette Coleman's prophetic *The Shape of Jazz to Come* – *Mingus Ah Um* stands out.

   4 1 2 3 5

C2 education
be smarter

5.   [1] You can find the ASP online at the Library of Congress website. [2] The American State Papers, or ASP, are an especially valuable resource for students of the Early Republic. [3] The ASP does not contain transcripts of congressional debates, but it includes messages to and from the presidents, reports on such milestones as the Lewis and Clark expedition, and valuable records on US-Native American relations. [4] Compiled and published in 38 volumes between 1831 and 1861, the ASP contains key legislative and executive branch documents created by and for Congress between 1789 and 1838. [5] The ASP is most important because it is the source for such documents created between 1789 and 1817, before Congress began publishing such records as they were created.

2 4 5 3 1

HOMEWORK EXERCISE 2:

I read much less than I used to **(1)** <u>do, I think much more</u>. Yet what is the use of thought which can no longer serve to direct life? Better, perhaps, to read and read incessantly, losing **(2)** <u>ones' self</u> in the activity of other minds.

This summer I **(3)** <u>have not taken up no new book</u>, but have renewed my acquaintance with several old ones which I had not opened for many a year. One or two have been books that mature men rarely read at all — books which it is one's habit to "take as read;" to presume sufficiently known to speak of, but never to open. Thus, one day my hand fell upon the *Anabasis,* the little Oxford edition which I used at school, with its boyish sign-manual on the fly-leaf, its blots and underlinings and marginal scrawls. To my shame I possess no other edition; yet this is a book one would like to have in beautiful form. I opened it, I began to read — a ghost of boyhood stirring in my heart — and from chapter to chapter was led on, until after a few days I had read the whole.

{4} I like to link childhood with these latter, warmer days, and no better way could **(5)** <u>I have been finding</u> than this return to a school-book, which, even as a school-book, was my great delight.

1. A) NO CHANGE
   B) do; I think
   C) do and I think
   D) do, in the fact that I think

2. A) NO CHANGE
   B) ones self
   C) oneselves
   D) one's self

3. A) NO CHANGE
   B) haven't taken up no new book
   C) have taken up any new book
   D) have taken up no new book

4. Which of the following serves as an effective transition between paragraph 2 and paragraph 3

   A) I am glad this happened in the summer-time.
   B) I often collect rare books.
   C) I was so fond of school as a child that, unlike my classmates, I never dreaded reading my schoolbooks.
   D) *Anabasis* was my favorite book at a schoolboy.

5. A) NO CHANGE
   B) I have been found
   C) I have found
   D) I found

[1] By some trick of memory I always **(6)** <u>mingle</u> school-boy work on the classics with a sense of warm and sunny days; rain and **(7)** <u>gloom</u> and a chilly atmosphere must have been far **(8)** <u>the more frequent conditions, but these things are forgotten.</u> [2] My old Liddell and Scott still serves me, and if, in opening it, I bend close enough to catch the scent of the leaves, I am back again at that day of boyhood (noted on the fly-leaf by the hand of one long dead) when the book was new and I used it for the first time. [3] In those days, I was a student who was frequently late for school. [4] It was a day of summer, and perhaps there fell upon the unfamiliar page, viewed with childish **(9)** <u>half apprehension and in addition half delight.</u>{10}{11}

6. Within the context of the passage, which of the following is the most precise replacement of the underlined word?

   A) NO CHANGE
   B) associate
   C) attach
   D) merge

7. Within the context of the passage, which of the following is the most precise replacement of the underlined word?

   A) NO CHANGE
   B) foreboding
   C) misery
   D) dejection

8. A) NO CHANGE
   B) The more frequent conditions when these things are forgotten.
   C) The more frequent conditions, and these things are forgotten.
   D) The more frequent conditions if these things are forgotten.

9. A) NO CHANGE
   B) half apprehension and, half delight
   C) half apprehension and half delight
   D) half apprehension and also half delight

10. Which of the following sentences would effectively conclude the paragraph?

   A) When recalling such times, I will forever be filled with feelings of warmth.
   B) Unfortunately, the rain and cold of my childhood crowd out any happy memory I may have of the time.
   C) Following this experience, I vowed to never dispose of books from my childhood.
   D) When my boyhood ended, I became a most avid reader, rarely taking time to even ponder my life circumstances.

11. Which of the following sentences should be eliminated in order to improve the focus of the paragraph?

   A) Sentence 1
   B) Sentence 2
   C) Sentence 3
   D) Sentence 4

Lesson wY10
Checkpoint

LET'S CHECK IN

Congratulations! We are now halfway through this book!

Today's lesson isn't really a lesson – it's a checkpoint to see how far we've come since the first lesson.

On the following pages, you'll find a series of writing passages and questions. Each set is designed to reflect the types of passages and questions that are common to the SAT writing section. Many of the questions will look familiar because they cover information we've already studied, but some of the questions may be new question types that we'll cover in later lessons.

As you work through each practice set, be sure to mark any questions that you find particularly challenging so that you and your teacher can review them in greater depth when you've finished this lesson.

Lesson wY10
Checking In
Practice Sets

PRACTICE PASSAGE 1

With its picturesque whitewashed buildings and its charming setting on the ruins of a Moorish mosque, the Spanish village of Genalguacil, population 522, seems like an ideal vacation destination. But its location along a winding road in a hilly region leads visitors to choose other, more accessible regions. In the 1990s, **(1)** the village launched an art festival, which hoped to attract more tourists. Now the village **(2)** increased its investment in the festival, hoping to bring in revenue despite the economic downturn.

Like many art festivals, Genalguacil's festival offers residency, subsidizing a place to stay for artists while they pursue their work. But the festival in Genalguacil is **(3)** a bizarre attempt to support Spanish artists while also bringing some measure of economic revival. Each artist attending the festival is required to donate at least one of **(4)** their works to the village. As many of these works are statues or other outdoor installations, the town has been transformed into a sort of "museum village."

The mayor, Miguel Ángel Herrera, said the bet on contemporary arts to draw tourists was already paying off. During the two weeks of the festival, about 8,000 people visited Genalguacil, out of a total of 20,000 visitors expected this year, according to estimates from the town hall. **{5}**

1. A) NO CHANGE
   B) the village launched an art festival hoping to attract more tourists.
   C) the village launched an art festival that hoped to attract more tourists.
   D) the village, hoping to attract more tourists, launched an art festival.

   [handwritten: my people]

2. A) NO CHANGE
   B) is increasing
   C) had increased
   D) was increasing

3. Which of the following is the most precise replacement for the underlined word?

   A) NO CHANGE
   B) an inconceivable
   C) an unusual
   D) a mysterious

4. A) NO CHANGE
   B) his or her
   C) one's
   D) its

5. Which of the following sentences, if added here, would best support the main idea of the paragraph?

   A) Other towns in the region saw a similar increase in visitors over the same time period.
   B) Furthermore, Mr. Herrera predicted that the town hall would close the year with a budget surplus.
   C) The festival, held every other summer, takes place during the height of the tourist season.
   D) Many of these visitors reported that they had not been aware of the festival before they arrived.

The investment in the arts benefits not only the town, but also the artists. Spending two weeks in an isolated village alongside other artists, several of the artists argued, is an experience that can be more enriching than having **(6)** their works on display at a major museum. **(7)** However, some of the artists said that taking part in the Genalguacil festival was a chance to meet not only other artists but also local residents. {8}

"I think that is much more rewarding than having my work inside a museum, as if it was put inside a box," Ms. Bueno said. "I really believe this festival should allow the village to breathe art in a way people here haven't done before."

{9} Like many other Spanish villages, however, Genalguacil has **(10)** an outdated farming population whose main preoccupation has not been admiring art. Francisco Izquierdo, a retired farmer, said that he did not have strong feelings about the murals and outdoor statues that now adorn his village, but that he appreciated the greater focus on aesthetics and the fact that "all this art has helped make this place a lot cleaner." While the art festival has benefited the town and helped balance its **(11)** budget, so it alone may not be enough to ensure the village's long-term economic success. "There is no longer enough farming," he lamented, "so the young continue to leave and the old stay."

6. A) NO CHANGE
   B) there
   C) you're
   D) they're

7. A) NO CHANGE
   B) Actually,
   C) Nevertheless,
   D) In fact,

8. For the sake of the logical flow of the passage, the preceding paragraph should be

   A) kept where it is.
   B) placed between the first and second paragraphs.
   C) placed between the second and third paragraphs.
   D) removed.

9. Which of the following most effectively establishes the main idea of the paragraph??

   A) Like the artists, the villagers appreciate the festival's positive effects.
   B) The festival has created new jobs in the village, bringing new hope to the population.
   C) Some village residents do not think the festival will be enough to save the village financially.
   D) Some residents see the art festival as a distraction from the town's real problems.

10. Which of the following is the most precise replacement for the underlined word?

    A) NO CHANGE
    B) a decaying
    C) an aging
    D) an ancient

11. A) NO CHANGE
    B) budget, it
    C) budget, but
    D) budget it

Lesson wY10
Checking In
Practice Sets

PRACTICE PASSAGE 2

Engineers at NASA's Marshall Space Flight Center in Huntsville, Alabama **(1)** has successfully tested the most complex rocket engine parts that it ever has created using additive manufacturing, or 3-D printing. NASA engineers pushed the limits of technology by designing a rocket engine injector – a highly complex part that sends propellant into the engine – with design features that took advantage of the 3-D printing technology.

To make the parts, the design was entered into the 3-D printer's computer. The printer then built each part by layering metal powder and fusing it together using a laser, a process known as selective laser melting.

[1] This additive manufacturing process allowed rocket designers to create an **(2)** injector. [2] The injector had 40 individual spray elements, all printed as a single component rather than **(3)** manufactured. [3] The entire injector was created from just two **(4)** parts, had they used traditional manufacturing methods, engineers would have needed to make and then assemble 163 individual parts. [4] The 3-D printing technology saved time and money, and it allowed engineers to build parts that enhance rocket engine performance **(5)** and are less prone to failure. [5] The injector was similar in size to injectors that power small rocket engines and similar in design to injectors for large engines, such as the engine that will power NASA's Space Launch System (SLS) rocket, the heavy-lift, exploration class rocket under development to take humans beyond Earth orbit and to Mars. {**6**}

1. A) NO CHANGE
   B) have successfully tested
   C) has been successfully testing
   D) is successfully testing

2. A) NO CHANGE
   B) injector with 40 individual
   C) injector, which having been constructed, had 40 individual
   D) injector of

3. A) NO CHANGE
   B) manufactured and produced as separate components
   C) manufactured individually
   D) manufactured individually as separate components

4. A) NO CHANGE
   B) parts had
   C) parts. Had
   D) parts, however, had

5. A) NO CHANGE
   B) or
   C) but
   D) yet

6. Which of the following sentences most effectively functions as the topic sentence of the paragraph?

   A) Sentence 1
   B) Sentence 3
   C) Sentence 4
   D) Sentence 5

"We wanted to go a step beyond just testing an injector and demonstrate how 3-D printing could revolutionize rocket designs for increased system performance," said Chris Singer, director of Marshall's Engineering Directorate. "The parts performed exceptionally well during the tests."

(7) <u>Additive manufacturing is more complicated than traditional manufacturing, yet it speeds up the entire design process.</u> Using Marshall's in-house capability to design and produce small 3-D printed parts quickly, the propulsion and materials laboratories can work together to apply quick modifications to the test stand or the rocket component. "Having an in-house additive manufacturing capability allows us **(8)** <u>to look at test data, to modify</u> parts or the test stand based on the data, **(9)** <u>materialize</u> changes quickly, and get back to testing," said Nicholas Case, a propulsion engineer leading the testing. "This speeds up the whole design, development, and testing **(10)** <u>process, allowing</u> us to try innovative designs with less risk and cost to projects."

7. Which of the following sentences would provide the best transition between the fifth and sixth paragraphs?

A) NO CHANGE
B) Additive manufacturing may have limited practicality now, but Marshall's engineers hope to expand its uses in the near future.
C) Additive manufacturing not only helps engineers create better rocket parts, but also enables them to test faster and more intelligently.
D) Additive manufacturing allows several teams to work together as part of the design process.

8. A) NO CHANGE
B) look at the test data, and to modify
C) to look at the test data, modifying
D) to look at test data, modify

9. Which of the following is the most precise replacement for the underlined word?

A) NO CHANGE
B) implement
C) actualize
D) make good on

10. A) NO CHANGE
B) process allowing
C) process; allowing
D) process: allowing

Marshall engineers have tested increasingly complex injectors, rocket nozzles and other components with the goal of reducing the time and cost of building and assembling future engines. {11}

11. Which of the following, if added, would provide the best conclusion for the passage?

A) Additive manufacturing is a key technology for advancing this goal, and may one day enable missions into deep space.

B) Additive manufacturing is a key technology for enhancing industrial productivity.

C) Who knows what additive manufacturing will let us accomplish in the future?

D) Additive manufacturing may eventually have an impact on NASA's development process.

Lesson wY10
Checking In
Practice Sets

PRACTICE PASSAGE 3

The legendary dragon has its roots in two main **(1)** <u>traditions,</u> the European dragon, which is derived from European folklore and ultimately tied to Greek and Middle Eastern myths, and the Chinese dragon, which takes varying forms in Japanese, Korean, and other East Asian cultures.

The antagonism between monstrous serpents and **(2)** <u>heroic deities have its roots</u> in the myths of the Ancient Near East, including **(3)** <u>Hebrew, Hittite, and Mesopotamian</u>. Humbaba, the fanged, fire-breathing beast first described in the Epic of Gilgamesh, is described as a dragon that is eventually overcome by the hero. The legless serpent *Chaoskampf* is found in Greek and Christian mythologies, although the serpent motif may already have been a part of prehistoric Indo-European mythology as well, based on comparative evidence of Indic and Germanic materials.

[1] Although dragons **(4)** <u>appear</u> in many legends around the world, different cultures have varying descriptions about beasts that have been grouped together under an encompassing "dragon" label. [2] Some are said to breathe fire or spew toxins, such as the monster in the Old English poem *Beowulf*. [3] Dragons are also frequently portrayed as having serpentine, reptilian, or even avian traits, hatching from eggs and **(5)** <u>to possess</u> typically scaly or feathered bodies. [4] Some myths endow them with spines along their backs. [5] "Spiny" dragons first appeared in Medieval literature, although such dragons may have existed in oral storytelling traditions long before then. [6] European **(6)** <u>dragons often winged,</u> while Chinese dragons resemble large snakes. [7] Early European literature describes dragons to have a variable number of limbs, ranging from none to six or more. {7}

1. A) NO CHANGE
   B) traditions:
   C) traditions;
   D) traditions being

2. A) NO CHANGE
   B) heroic deities have their roots
   C) heroic deities has their roots
   D) heroic deities has its roots

3. A) NO CHANGE
   B) those of the Hebrews, Hittites, and Mesopotamians
   C) Hebrew, Hittite, and Mesopotamian ones
   D) Hebrew myths, Hittites myths, and Mesopotamian myths

4. Within the context of the passage, which of the following is the most precise replacement of the underlined word?

   A) NO CHANGE
   B) happen
   C) live
   D) roam

5. A) NO CHANGE
   B) they possess
   C) possessing
   D) possess

6. A) NO CHANGE
   B) dragons, though they are winged
   C) dragons winged often
   D) dragons are often winged

7. Which of the following sentences should be eliminated in order to improve the focus of the paragraph?

   A) Sentence 2
   B) Sentence 4
   C) Sentence 5
   D) Sentence 7

[1] Dragons have major spiritual significance in many religions and around the world. [2] In several Asian cultures dragons **(8)** <u>were before and now in some cultures still are</u> revered as representative of the primal forces of nature. [3] Stories tell of men embarking on long treks to seek knowledge from these creatures. [4] They are almost always portrayed as possessing some sort of supernatural power. [5] Multiple traditions cite dragons' capability of speech, some even suggesting that these great beasts taught language to humans. [6] In some cases, dragons are associated with great wisdom and prophetic abilities. {9}

{10} The blood of a slain dragon is consistently a topic of interest in folklore. In German legends, dragon blood has the power to render invincible any object that is bathed in it, as is the case with Siegfried's skin or Ortnit's armor. In Slavic myths, Mother Earth considers dragon blood so vile that she refuses to consume it, forcing it to remain above ground. The blood of the dragon in *Beowulf* has an acidic quality, **(11)** <u>allowing it to therefore eat through iron</u>. Heinrich von Winkelried slays a dragon but is killed when its blood drips on him.

8. A) NO CHANGE
    B) were before, like now in some cultures, are
    C) were, and now still are in some cultures,
    D) were, and in some cultures still are,

9. To improve the logical flow of the paragraph, sentence 3 should be relocated

    A) NO CHANGE
    B) after sentence 1
    C) after sentence 5
    D) after sentence 6

10. Which of the following best establishes the main idea of the paragraph?

    A) Dragon blood is regarded as precious in several cultures.
    B) The cultural associations with dragon blood are many and varied.
    C) Heinrich von Winkelried was a brave yet unfortunate character.
    D) The earth was considered an enemy of dragons.

11. A) NO CHANGE
    B) this allowing iron to be eaten through by it
    C) which allows it to eat through iron
    D) iron which is eaten through because of this

Lesson wY10
Checking In
Homework Sets

HOMEWORK PASSAGE 1

I am convinced that if NASA were to disappear tomorrow, people in this country would be profoundly distraught. Americans would feel that we had lost something that matters, and we would feel ourselves somehow diminished. Yet I think most would be unable to say why.

There are many good reasons to continue to explore space. Some of these reasons have been debated in public policy circles and evaluated on the basis of financial investment. In announcing his commitment to send the country back to the moon, **(1)** the speech by President Bush stated that we do it for scientific discovery, economic benefit, and **(2)** securing the nation. These are all great reasons. But these are not what would make us miss exploring space. They are only the reasons we are comfortable discussing. These are the "acceptable reasons" because they can be logically defended. When we contemplate committing large sums of money to a project, we tend to dismiss reasons that are emotional or value-driven or unquantifiable. But when it comes to space, these are the reasons— the "real reasons"—that are truly important.

When Charles Lindbergh was asked why he crossed the Atlantic, he didn't say **(3)** he wanted to so that he could win the $25,000 prize. Burt Rutan and his backer, Paul Allen, certainly didn't develop a private spacecraft just to win the Ansari X-Prize. They spent double the money they won. Sergei Korolev's team wasn't asked to launch Sputnik; **(4)** they had to fight for the honor and the resources to do it. These people didn't want money; they wanted to achieve something that no one before them had.

{5} [1] I think we all know why we want to accomplish great things. [2] We do so for reasons that are intuitive and compelling but

1. A) NO CHANGE
   B) President Bush stated that
   C) it was stated by President Bush that
   D) we were informed by President Bush that

2. A) NO CHANGE
   B) security of the nation
   C) to secure the nation
   D) national security

3. A) NO CHANGE
   B) it was because of the $25,000 prize
   C) because he wanted to win the $25,000 prize
   D) so that he could win the $25,000 prize

4. A) NO CHANGE
   B) he
   C) it
   D) Korolev's team

5. Which of the following sentences should be removed in order to improve the focus of the paragraph?

   A) Sentence 2
   B) Sentence 5
   C) Sentence 7
   D) Sentence 10

6. Within the context of the passage, which of the following is the most precise replacement of the underlined word?

   A) NO CHANGE
   B) bracing
   C) inspiring
   D) stimulating

not necessarily logical. [3] The logical reason is safe, defendable, and sensible. [4] But it's not emotionally engaging or **(6)** refreshing. [5] We want to be the first or the best in something. [6] This is our natural impulse. [7] It's this inherent trait that causes us **(7)** to wonder, explore, and conquer. [8] Who among us hasn't had the urge to discover what's over the next hill? [9] What child has not been drawn to explore beyond the familiar streets of his neighborhood? [10] Exploration may be dangerous when we're young, but it is essential to our maturation. **{8}**

Since the earliest times, humans **(9)** had constructed monuments. We've always wanted to leave something behind for posterity. By doing this, we validate our time here on earth. This is the impulse behind castles and pyramids, bridges and skyscrapers. **{10}**

Cathedral builders would understand what I mean by "real reasons." The monuments they erected required far greater portions of their resources than what we've put into the space business. But when we look back, we are **(11)** still awestruck by what they accomplished. These builders did much more than construct impressive monuments. They sparked the imaginations of their countrymen. They rekindled the passion for art so greatly that centuries later entire collegiate programs are dedicated to the study of their work. And perhaps unknowingly, they also catalyzed progress, expanded knowledge, inspired discovery. As we learned to harness fire, and then electricity, we will learn to harness the power of the sun, the resources on Mars, the mysteries of dark matter. But not because we thought these pursuits to be economically sensible or logically sound. We will have accomplished these things because we will have been curious, passionate, and foolishly ambitious, just as we've always been.

7. A) NO CHANGE
   B) to wonder, explore, and to conquer
   C) to wonder, explore, and also to conquer
   D) to wonder, explore, and conquering

8. Which of the following best establishes the main idea of the paragraph?

   A) People have a natural impulse to explore.
   B) People are naturally repulsed by logic.
   C) Without emotional stimulation, people cannot achieve success.
   D) Children need to be exposed to larger environments than just their neighborhoods.

9. A) NO CHANGE
   B) constructed
   C) will have constructed
   D) have constructed

10. Which of the following examples would best support the ideas in the paragraph?

    A) A father builds a tree house for his children.
    B) A physics student builds a robot for a science fair.
    C) A toddler constructs a tower of toy blocks.
    D) An architect erects a tower of record-breaking height.

11. A) NO CHANGE
    B) still awestruck even now by what they accomplished
    C) still awestruck by what they accomplished even today
    D) awestruck by what they accomplished even still

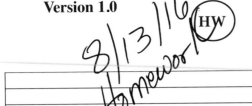

Lesson wY10
Checking In
Homework Sets

HOMEWORK PASSAGE 2

Anyone can build a house. All you need **(1)** <u>being</u> a plan, a few bids and the price — and there you are. But that wasn't the kind of a house we wanted. We hoped to build a home that we would like **(2)** <u>more better</u> every year we lived in it — something that we could point to with pride instead of viewing with alarm.

We hoped to **(3)** <u>finish</u> that "white house with green blinds" effect that you see so often in your imagination and so seldom by the roadside. It was risky to attempt a type of house that none of our local carpenters or masons was **(4)** <u>familiar with, the houses</u> we had in mind became obsolete a hundred years before present-day operators were born. It was also risky for a layman to attempt to design such a house without benefit of clergy or architects. It is easy to fall prey to tricky details when you design your own house no matter what type it may be.

1. A) NO CHANGE
    B) are
    C) is
    D) was

2. A) NO CHANGE
    B) most better
    C) most well
    D) better

3. Within the context of the passage, which of the following is the most precise replacement for the underlined word?

    A) NO CHANGE
    B) manage
    C) deliver
    D) achieve

4. A) NO CHANGE
    B) familiar with. The houses
    C) familiar with, also the houses
    D) familiar with. However, the houses

{5} [1] Then there are those narrow, curving cellar stairs, which — because they lack sufficient headroom — make you lift your voice to high heaven every time the floor beam above cracks you in the skull. [2] Some of the favorite tricks of amateur house planners are unexpected steps up or down that make a visitor lucky to escape with a bruised shin **(6)** <u>instead of</u> a broken neck. [3] There are doors that swing the wrong way, electric light switches you paw over a half acre of wall to find. [4] Finally, there are rooms so poorly lighted that they resemble an Egyptian tomb. {7}

5. To improve the logical flow of the paragraph, Sentence 2 should be moved

    A) NO CHANGE
    B) Before Sentence 1
    C) Between Sentence 2 and Sentence 3
    D) To the end of the paragraph

6. A) NO CHANGE
    B) rather than of
    C) instead of,
    D) in the matter of

7. Which of the following best describes the main purpose of the paragraph?

    A) To provide examples that illustrate the problem presented in the previous paragraph.
    B) To describe the quirks that are often found in old houses.
    C) To convince the reader of the necessity of an architect in planning and building a home.
    D) To provide a complete list of mistakes to avoid when planning a house.

Planning to avoid these things is usually the job of an architect. **(8)** Because I had already planned and built nineteen houses, so I decided that the twentieth house wasn't exactly **(9)** a newcomer performance. Many people decide to design their own homes even without the benefit of prior experience or an architect, but whether one plans his own house or not, anyone can decide on the type of house he wants. **(10)** The fact is that millions of people are dissatisfied with homes that someone else has planned. Are you satisfied with yours? {**11**}

8. A) NO CHANGE
   B) However, I
   C) So I
   D) In light of the way I

9. Within the context of the passage, which of the following is the most precise replacement of the underlined word?

   A) an apprentice
   B) a practice
   C) a recruit
   D) an amateur

10. Which of the following, if added here, would best support the claim presented in the previous sentence?

    A) Architects are completely unnecessary when building a home.
    B) Architects bring a creative perspective to home design, so people who lack an eye for design would do well to hire an architect.
    C) A good architect works closely with homeowners to create a plan that incorporates their needs and wants.
    D) Because architects are so knowledgeable, they often tell homeowners what they should and should not include in their homes.

11. Which sentence would be the best conclusion to the passage?

    A) It's up to you to make the answer "yes."
    B) I hope so, because you have no control over it.
    C) Think of three reasons why or why not.
    D) Satisfaction is one measure of success.

Lesson wY11
Introductions, Conclusions, and Transitions
Getting Your Feet Wet

Directions: Read the paragraphs below, then answer the questions that follow.

{1} During last year's harvest, banana farmers in Jordan and Mozambique made a chilling discovery: Instead of the soft, creamy fruits they'd been growing for decades, they found a rotting, fibrous mass. Scientists first discovered the fungus behind this problem in Southeast Asia in the 1990s. Since then the pathogen, known as the Tropical Race 4 strain of Panama disease, has ravaged banana crops throughout Asia.

That the vicious fungus has now leapt to Mozambique and Jordan is frightening, in part because this brings the disease closer to Latin America, where more than 70% of the world's bananas are grown. In fact, Randy Ploetz, professor of plant pathology at the University of Florida, says Tropical Race 4 may already be in Latin America. Some have theorized that Race 4 was carried to Mozambique by Latin American workers who were brought over to help establish banana plantations. If that is true, then Race 4 is already in the heart of banana country. At least thus far, Latin American banana growers have not reported the devastation of Tropical Race 4.

{2} After all, this scenario has happened before. Starting in 1903, Race 1, an earlier variant of today's pathogen, ravaged the banana plantations of Latin America and the Caribbean. Within 50 years, Race 1 caused the world's only export banana, the Gros Michel, to near extinction. **(3)** <u>On the contrary</u>, most of the bananas eaten today are Cavendish bananas, the only export-suitable banana that was able to withstand Race 1.

Compared to its 20th-century predecessor, Tropical Race 4 is a killing machine. In addition to destroying Cavendishes, the pathogen has affected several other species that are immune to Race 1 but seem to have no defenses against Race 4. Ploetz predicts that Tropical Race 4 is capable of killing at least 80% of the bananas and plantains produced each year.

A shortage of bananas may seem unimportant, but at just $8.9 billion, banana exports are just a fraction of the $44.1 billion worth of bananas and plantains produced each year. The majority of bananas and plantains are not exported; they provide roughly one-fourth of the daily calories for at least 400 million people in the world's poorest countries. In the decades since the utter destruction caused by Race 1, bananas have become a vital source of sustenance, and if modern bananas go the way of the Gros Michel, there are no back-up varieties to grow in their place. {4}

1. Which of the following, if added to the beginning of the first paragraph, would provide the best introduction to the passage?

   A) There is nothing worse than a rotten banana, especially for a banana farmer.
   B) It's possible that the spread of a new banana disease could result in widespread starvation in many banana-growing countries.
   C) A pathogen capable of destroying whole crops of bananas has, at least until recently, seemed to be isolated to Asia.
   D) It is entirely possible that we may soon experience a banana apocalypse.

Joke answer

2. If inserted at the beginning of this paragraph, which of the following sentences would provide the best transition from the second to the third paragraph?

A) Even if the disease takes years to appear in Latin America, the destruction of the commercial banana may be inevitable.
B) It's most likely that Tropical Race 4 is already in Latin America, silently infiltrating banana plantations.
C) Regardless, Tropical Race 4 will almost certainly cause a global banana crisis, potentially killing millions of people who rely on bananas for sustenance.
D) Although it is hard to take a disease that sounds like a video game title seriously, Tropical Race 4 is probably going to kill the world's bananas, resulting in serious problems.

3. A) NO CHANGE
   B) For example
   C) Currently
   D) As a result

4. Which of the following, if added here, would best conclude the passage?

A) This devastation is in addition to the economic devastation that will likely result, as many nations rely almost exclusively on banana exports for economic stability.
B) People in developed countries should stop consuming bananas in such large numbers in order to ensure that the world's poorest people have access to this important fruit.
C) This single fungal disease, which did not even exist a mere twenty years ago, may well kill millions by causing widespread starvation.
D) Countries that grow bananas should start looking for new crops to grow.

Lesson wY11
Introductions, Conclusions, and Transitions
Wading In

TOPIC OVERVIEW – INTRODUCTIONS, CONCLUSIONS, AND TRANSITIONS

As we discussed in Lesson 9, the SAT writing section tests organization in addition to grammar knowledge. In this lesson, we'll learn about some of the other types of organization questions: introduction questions, conclusion questions, and transition questions. Much like logical sequence questions, these questions ask us to improve the logic and flow of the passage.

TOPIC OVERVIEW – INTRODUCTIONS

A good introductory sentence will introduce the main topic of the passage without giving away the details of the passage.

RECOGNIZING INTRODUCTION QUESTIONS

Introduction questions ask us to either add a sentence to the beginning of the passage or to change a sentence that already appears in the beginning of the passage. Look for the key words "introduction" or "introduce" to help identify these questions.

ANSWERING INTRODUCTION QUESTIONS

After identifying a question as an introduction question, follow these steps to find the correct answer:

1. Consider the tone and style of the passage as a whole. Eliminate any answer choices that do not fit with the tone or style of the passage.
2. Eliminate any answer choices that refer to information that is not at all related to the main ideas of the passage as a whole.
3. Carefully read the first paragraph. Eliminate any answer choices that are not at all related to the information in the first paragraph.
4. Examine the remaining answer choices. Choose the choice that is most closely related to the information in the first paragraph and that provides the most natural introduction to the passage.
5. Reread the beginning of the passage with your chosen answer inserted. If the new introduction flows naturally and makes logical sense, move on to the next question.

TOPIC OVERVIEW – CONCLUSIONS

Conclusions should summarize the main ideas of the passage. Depending on the passage, a conclusion might also restate the author's main claim.

RECOGNIZING CONCLUSION QUESTIONS

Conclusion questions ask us to either add or change a sentence at the end of the passage in order to create a strong conclusion for the passage as a whole. The words "conclusion" or "conclude" can help identify conclusion questions.

ANSWERING CONCLUSION QUESTIONS

Once you've identified the question as a conclusion question, follow these steps to arrive at the correct answer:

1. As with introduction questions, eliminate any choices that do not suit the overall tone and style of the passage.
2. Consider the main claim, purpose, or idea of the passage. Eliminate any answer choices that do not relate to or agree with the main claim of the passage.
3. Eliminate any answer choices that make claims that cannot be supported by information in the passage.
4. Examine the remaining answer choices. Choose the one that best summarizes the main ideas of the passage or that makes a claim that is most clearly supported by the information and tone of the passage.
5. Reread the end of the passage with your chosen answer inserted. If the new ending of the passage flows naturally and makes logical sense, move on to the next question.

TOPIC OVERVIEW -- TRANSITIONS

Transition questions ask us to utilize transitional strategies to create a smooth progression of ideas within a passage. It's important to note that the phrase "transitional strategies" includes more than just the transitional words and phrases that we are most familiar with. Transitional strategies also include the use of whole sentences to link the ideas in two paragraphs.

RECOGNIZING TRANSITION QUESTIONS

Transition questions appear in two forms.

The first form is similar to that of many grammar or convention questions on the SAT; these questions have a transitional word of phrase underlined within the passage and ask us to select the best transition for that particular sentence. These questions usually focus on transitions between *sentences* rather than between *paragraphs*.

The second form asks us to either add or replace a sentence to provide a smooth transition from one paragraph to another. Sometimes the question refers to a place in the passage where a transitional sentence does not yet exist; other times, the question will refer to an underlined sentence and ask us to either change that sentence or replace it with a better sentence. These questions often include the word "transition," but other key terms include "flow" or "progression of ideas."

ANSWERING TRANSITION QUESTIONS

Below is a table containing some of the common transitions and their functions:

FUNCTION	TRANSITIONS
Similarity	also, in the same way, just as…so too, likewise, similarly
Contrast	but, however, in spite of, on the one hand…on the other hand, nevertheless, nonetheless, notwithstanding, in contrast, on the contrary, still, yet
Sequence	first, second, third, next, then, finally, after, afterward, at last, before, currently, during, earlier, immediately, later, meanwhile, now, recently, simultaneously, subsequently, then
Example	for example, for instance, namely, specifically, to illustrate
Emphasis	even, indeed, in fact, of course, truly
Position	above, adjacent, below, beyond, here, in front, in back, nearby, there
Cause/Effect	accordingly, consequently, hence, so, therefore, thus
Support or Evidence	additionally, again, also, and, as well, besides, equally important, further, furthermore, in addition, moreover
Conclusion	finally, in a word, in brief, in conclusion, in the end, in the final analysis, on the whole, thus, to conclude, to summarize, in sum, to sum up, in summary

It's important to understand the functions of transitional words and phrases so that we can identify the best transition to use in the context of the passage. After all, transitions help to link ideas by explaining the relationship between those ideas. For example:

Example 1: Opponents to the widespread implementation of wind energy point to statistics that suggest that wind turbines kill up to 368,000 birds each year. **For example**, cats kill an estimated 1.4 to 3.7 billion birds each year, suggesting that wind turbine-related deaths are unlikely to cause lasting harm to bird populations.

In this example, the transitional phrase "for example" does not properly identify the relationship between the two sentences. Even without the broader context of a passage, we can see that the second sentence provides information that disputes the claim made in the first sentence, so we need a transition that shows contrast. A better option would be:

Example 2: Opponents to the widespread implementation of wind energy point to statistics that suggest that wind turbines kill up to 368,000 birds each year. **However**, cats kill an estimated 1.4 to 3.7 billion birds each year, suggesting that wind turbine-related deaths are unlikely to cause lasting harm to bird populations.

"However" provides a much clearer relationship between the two sentences. These examples show that it's important to recognize the relationships indicated by specific transitions – not just any transition will do!

For questions that ask you to choose the best transitional word or phrase for an underlined portion of a sentence, follow these steps to find the correct answer:

1. Carefully read the sentence containing the transition and the sentences immediately before and after that sentence. Determine which two sentences are being connected by the transition.
2. Once you've identified the two sentences being connected, consider the relationship between the two sentences. Eliminate any answer choices that don't reflect that relationship. For example, if the two sentences are in agreement with each other, you would eliminate transitions that suggest contradiction, such as "on the other hand" or "however."
3. Examine the remaining answer choices. Select the transition or transitional phrase that best reflects the relationship between the two sentences.

For questions that ask you to select the best sentence to transition between two paragraphs, follow these steps to find the correct answer:

1. Consider the style and tone of the passage as a whole. Eliminate any answer choices that do not suit the style or tone of the passage.
2. Identify the main ideas of each of the paragraphs being connected. Eliminate any answer choices that either disagree with those ideas or are completely unrelated to those ideas.
3. Sometimes the ideas in each paragraph will have a specific relationship. For example, two paragraphs may present conflicting ideas. If you can identify a clear relationship between two paragraphs, eliminate any choices that create a relationship that is not reflected by the passage.
4. Look at the remaining answer choices. Eliminate any choices that reference information found in paragraphs other than the two paragraphs being connected.
5. Examine the remaining answer choices. Select the option that most logically and clearly connects the information in the two paragraphs.

Lesson wY11
Introductions, Conclusions, and Transitions
Learning to Swim

CONCEPT EXERCISE:

Directions: Use the passage to answer the questions below.

A Chauffeur's Tale

{1} Rumors flew about how much money we could make. One driver had a friend who had been invited to travel with Saudi Arabians after driving them around Los Angeles for only a few weeks. They paid for him to fly with them to London, New York, and Paris for months, all first class. He didn't even have to drive. They just liked his company and wanted him around. Charles, an experienced driver friend from the East Coast, said he drove some Saudi Arabian royals for only thirty days, **(2)** <u>so</u> at the end of the job he'd received his pay, a gold Rolex, and a $10,000 tip.

1. Which of the following provides the best introduction to the passage?

   A) I was immediately excited about the money I could make.
   B) All of the other limousine drivers at the company where I worked were talking about the Saudi Arabians who were coming to town.
   C) After a couple of months on the job, I couldn't help but acknowledge that the whole driving thing was not working out on any front.
   D) This driving job was now becoming a problem, not a solution, for my financial situation.

2. A) NO CHANGE
   B) and
   C) because
   D) while

{3} The interviewing process for the Saudi Arabian job was odd. No one ever asked me about my professional chauffeuring experience. I assumed this was because Fausto, the lead driver, had recommended me for the job, **(4)** but to this day I don't know for sure. I can't say it demonstrates good business practice. **(5)** But I received a series of perplexing phone calls over several days. The security firm hired by the family to do advance work called me and asked how I had learned about the job, who else I knew on the detail, and who referred me. **(6)** I had no way of knowing who else was on the job.

3. Which of the following, if added here, would provide the best transition from the first paragraph to the second paragraph?

   A) The rumors kept flying among the drivers.
   B) Having heard about these stories, I had every reason to believe that I could earn tips like that as well, if only I were given the chance.
   C) Knowing that the job could pay very well, I was excited when I received a call informing me that I had been recommended for the job.
   D) I began to fear I would never get a chance to interview for the Saudi Arabian job.

4. A) NO CHANGE
   B) despite
   C) since
   D) additionally

5. A) NO CHANGE
   B) Then
   C) Regardless
   D) Therefore

6. Which of the following changes to the underlined sentence would create the best transition between the second and third paragraphs?

   A) Delete the sentence because it is not necessary to create a smooth transition.
   B) Move the sentence to the beginning of the second paragraph.
   C) Move the sentence to the beginning of the third paragraph.
   D) Replace it with a sentence containing more information about how much money drivers make.

I knew they knew that Fausto had told me about the job and that he had referred me. When I reminded them of this, they confirmed that this was so. So, were they testing my memory of the last two days? Were they thinking I might lie? Were they giving me a hard time because I was a woman? It was truly peculiar. I began to wonder whether the job even truly existed **(7)** therefore the entire process was very secretive and mysterious.

{8} I was asked to fax my license to different numbers whose area codes I didn't recognize. I then spent hours in line at the DMV to obtain a printout that lists all traffic accidents or infractions in the past ten years. I faxed the printout and my license again, this time to different numbers. I spoke with many people a day about when the family was arriving and when I would be needed. Suddenly the job was off, and then back on again. The details changed on an hourly basis, and the dates were postponed repeatedly. Fausto finally said it was a go, but first I had to meet the family's security staff in person.

{9} After such a long and confusing application process, I was surprised when the security staff asked only one or two basic questions. That was the whole screening process. There were no background checks, no references called, nothing. I did have a clean DMV record, **(10)** however I am sure that counted for something. I was surprised at the lack of due diligence given how much concern there had been over basic details.

7. A) NO CHANGE
   B) if
   C) however
   D) because

8. Which sentence provides the best transition between the third and fourth paragraphs?

   A) NO CHANGE
   B) I wanted to meet the family members in person before I was hired to work for them.
   C) A couple of more days went by, and I received some more puzzling calls and requests.
   D) I began to grow tired of faxing my license to so many different numbers.

9. Which of the following, if added here, would provide the best transition between the fourth and fifth paragraphs?

   A) I was reluctant to meet the security staff after the confusing interview process.
   B) I hoped to see the family, not just the security staff, at the meeting.
   C) I flatly refused to meet the security staff after the maddening interview process.
   D) I met a small group of superhero action-type figures briefly at a hotel in Beverly Hills.

10. A) NO CHANGE
    B) so
    C) especially
    D) otherwise

C2 education
be smarter

So I got the job to drive for a family of Saudi Arabian royals—Princess Zaahira, her children, the family's security, and their entourage. {11}

11. Which of the following provides the best conclusion to the passage?

A) I was glad that the interviewing process was finally over.

B) It was likely that I would have to travel to Saudi Arabia to work for this family.

C) Thankfully, the family was able to remain in the States for a long time.

D) After such a strange hiring process, I had no idea what to expect; the experience would turn out to be one of the most interesting jobs I've ever had.

Lesson wY11
Introductions, Conclusions, and Transitions
Diving into the Deep End

PRACTICE EXERCISE:

Directions: Use the passage to answer the following questions.

Cats in the Muslim Tradition

{1}From antiquity to the present, Muslims have admired cats for their cleanliness, usefulness, and companionship. Reverence for cats in the Near-East has a long history, predating the establishment of Islam. **(2)** <u>Nevertheless,</u> Islam's unique regard for cats largely stems from Muhammad, the founder of the religion, who purportedly prized the company of these furry creatures.

1. Which of the following, if inserted here, would best introduce the passage?

   A) Born in 570 CE in Mecca, Muhammad was the founder of Islam and an avid cat lover.
   B) Although most people are familiar with Islam, a monotheistic faith originating in the Middle East, few know that cats have long had a special place in Muslim tradition.
   C) Cats have long been a major part of Islamic culture due to Muhammad's influence and the many uses Muslims have gotten out of the creatures.
   D) Domestic cats are the most popular pets in the world, known for their cuteness and fast reflexes.

2. A) NO CHANGE
   B) Indeed,
   C) Consequently,
   D) In a word,

{3} Muhammad's most famous pet cat, Muezza, could often be found on the religious leader's lap when giving sermons. One example of Muhammad's affection for Muezza is a story in which the cat fell asleep in a sleeve of one of Muhammad's robes. Reportedly, Muhammad was so opposed to disturbing the feline, that he cut off the sleeve so he could wear the robe and avoid waking the cat. Moreover, additional references to cats connected to Muhammad exist in the Islamic tradition—from a story involving a cat saving Muhammad's life to an instance of his widow A'isha despairing that her cat had abandoned her.

(4) Considering their practical uses, it is unsurprising cats have become integrated into Muslim culture. In fact, ancient art depicting cats has been recovered from the Ottoman Empire, Afghanistan and Iran. While Christians were killing cats in Medieval Europe for being pests or witches' familiars, Muslims in the Middle East were establishing cat hospitals and sanctuaries. For example, in 13th Century Cairo, Sultan Baybars made the garden of his palace a cat haven, where cats were given food and care—a tradition that continued for at least 500 years. Today, countless cats roam the streets of predominantly Muslim cities such as Damascus, Istanbul, and Kairouan.

3. Which of the following, if added here, would provide the best transition from the first paragraph to the second?

   A) The domestic cat is an adorable and charming species, so why wouldn't it be popular?
   B) The domestic cat would later become a common feature of Muslim life.
   C) Muhammad's love of cats was quite evident: he explicitly prohibited abuse or killing of these animals and owned several as pets.
   D) Muhammad loved cats so much that he nicknamed an advisor of his, who cared for a cat, Abu Hruyrah, meaning "father of kittens."

4. Which of the following provides the best transition between the two paragraphs?

   A) NO CHANGE
   B) Muslims immortalized Muhammad's love of cats through art and many other gestures.
   C) Considering Muhammad's bond with Muezza, it is unsurprising cats became integrated into Muslim culture throughout history.
   D) Muhammad's love of cats inspired their integration into Muslim culture throughout history.

{5} Cats have long served the practical purpose of killing pests to protect food in storage. In Medieval times, they also proved useful for protecting books, essential to paper-based Arab-Islamic cultures, from mice that would damage them. (6) As a result, cats were often depicted in paintings alongside Muslim scholars. {7}

5. Which of the following, if added here, would provide the best transition between the third and fourth paragraphs?

A) Although Muslim cat lovers like Sultan Baybars have historically cared for cats as pet, cats have also been valued for practice reasons.

B) Even though having a cat can be hard work, they can also be useful

C) Cats may be small and cute, but they are carnivorous creatures that constantly stalk prey.

D) Although in Medieval Europe cats were seen as pests themselves, around the same time period in Muslim countries they were used to hunt pests down.

6. A) NO CHANGE
   B) In addition,
   C) In conclusion,
   D) Despite this fact,

7. Which of the following, if added here, would provide the best transition between the fourth and fifth paragraphs?

A) Aside from hunting pests, cats are also useful in that they are incredibly clean creatures and don't require much grooming.

B) In addition to being included in Muslim scholarly life, cats have also been included in religious rituals.

C) In addition to, historically, being very practical for Muslims, cats have also been considered ritually pure according to the Muslim tradition due to their cleanliness.

D) Feline behavior has, indeed, coincided with Muslims' needs and values in many fortuitous ways.

In fact, cats are also compatible with the Islamic emphasis on cleanliness. One crucial aspect of a devout Muslim's daily routine is praying to God five times a day, which requires being clean for God. Muslims, **(8)** in spite of this fact, engage in a cleansing ritual known as Wudu or ablutions, i.e., rinsing the body with clean water. Muhammad, who founded this ritual, would still use water a cat had drunk from for his ablutions, considering such water pure. **(9)** In a similar way, cats are seen as ritually clean in the Islamic tradition. Thus, they are allowed to enter mosques, Muslim places of worship.

Despite the permissibility of felines in Islamic ritual, many have overlooked Muslims' affinity with cats, since Islam encourages goodwill toward all animals. **(10)** In contrast, cats seem to hold a special place in Muslim culture and history. {11}

8. A) NO CHANGE
   B) as an example of this,
   C) in the same way,
   D) to fulfill this requirement,

9. A) NO CHANGE
   B) Perhaps as a result of Muhammad's high opinion of them,
   C) Despite the fact Muhammad exhibited these peculiar behaviors in his treatment of cats,
   D) Because they have such good hygiene,

10. A) NO CHANGE
    B) However,
    C) Likewise,
    D) In conclusion,

11. Which of the following would best conclude the passage as the last sentence of the paragraph?

    A) Given Muhammad's love of cats and the substantial inclusion of them in Muslim culture, Islam is the most cat-friendly religion in the world.
    B) The love of cats in Islamic cultures is not surprising considering the universal appeal of this amazing animal.
    C) Much of this reverence is attributable to Muhammad's love of felines, but cats have also proven apt companions to Muslims throughout the centuries.
    D) Accordingly, despite all the evidence, it becomes obvious cats aren't nearly as special to Muslims as many have thought.

TEST EXERCISE:

With about 50,000 flights in America every day, air travel is becoming **(1)** <u>increasingly ordinary and commonplace</u>. Most people, however, do not view it as a pleasant experience. Long security lines, delayed flights, cramped seating, and **(2)** <u>when they lose your</u> <u>baggage</u> are just a few of the inconveniences. Nevertheless, new technology is helping to reduce at least one of the discomforts of flying: air turbulence.

Not that long ago, pilots would study printed weather reports before taking off, comparing the forecasts with their flight plans. Once they were in the air, they depended on radio communications and rudimentary radar to avoid bad weather. Now, pilots can download detailed flight plans and weather reports onto tablet devices. Flight dispatchers track aircraft in real time and **(3)** <u>provides</u> up-to-the minute weather data, and new radar systems allow for easy in-flight adjustments. As a **(4)** <u>result, fewer</u> of the bumps, jolts and spilled drinks that have been a part of flying ever since the Wright Brothers.

[1] Weather conditions, which accounted for 36 percent of all airline delays in 2013, have always been a major concern for airlines and their customers. [2] Planes are also delayed by congested airspace, limited runway capacity, or mechanical problems. [3] Fortunately, stronger computing power, improved satellite and radar technology, and more advanced scientific models have all given airlines a more detailed understanding of flying conditions. [4] This means they can better plan their operations before flights—for instance by canceling flights early and avoiding stranding passengers at airports. [5] During flights, they can better navigate around storms and **(5)** <u>skip</u> turbulence. {6}

1. A) NO CHANGE
    B) ordinary and more commonplace
    C) increasingly commonplace
    D) ordinary and commonplace

2. A) NO CHANGE
    B) lost baggage
    C) your baggage gets lost
    D) baggage having been lost

3. A) NO CHANGE
    B) providing
    C) provide
    D) is providing

4. A) NO CHANGE
    B) result are fewer
    C) result of few
    D) result, there are fewer

5. Which of the following is the most precise replacement for the underlined word?

    A) NO CHANGE
    B) shun
    C) remove
    D) avoid

6. Which of the following sentences should be removed in order to improve the focus of the paragraph?

    A) Sentence 2
    B) Sentence 3
    C) Sentence 4
    D) Sentence 5

Unauthorized copying or reuse of any part of this page is illegal.

Turbulence presents a particular challenge to **(7)** <u>airlines; because</u> it cannot be seen by satellite or radar. Meteorologists use complex weather models and reports from pilots to predict areas of heavy turbulence. **(8)** <u>In addition,</u> sensors on some planes can automatically relay turbulence information to dispatchers who look for alternative routing for later flights. "We can reliably identify potential areas for turbulence," said Tom Fahey, who heads a team of 27 meteorologists at a major airline. "Where it gets difficult is identifying exact locations at a given instant, since by definition turbulence is in motion."

{9} Some airlines are developing real-time weather maps in the cockpit to give pilots access to the same information available to dispatchers on the ground. Others are equipping their planes with sensors that measure water vapor in the air to determine the location of fog, cloud formation, and cloud ceilings. **(10)** <u>Meteorologists also expect that new satellites will provide a better reading of low-ceiling clouds and low-visibility environments, to be launched in early 2016.</u>

7. A) NO CHANGE
    B) airlines because
    C) airlines; because,
    D) airlines because,

8. A) NO CHANGE
    B) In contrast
    C) Nonetheless
    D) Therefore

9. Which choice most effectively establishes the main topic of the paragraph?

    A) Airlines are constantly looking for ways to better understand and respond to weather conditions.
    B) Turbulence is not the worst thing airlines have to deal with.
    C) Satellites may provide the best solution to weather problems.
    D) Airlines need to do more to make passengers more comfortable.

10. A) NO CHANGE
    B) To be launched in early 2016, meteorologists also expect that new satellites will provide a better reading of low-ceiling clouds and low visibility environments.
    C) Meteorologists expect to be launched in early 2016, new satellites will provide a better reading of low-ceiling clouds and low visibility environments.
    D) Meteorologists also expect that new satellites, to be launched in early 2016, will provide a better reading of low-ceiling clouds and low visibility environments.

Of course, weather can still be unpredictable, and a hassle-free flying experience may still be a long way off. {11}

11. Which of the following would provide the best conclusion to the passage?

A) Hopefully technology can soon be used to solve other flying discomforts as well.

B) Still, at least airlines are doing what they can to make us comfortable.

C) However, with the help of innovative technology, airlines are working toward a smoother future for flight.

D) Nevertheless, technology will someday allow airlines to completely eliminate weather-related delays.

HW 8/27 Start

Lesson wY11
Introductions, Conclusions, and Transitions
Race to the Finish

HOMEWORK EXERCISE 1:

Directions: Use the passage to answer the following questions.

A Story Worth Telling

Though perhaps not the first name that comes to mind in connection with the Civil Rights movement of the 1960s, Ezra Jack Keats **(1)** was a famous children's book author. Keats did not participate in marches or public protests. **(2)** Instead, in 1962, he published *The Snowy Day*, the first full-color picture book to feature a black child as its protagonist. Throughout his career, Keats continued to write and illustrate children's books featuring minorities as the central characters. **(3)** In addition, he gave a voice to those whose stories had never before been told.

{4} Keats was born in 1916 to Jewish-Polish immigrants. In addition to suffering from poverty, his family dealt with discrimination as a result of widespread anti-Semitism at the time. **(5)** Nevertheless, he felt a deep connection with others who similarly experienced life on the fringes of society. This helped fuel the injustice he later felt over the absence of minority children in the books he was asked to illustrate.

1. Which of the following changes would provide the best introduction to the passage?

   A) NO CHANGE
   B) became quite successful in spite of growing up in poverty
   C) played his part in bringing about social change in a quiet but profound way
   D) wrote and illustrated many books directly arguing for equal rights for all

2. A) NO CHANGE
   B) Also
   C) Thus
   D) Earlier

3. A) NO CHANGE
   B) In spite of difficulties
   C) Nevertheless
   D) Through this work

4. If inserted at the beginning of this paragraph, which of the following would provide the best transition from the first to the second paragraph?

   A) One might wonder why Keats cared about social change. That is a good question.
   B) The road to fame was not an easy one for Keats.
   C) In spite of many hardships growing up, Keats always dreamed of writing children's books.
   D) Keats's desire to give life to the stories of the socially disadvantaged arose from his own experiences growing up.

5. A) NO CHANGE
   B) As a result
   C) Finally
   D) For example

Keats did not initially intend to become a children's illustrator. He began his career as a painter working in the comic industry, but in 1954 when Elizabeth Riley of Crowell Publishing invited him to illustrate children's books, he made the most of the opportunity. Over the next eight years, he illustrated three dozen books.

(6) Furthermore, none of these books featured a minority as a major character. Keats knew that this did not fit with his own experience and did not accurately portray the stories of American children.

(7) For example, in 1962 he wrote and illustrated his own book, *The Snowy Day*. Using beautiful layers of collage illustrations (one of the first books to do so), the book depicts the snow day adventures of Peter, a little boy who lives in the city. The book won the 1963 Caldecott Medal and went on to become an icon of children's literature.

{8} The publishing industry at the time was not interested in stories featuring minorities because it did not think such books would sell well. **(9)** In spite of these expectations, *The Snowy Day* was immediately welcomed by educators and critics and embraced by the public, opening the door for increased multiculturalism in children's literature.

6. A) NO CHANGE
   B) Similarly
   C) However
   D) Consequently

7. A) NO CHANGE
   B) Thus
   C) Still
   D) Meanwhile

8. If inserted at the beginning of this paragraph, which of the following sentences would provide the best transition from the third to the fourth paragraph?

   A) What Keats accomplished with this book was a break in the color barrier in children's literature.
   B) Keats won instant fame after publishing *The Snowy Day*.
   C) Keats never realized the full significance of his works.
   D) The public's response to *The Snowy Day* was not as enthusiastic as the critics'.

9. A) NO CHANGE
   B) Because of
   C) Besides
   D) Resulting from

(10) <u>As a result,</u> Keats never had children of his own—he is said to have considered his characters to be his children—he continued to write and illustrate picture books through the remainder of his life. His works have proved to have a universal appeal and have been translated into some 20 languages, including Japanese, French, Spanish, Italian, Portuguese, Turkish, German, Swedish, Thai, Chinese, and Korean. **{11}**

10. A) NO CHANGE
    B) Because
    C) Accordingly
    D) Although

11. Which of the following would provide the best conclusion to the passage?

    A) In addition to *The Snowy Day,* Keats later wrote several more books that featured the same child, Peter, as the main character.
    B) Although writing children's books may not seem like the most influential work, Keats was very successful in what he did.
    C) Truly, Keats has done his part to instill children of all races and ethnicities with the knowledge that their stories are worth telling.
    D) This shows that Keats really was very popular around the world.

HOMEWORK EXERCISE 2:

Rethinking Nero

Given that modern history remembers Emperor Nero as evil incarnate, many would be surprised to learn that Nero was beloved by many of his subjects. This historical revision came about because the dead do not write **(1)** his own history. Nero's first two biographers, Suetonius and Tacitus, had ties to the elite Senate and recorded his reign with contempt, setting the tone for future historians' interpretation of Nero's reign. Later, the notion of Nero's fabled return **(2)** became negative overtones in Christian literature with Isaiah's warning of the coming Antichrist. Then came the condemnations: comic Ettore Petrolini's Nero as a babbling lunatic, Peter Ustinov's Nero as a cowardly murderer, and the well-known, enduring **(3)** appearance of Nero playing his fiddle while Rome burned. What occurred over time was hardly erasure but instead vilification. A complex ruler **(4)** was now simply a "bad guy."

"Today we condemn his behavior," says archaeological journalist Marisa Ranieri Panetta. "But look at the great Christian emperor Constantine. He had his first son, his second wife, and his father-in-law all murdered. **(5)** You can't be a saint and the other a devil. Look at Augustus, who destroyed a ruling class with his blacklists. Rome ran in rivers of blood, but Augustus was able to launch effective propaganda. He understood the media. And so Augustus was great, they say. Not to suggest Nero was a great emperor, but he was no worse than those who came before and after him." {6}

1. A) NO CHANGE
   B) her
   C) its
   D) their

2. A) NO CHANGE
   B) took on
   C) evolved
   D) transitioned

3. A) NO CHANGE
   B) replica
   C) image
   D) photograph

4. A) NO CHANGE
   B) has been
   C) had been
   D) were

5. A) NO CHANGE
   B) One
   C) They
   D) Both

6. Which of the following most effectively establishes the main idea of the paragraph??

   A) Augustus learned how to effectively employ propaganda.
   B) Nero should have learned how to use propaganda like Augustus did.
   C) Nero was actually a fairly effective emperor.
   D) In the context of history, Nero was no worse than other emperors.

[1] Ranieri Panetta is among the multiplying voices who support a reconsideration of Nero. [2] "This rehabilitation—this process of a small group of historians trying to transform aristocrats into gentlemen—seems stupid to me," says the famed Roman archaeologist Andrea Carandini. [3] "For instance, there are serious scholars who now say that the fire was not Nero's fault. But how could he build the Domus Aurea without the fire? Explain that to me. Whether or not he started the fire, he certainly profited from it." [4] Not everyone is on board. {7}

It's worth lingering on Carandini's logic because the fire is central to Nero's mythology. Nero benefitted from the fire, so **(8)** <u>yet</u> he caused the fire.

"Even Tacitus, the great accuser of Nero, writes that no one knows whether Rome burned by arson or **(9)** <u>by chance</u>," counters Ranieri Panetta. "Rome in Nero's time had very narrow streets and was full of tall buildings with wooden upper stories. Fire was essential for lighting, cooking, and heating. Consequently almost all the emperors had big fires during their reigns." Regarding the story of Nero playing the fiddle while Rome burned, there is some evidence that Nero enjoyed playing a stringed instrument called a kithara. {10}

7. In order to improve the logic of the paragraph, where should Sentence 4 be placed?

   A) Where it is now
   B) Before Sentence 1
   C) After Sentence 1
   D) After Sentence 2

8. A) NO CHANGE
   B) therefore
   C) despite
   D) unfortunately

9. A) NO CHANGE
   B) it was destined
   C) because of luck
   D) by design

10. Which of the following sentences, if added here, would best conclude the paragraph?

   A) Yet the idea of Nero doing so during the fire has not reached popular acceptance today.
   B) However, the first historical account stating he played during the fire was written a century and half after it supposedly occurred.
   C) But Roman emperors were all logical men, so it seems strange that he would play an instrument while a city burned.
   D) However, every single modern-day archaeologist believes that he did so during the fire.

Version 1.0

Though by the end of his reign Nero had, as Ranieri Panetta puts it, "lent himself to the label of a monster," Nero began his reign as a beloved man of the people. {11}

11. Which of the following would best conclude the passage?

A) As with many rulers, Nero was neither a saint nor a devil, but a complex figure oversimplified by history.
B) It is important to remember that Nero was not an evil man, but a great ruler.
C) All historians should band together to rehabilitate Nero's reputation.
D) Still, it's how one ends one's life that matters most, so Nero should continue to be remembered for his evil deeds.

Lesson wY12
Parallelism
Getting Your Feet Wet

Directions: Use the paragraph below to answer the questions.

As banks, technology giants, and start-ups like Square fight to create the payment system of the future, German consumers seem perfectly satisfied with the payment system of the past. In fact, Germany remains one of the most cash-centered advanced economies in the world.

On average, German citizens carry roughly twice the amount of cash carried by citizens **(1)** of the Netherlands, France, Canada, Australia, and in the U.S. Roughly 80% of all transactions in Germany are conducted in cash, compared to just 50% in the U.S.

Many believe that a unique set of cultural values have created this preference for cash. **(2)** As a group, Germans value privacy, aversion to debt, and fear monetary instability.

Perhaps in response to a troubled national history, German citizens are strong advocates for privacy protections. When asked about monetary preferences, German survey respondents reported that they enjoyed the anonymity that cash provides, reflecting this national concern for personal privacy.

In addition, Germans show a marked aversion to debt. In fact, the German word for debt, *Schulden*, comes from the word for guilt, *Schuld*. This anthropological factoid helps to explain why just 18% of transactions in Germany were made via credit card, compared to **(3)** 50% in France and 59% of transactions in the UK. In general, Germans **(4)** prefer saving to debt.

Due to their rocky economic past, Germans have greater reason to hold onto cash than citizens of many other nations. Throughout the last century, Germany has experienced multiple episodes of hyperinflation, which caused banking crises and sky-high prices.

1. A) NO CHANGE
   B) of the Netherlands, of France, of Canada, of Australia, and of the U.S.
   C) of the Netherlands, France, Canada, Australia, and the U.S.
   D) of the Netherlands, the French, Canadians, Australians, and Americans.

2. A) NO CHANGE
   B) As a group, Germans value privacy, debt, and monetary instability.
   C) As a group, Germans value privacy, have an aversion to debt, and fear monetary instability.
   D) As a group, Germans are private, debt-free, and unstable.

3. A) NO CHANGE
   B) 50% of French transactions and 59% in the UK
   C) 50% and 59% in France and the UK
   D) 50% in France and 59% in the UK

4. A) NO CHANGE
   B) prefer saving to accumulating debt
   C) prefer to save than debt
   D) prefer save to debt

Lesson wY12
Parallelism
Wading In

TOPIC OVERVIEW – PARALLELISM

In the world of grammar, parallelism requires that different elements in a sentence (or in related sentences) share the same form. This prevents awkwardness, makes writing clearer, and improves overall writing style. Notice that each of the verbs in the previous sentence are in the same form – that's parallelism.

RECOGNIZING PARALLELISM QUESTIONS

Parallelism questions ask us to ensure that parts of a sentence that serve the same function also use the same form. As with other grammar or convention questions, these questions will include an underlined portion of a sentence and several alternate answer choices.

PARALLELISM WITH COORDINATING CONJUNCTIONS

In Lesson 2, we learned about coordinating conjunctions, which we can remember by using FANBOYS (for, and, nor, but, or, yet, so). In that lesson, we used coordinating conjunctions to combine sentences, but these conjunctions are also often used to connect *parts* of sentences. When we join elements of a sentence with a coordinating conjunction, those elements must be in the same form.

Let's look at some examples:

Example 1: I do not like swimming **or** to sunbathe.

This sentence sounds very awkward because of its lack of parallelism. "Swimming" and "to sunbathe" serve the same purpose in the sentence and they are connected using a coordinating conjunction, so they need to be in the same form:

Example 2: I do not like swimming or **sunbathing**.
Example 3: I do not like **to swim** or sunbathe.

It doesn't really matter which form we use, as long as both elements are in the same form, so either Example 2 or Example 3 would be considered correct.

PARALLELISM WITH ITEMS IN A SERIES

The same rules apply to items in a series: items in a series must be in the same form.

Let's look at some examples:

Example 4: He wanted three things: money, power, and to be successful.

"Money" and "power" are both nouns, but "to be successful" isn't. This is an example of faulty parallelism. The simplest solution is to make "to be successful" into a noun:

Example 5: He wanted three things: money, power, and **success**.

We can see the same type of error with other parts of speech, including verbs, prepositional phrases, or clauses. For example:

Example 6: When Fluffy went missing, Hannah looked for the dog in the closet, the garage, and under the bed.

In this example, the faulty parallelism has to do with prepositional phrases. "In the closet" and "under the bed" are both prepositional phrases, but "the garage" is not. We can fix this by changing "the garage" to a prepositional phrase:

Example 7: When Fluffy went missing, Hannah looked for the dog in the closet, **in the garage**, and under the bed.

Although it might seem like adding "in the" to the sentence for a second time makes the sentence redundant, this is one case in which grammar rules require redundancy.

PARALLELISM IN COMPARISONS

When we compare two things, we need to make sure that both items appear in the same form. For example:

Example 8: *Driving* to Canada takes far more time than *to fly* there.

In this sentence, we are comparing driving and flying, so both verbs need to be in the same form:

Example 9: Driving to Canada takes far more time than **flying** there.

ANSWERING PARALLELISM QUESTIONS

The SAT presents parallelism errors in two ways: Either the underlined portion contains all of the items that need to have parallel structure, or the underlined portion needs to be changed to match something found elsewhere in the passage. The steps below address both of these situations:

1. Locate the items that need to have parallel structure.
2. If they are all in the underlined portion, eliminate any answer choices that contain more than one structure.
3. If one is not in the underlined portion, then the underlined item needs to have the same form as the item that is not underlined. Eliminate any answer choices that contain a different form.
4. Choose the best answer from the remaining choices.

<u>Example 10:</u>

Jina always <u>completed her homework, studies for tests, and pays attention in class</u>.

A) NO CHANGE
B) completed her homework and tests, and pays attention in class
C) completed her homework, studied for tests, and pays attention in class.
D) completes her homework, studies for tests, and pays attention in class.

1. The three terms in the list are *completed her homework, studies for tests,* and *pays attention in class.*
2. In the given sentence, all three are in the underlined portion. We can eliminate choices A, B, and C because they contain different structures.
3. Because all three items are in the underlined portion, we can skip this step.
4. Choice D is the only answer remaining.

<u>Example 11:</u>

My English teacher taught us to avoid faulty parallelism and <u>that we should properly revise our essays</u>.

A) NO CHANGE
B) to properly revise our essays
C) how we should properly revise our essays
D) how to go about properly revising our essays

1. The related items are *to avoid faulty parallelism* and *that we should properly revise our essays.* In this sentence, they are connected by "and" – clauses or phrases joined by coordinating conjunctions should be parallel.
2. Because only one item is included in the underlined portion, we can skip this step.
3. We know that the underlined portion needs to be in the same structure as "to avoid faulty parallelism." We can eliminate A and C because they do not follow the "to verb" (also known as *infinitive*) structure.
4. Although choice D does include "to go about," which seems close to "to avoid," this answer choice is very awkward and wordy. Choice B matches the structure of "to avoid faulty parallelism" much more closely.

WRAP-UP

Parallelism questions can be answered using the following steps:

1. Identify the items that need to contain parallel structure.
2. If they are all in the underlined portion, eliminate any answer choices that contain more than one structure.
3. If one is not in the underlined portion, eliminate and answer choices that contain a different structure from that.
4. Choose the best answer from the remaining choices.

Lesson wY12
Parallelism
Learning to Swim

CONCEPT EXERCISE:

Correct the error involving parallelism in each of the following sentences. If you believe there is no error, write *No Error*.

1. I believe we can learn far more from our mistakes than ~~that of~~ our victories.

   from

2. Carefully pour the acid into the beaker, and then, using a medicine dropper, adding four drops of the indicator solution and waiting for it to change color.

3. Once Theo had bought a train ticket, he found himself looking forward to the trip, meeting his friends, and to head to the nearby sulfur springs.

   ing

4. Please dispose of food waste and napkins in the green compost bin, recyclables in the blue bin, and ~~you can put~~ anything left over in the black garbage ~~can~~. *bin*

5. Lottery winners can elect to take either a lump sum up front or ~~to take a~~ larger amount in installments over time.

6. The founder's benevolence toward his own employees was matched only by ~~how he could~~ *his* ~~be~~ ruthless in dealing with business competitors. *ness*

7. A genuine 16th century gold doubloon, a fully functional cannon, and a sword reputed to have belonged to Blackbeard are among the treasures on display at the Pirate Museum.

8. The pianist's fingers swept nimbly, gracefully, and ~~with no effort~~ across the keys.

   effortlessly

9. Do you agree with the saying that it is better to have loved and lost than never ~~having~~ loved at all?

   to have

10. The two things keeping Violet from finishing assignments on time were procrastination and ~~being a~~ perfectionist *ism*.

11. Although Clarence was hardly optimistic that the upstart candidate would be able to run a competitive race against the veteran senator, he made a donation because he hoped that her presence in the race would broaden the scope of the debate.

12. As Whitney pondered her upcoming experiment in living off the grid in Alaska, she realized that finding food and water and generating her own electricity were not nearly as daunting to her as ~~that she would spend~~ so many months without human companionship. *spending*

13. Imagination is less important in being a successful poet than ~~if one is~~ perceptive or not. *having*

14. The relentless drought had again ruined Norm's crop and his livelihood, but one look at his weathered face and you understood that he would rather die on this patch of ground than ~~the thought of giving~~ up farming. *give*

15. You have two options at the end of the semester: you may either take the final exam or ~~you may~~ write a fifteen-page term paper.

16. Napoleon's armies came within a hair's breadth of conquering Europe, with only his defeat at Waterloo ending the series of wars that had swept the continent and ~~which~~ ~~that had~~ ~~brought~~ an era of relative peace.

    bringing

17. Neither a raging blizzard nor ~~if my car breaks~~ ~~down~~ will keep me from getting home for the holidays.

    a automotive breakage breakdown

18. After further examination of the results and ~~failing~~ *failure* to replicate them, the team of physicists began to suspect that the previously published findings had been in error.

19. Would you be so kind as to bring your mother a glass of water, let the dog out for a while, and ~~could you~~ take out the trash?

20. Predicting the behavior of complex systems an inherently uncertain business; we should greet with skepticism both guarantees of the condition of the stock market in five months and pronouncements of what the weather will be in five days.

    No Error

good shading

you're not quite even with your symmetry!

nice lines, good intricacy

*9/20/16
Homework*

Lesson wY12
Parallelism
Diving into the Deep End

PRACTICE EXERCISE:

The Value of Grassland Ecosystems

The Forest Service currently administers twenty National Grasslands, consisting of 3.8 million acres of public land. These grasslands are managed for a variety of purposes including forage, fish and wildlife, **(1)** timber, water, and recreation resources. National Grasslands are valued both for these basic goods and **(2)** to deliver other important services that may be perceived as free and limitless. As a result, their critical contributions are overlooked in public, corporate, and **(3)** by individual decision-makers. The Forest Service is working to promote public awareness of the importance of forests and grasslands to human well-being.

The health and **(4)** being well of human populations depend on the services provided by ecosystems and their components: the organisms, soil, water, and nutrients. Ecosystem services are the process by which the environment produces resources such as clean water, forage, and range; habitat for wildlife; and **(5)** pollinate of native and agricultural plants.

Aesthetic beauty is one example of an ecosystem service provided on the grasslands for which there is no substitute. For many, nature is a source of inspiration, **(6)** peace, of beauty, and rejuvenation. Our National Grasslands provide aesthetic beauty in many forms including wildlife viewing by being home to a diversity of species including golden eagles, grouse, pronghorn, elk, prairie dogs, and **(7)** they are also home to bison. National Grassland units contain the largest representation of threatened and endangered species. In addition, our grasslands contain thousands of species of wildflowers and **(8)** stunning grass-filled vistas that are available year-round for the viewing enjoyment of our public.

1. A) NO CHANGE
   B) a source of timber
   C) cutting down trees for timber
   D) for timber

2. A) NO CHANGE
   B) deliver
   C) delivering
   D) for delivering

3. A) NO CHANGE
   B) by individual decision-making
   C) in individual decision-makers
   D) individual decision-making

4. A) NO CHANGE
   B) to be well
   C) well-being
   D) is well

5. A) NO CHANGE
   B) pollinate native and of agricultural plants
   C) pollinating native and of agricultural plants
   D) pollination of native and agricultural plants

6. A) NO CHANGE
   B) peace, beauty,
   C) of peace, beauty,
   D) of peace, of beauty,

7. A) NO CHANGE
   B) also home to
   C) are also home to
   D) DELETE the underlined portion

8. A) NO CHANGE
   B) are stunned by grass-filled vistas
   C) filling grass, stunning vistas
   D) visitors will be stunned by grass-filled vistas

The plants and animals both living within grassland ecosystems and otherwise **(9)** depending on those ecosystems provide humans with services that would be very difficult to duplicate. For example, pollination is a service for which there is no technological substitute. Our National Grasslands provide habitat for thousands of species of pollinators. Over 100,000 different animal species—including bats, bees, flies, moths, beetles, birds, and butterflies—provide free pollination services. One third of human food comes from plants pollinated by these wild pollinators. The value of pollination services from wild pollinators in the United States alone is estimated at four to six billion dollars per year.

Grassland ecosystem services help sustain, support, and **(10)** they help fulfill human life. Though many of these services are intangible, and **(11)** though hard-to-quantify in value, they are nevertheless critical for sustaining human well-being.

9. A) NO CHANGE
   B) to depend on those
      ecosystems
   C) dependence on those
      ecosystems
   D) on dependent ecosystems

10. A) NO CHANGE
    B) fulfillment of
    C) fulfilling
    D) fulfill

11. A) NO CHANGE
    B) hard to quantify their value,
       though
    C) though their value can be
       hard to quantify
    D) their value can be hard to
       quantify, though

TEST EXERCISE:

Researching Asthma: Causes, Treatments, and Risk Factors

Asthma is a disease of the lung in which the airways are inflamed, making them vulnerable to narrowing, which results in symptoms such as wheezing, chest tightness, and difficulty breathing. **(1)** Estimated to cause millions of urgent medical visits and missed school and work days each year, asthma impacts roughly 8 percent of adults and more than 9 percent of children in the United States, according to the Centers for Disease Control and Prevention. In some cases, the disease can be fatal. However, **(2)** significant progress is being made in asthma research, from basic science, such as how lung cells work, to clinical trials on current and future treatments. Asthma research focuses on environmental factors, mechanisms of disease severity, therapies and prevention, and **(3)** learning about the role of the immune system.

1. A) NO CHANGE
   B) Estimated to cause millions of urgent medical visits and missed school and work days each year,
   C) Millions of urgent medical visits and missed school and work days are caused each year by asthma, and impacts
   D) Asthma causes millions of urgent medical visits and missing school and work days each year; and impacts

2. A) NO CHANGE
   B) experts are making significant progress in asthma research
   C) significant progress is currently being made today in the field of asthma research
   D) much progress is made in asthma research

3. A) NO CHANGE
   B) the role of the immune system.
   C) about the role of the immune system.
   D) information and discoveries about the role of the immune system.

{4} [1] New research has shown that various kinds of air pollution affect asthma differently. [2] **(5)** Therefore, ultra-fine particles from vehicle emissions get deeper into the lungs where the effects may be more significant than many other emissions. [3] In those cases, reducing exposure and improving standards on vehicular emissions has helped reduce asthma symptoms. [4] Understanding how immune cells respond to different environmental triggers may lead to therapies targeting specific types of asthma. [5] Scientists have also found that allergic responses to specific environmental agents, such as allergens from pets and molds, involve many different types of immune cells in the lung. {6}

Research into asthma also includes mechanisms of disease susceptibility and severity, including racial background, genetics and other biological factors. Current priorities include **(7)** clinical studies, such as the Best African American Response to Asthma Drugs trial; new research frontiers, such as studying microbial organisms in the lung; and genetic research, such as looking at the heritability of asthma. The National Asthma Education and Prevention Program translates research discoveries into improved clinical practice and quality of life for patients with asthma.

4. Which choice effectively establishes the main topic of the paragraph?

   A) Increasing standards for car emissions has improved symptoms of asthma for many people.
   B) Different environmental factors impact asthma users in various ways.
   C) Immune cells in lungs react to different environmental agents in a variety of ways.
   D) Studying the effects environmental factors have on asthma is necessary for improving treatments of the condition.

5. A) NO CHANGE
   B) Regardless,
   C) For example,
   D) Similarly,

6. Which of the following would create the most logical and coherent paragraph?

   A) Eliminate sentence 4.
   B) Add a sentence to the end of the paragraph explaining immune cells.
   C) Add a sentence after sentence 4 explaining immune cells.
   D) Switch sentences 4 and 5.

7. A) NO CHANGE
   B) clinical studies, such as the Best African American Response to Asthma Drugs trial, new research frontiers, such as studying microbial organisms in the lung, and study of the genetic research, such as looking at the heritability of asthma.
   C) clinical studies, new research frontiers, and studying genetic research.
   D) clinical studies; new research frontiers; and genetic research.

(8) <u>Also, the immune system is super important when it comes to asthma, so scientists are really interested in understanding it.</u> Normally, the immune system fights off harmful invaders, such as viruses and contagious diseases. However, the immune system also plays a primary role in asthma attacks, since, in asthma sufferers, it treats allergens like pet dander as "invaders" when they enter the lungs, triggering coughing, inflammation, **(9)** <u>and the body to produce mucus.</u> Scientists are still researching why this reaction **(10)** <u>originates</u> in those who have asthma.

Despite the fact scientists have much to learn about asthma, which causes severe symptoms and even death in many people, the condition is still often manageable with proper medication and treatment. Scientists also continue to research various environmental, genetic, and biological factors. {11}

8. Which choice best suits the style and tone of the passage?

   A) NO CHANGE
   B) Largely responsible for asthma attacks is the immune system, which, ironically, is meant to protect the body.
   C) Additionally, the immune system, which plays a major role in asthma, is an important focus of study.
   D) What you might be surprised to know is that scientists are interested in studying the immune system because it plays an important role in asthma.

9. A) NO CHANGE
   B) mucus production
   C) and producing mucus
   D) and mucus production

10. A) NO CHANGE
    B) exists
    C) establishes
    D) occurs

11. Which of the following would best conclude the passage?

    A) Fortunately, experts are constantly making more discoveries, which help improve the efficacy of treatment and prevention strategies for this disease.
    B) Given all the discoveries scientists have been making, a cure for asthma should be just around the corner.
    C) Even though scientists have made many breakthroughs, the possibility of things improving for asthmatics is unlikely.
    D) All these discoveries point to scientists continuing to make breakthroughs for years to come.

Lesson wY12
Parallelism
Race to the Finish

HOMEWORK EXERCISE 1:

Directions: Identify and fix the errors in each sentence for parallelism/parallel structure.

1. Julius Caesar famously came to Gaul, saw the warriors, and was victorious over them. *conquered*

2. Caesar was both an excellent general and he was a great writer.

3. I don't remember whether the tailor said the wool was Scottish, Italian, or came from China. *Chinese*

4. Patience, an eagle eye, and thinking logically are key qualities of a good programmer. *logical thinking*

5. The consultant's report was written quickly, accurately, and with plenty of detail. *thoroughly*

6. In this case, seeing really is to believe. *believing*

7. When he couldn't find his keys, he checked the living room and in the kitchen.

8. The coach told the players that they should get plenty of sleep, eat lightly, and then warm up just before the game.

9. The smell was so bad that death seemed preferable to breathing. *same*

10. We need your approval, verbal or in writing. *verbally* *written*

11. His favorite activities were hiking, biking, and **playing** football.

12. The weather in California is warmer than *in* Washington.

13. The frolicsome puppy dashed into the yard, eagerly dug up his bone, and down the road it ran.

14. To ride around on a Segway—ridiculous as it looks—is a much easier way to sightsee than going on foot. *to walk*

15. When you cough into your hand, it's far less *Coughing* sanitary than coughing into your sleeve.

16. Walking to school allows you both to get some exercise and you can clear your head. *to*

17. To be honest, eating the dried crickets sprinkled on the guacamole was like swallowing stale sunflower seeds.

18. Harold enjoys going for long walks and the *watching the* symphony.

19. Whether at rest or when at work, he always seems relaxed.

20. Football is more popular in Europe than the United States. *in*

HOMEWORK EXERCISE 2:

How Caffeine Gives an Evolutionary Edge

By the time you finish reading this sentence, more than 26,000 cups of coffee **(1)** <u>will been drunk</u> worldwide. Some people might drink it for flavor, but many more of us use coffee as a means **(2)** <u>of delivering</u> caffeine into the bloodstream. Hands down, caffeine is the most widely consumed psychoactive substance.

Caffeine may be a drug, but it's not the product of some underworld chemistry **(3)** <u>lab, rather,</u> it's the result of millions of years of plant evolution. Despite our addiction to caffeine, scientists know little about how and why plants make it.

{4} By sequencing the genome of the coffee bean *Coffea canephora*, a team of scientists has reconstructed how coffee **(5)** <u>received</u> its caffeine-making capacity. Their report also suggests that plants use caffeine to influence the behavior of animals—and, indirectly, us.

1. A) NO CHANGE
    B) will be drank
    C) will have been drunk
    D) have been drunk

2. A) NO CHANGE
    B) to deliver
    C) for delivering
    D) by which to deliver

3. A) NO CHANGE
    B) lab; rather,
    C) lab: rather,
    D) lab; rather

4. Which of the following would be the best transition from the previous paragraph?

    A) The hows and whys of caffeine production are the subject of a new study that's been recently released.
    B) Drugs may be bad for people but not for plants, according to a new study.
    C) DNA experts have now released a report on caffeine production in coffee plants.
    D) A new study is helping to change that.

5. A) NO CHANGE
    B) acquired
    C) earned
    D) garnered

In coffee plants, caffeine starts out as a precursor compound called xanthosine. A certain enzyme in coffee detaches a dangling arm of atoms from the xanthosine, while a second enzyme adds a cluster of atoms at another location. The plant then **(6)** <u>employs</u> two additional enzymes to add two more clusters. What started as xanthosine is now caffeine.

The enzymes that produce caffeine in coffee belong to a group called N-methyltransferases. Scientists had already determined that N-methyltransferases are also responsible for the caffeine in tea and cacao. **(7)** <u>Moreover,</u> one surprise in the new report, is that the specific caffeine-manufacturing enzymes in coffee and cacao are different. They did not evolve from the same ancestors.

In other words, coffee and cacao took different evolutionary paths to reach the same destination. Evolutionary biologists call this process "convergent evolution."

When **(8)** <u>it</u> produces the same complex trait more than once, this is usually a sign of a powerfully useful adaptation. So what's so useful about caffeine?

At high doses, the substance is toxic, so coffee plants may use the caffeine to repel insects or **(9)** <u>for killing off</u> competing plants. But coffee and a number of other plants also lace their nectar with low doses of caffeine, and, in that form, it seems to benefit the plants in a different way.

{10} [1] When insects feed on caffeine-spiked nectar, they get a beneficial <u>buzz</u>. [2] Thus they become much more likely to remember the scent of the flower. [3] Plants make nectar to attract insects so they'll spread their pollen. [4] This enhanced memory may make it more likely that the insect will revisit the flower and spread its pollen further.

(11) <u>We humans</u> are just as susceptible to caffeine's chemical manipulation. Every time we plant more coffee, we're unwittingly advancing the plant's evolutionary strategy.

6. A) NO CHANGE
    B) exploits
    C) uses
    D) manipulates

7. A) NO CHANGE
    B) However
    C) On the other hand
    D) Despite that

8. A) NO CHANGE
    B) this
    C) convergent evolution
    D) nature

9. A) NO CHANGE
    B) for the killing off of
    C) killing off
    D) kill

10. Which of the following revisions would best improve the coherence of paragraph 9?

    A) Delete sentence 2.
    B) Move sentence 2 after sentence 4.
    C) Move sentence 3 before sentence 1.
    D) Delete sentence 4.

11. A) NO CHANGE
    B) Us humans
    C) We, humans,
    D) Humans like ourselves

Lesson wY13
Other Punctuation Errors
Getting Your Feet Wet

Directions: Use the paragraphs below to answer the questions.

The sound of soft, scattered cowbell clunks brings to mind a beautiful countryside. It's a sound that makes us feel **(1)** <u>peaceful, calm, and perhaps just a bit nostalgic</u>. After all, who doesn't enjoy the sound of a cowbell floating through the grass-scented **(2)** <u>air.</u>

As it turns out, the cows don't.

A new study from researchers at the Swiss Federal Institute of Technology in Zurich found that cows wearing cowbells ate and chewed less than cows without the bells. Researchers noted that it was unclear whether it was the noise or the **(3)** <u>weight because standard cowbells weigh five-and-a-half pounds that</u> bothered the cows.

This news should hardly be **(4)** <u>surprising, since</u> cows are known to have more sensitive hearing than humans. Although we may consider cowbells to be a peaceful **(5)** <u>noise. They</u> can generate sounds louder than 100 decibels.

1. A) NO CHANGE
   B) peaceful calm and perhaps just a bit nostalgic
   C) peacefully calm, and perhaps just a bit nostalgic
   D) peaceful, and calm, and perhaps just a bit nostalgic

2. A) NO CHANGE
   B) air!
   C) air?
   D) air?!

3. A) NO CHANGE
   B) weight (standard cowbells weigh five-and-a-half pounds) that
   C) weight, standard cowbells weigh five-and-a-half pounds, that
   D) weight, because standard cowbells weigh five-and-a-half pounds that

4. A) NO CHANGE
   B) surprising after all
   C) surprising. Since
   D) surprising since

5. A) NO CHANGE
   B) noise? They
   C) noise, they
   D) noise they

C2 education
be smarter

Lesson wY13
Other Punctuation Errors
Wading In

TOPIC OVERVIEW: OTHER PUNCTUATION ERRORS

In Lesson 4, we reviewed rules for commas, semicolons, and colons, but the SAT will test our knowledge of other punctuation errors as well. In this lesson, we will discuss some of the other common punctuation error questions that will appear on the SAT.

END-OF-SENTENCE PUNCTUATION ERRORS

The punctuation used at the end of a sentence includes periods, exclamation points, and question marks. These tend to be the easiest punctuation error questions to recognize because the question will include the end-of-sentence punctuation in the underlined portion. The answer choices might include alternative end-of-sentence punctuation marks or the option of combining the sentence with the next sentence using a comma, colon, or semicolon.

In Lessons 1, 2, and 4 we discussed different methods for combining sentences. Remember these rules:

1. When combining sentences using semicolons: Use a semicolon to combine two sentences that are clearly related. Do not use a coordinating or subordinating conjunction with a semicolon.
2. When combining sentences using colons: Use a colon to combine two sentences when the second sentence summarizes or explains the first sentence. Do not use a coordinating or subordinating conjunction.
3. When combining sentences using subordination: Only use a comma if the first sentence becomes a dependent clause. If the second sentence becomes a dependent clause, do not use a comma.
4. When combining sentences using coordination: Separate the sentences by placing a comma before the coordinating conjunction.

Other answer choices might provide alternative end-of-sentence punctuation. The rules for end-of-sentence punctuation are likely very familiar:

1. A complete sentence must include a subject and a verb and must communicate a complete idea. End-of-sentence punctuation should only be used for complete sentences.
2. Sentences that ask a question end in question marks.
3. Sentences that make a statement or demand end in periods.
4. Exclamation points are very rarely used in formal writing. If an exclamation point is provided as an answer choice, examine the tone of the passage to determine whether an exclamation point would be appropriate.

ANSWERING END-OF-SENTENCE PUNCTUATION QUESTIONS

Many times, we can answer end-of-sentence punctuation questions quite easily. Sometimes, a question might be slightly tricky of confusing. When that happens, use this strategy for questions involving end-of-sentence punctuation:

1. If the underlined portion includes the end of one sentence and the beginning of another, determine whether the sentences should be combined. If they should be combined, eliminate any answer choices that do not combine the sentences and follow the rules for combining sentences to choose the correct answer.
2. If the question does not include sentences that should be combined, eliminate any answer choices that combine sentences. All remaining answer choices should contain potential endings to the sentence.
3. Determine whether the sentence is asking a question. Be careful because some sentences will contain phrasing that *looks* like a question but is really a clause that acts as part of a sentence. Eliminate answer choices based on whether a question mark should be used.
4. If an exclamation point is included as an option, examine the tone of the surrounding paragraph to determine whether an exclamation point would be appropriate. Eliminate answer choices based on whether an exclamation point should be used.
5. Closely examine the remaining answer choices. Choose the answer that best suits the sentence.

Let's look at some examples of this type of question. Each of the examples is based on this brief passage:

In the late 1800s, the average American worked 12-hour days, seven days a week. Children as young as five worked in factories and mines, often under the same conditions as **(1)** adults! Although these practices led to the fastest rate of economic growth in U.S. **(2)** history. There was a significant human cost attached to this growth, as U.S. industry had the highest rate of accidents in the world. At the time, the U.S. was the only industrial power in the world to offer no workman's compensation program to support injured workers. Many people wondered how one of the most powerful nations in the world could leave its workers **(3)** behind?

Example 1:

A) NO CHANGE
B) adults? Although
C) adults although
D) adults. Although

Let's follow the steps outlined above to answer the question.

1. First we must determine whether the sentences should be combined at the underlined portion. Although the two sentences are slightly related, combining them would not result in a logical thought.
2. We should eliminate answer choice C, which would combine the sentences.
3. The sentence is not asking a question. We can eliminate answer choice B.
4. The paragraph as a whole is written in a formal style and has a serious tone. Although the fact that children worked under harsh conditions might seem like something that should be emphasized with an exclamation point, the surrounding passage makes an exclamation point inappropriate. We can eliminate choice A.
5. This leaves us with only choice D. D is the correct answer.

Example 2:

A) NO CHANGE
B) history, there
C) history there
D) history; there

1. The first sentence begins with the subordinating conjunction "although." This makes the first sentence a fragment, so we know that it should be combined with another sentence. We can eliminate answer choice A. This now becomes a coordination/subordination question.

We know that when we combine sentences where the first sentence is a dependent clause, we put a comma after the dependent clause. Thus B is the correct answer, and we can skip the remaining steps.

Example 3:

     A) NO CHANGE
     B) behind.
     C) behind!
     D) behind everyone else?

1. There is no sentence to combine.
2. We can skip this step.
3. The word "how" suggests that a question is being asked, but in this sentence, the question is turned into a clause: "how one of the most powerful nations in the world could leave its workers behind" is *what* the people wondered. Since a question is not being asked, we can eliminate choices A and D.
4. Although the sentence suggests that many people were angry or frustrated, which might justify using an exclamation point, the rest of the paragraph is formal, informative, and generally unemotional, so an exclamation point would be inappropriate. We can eliminate choice C.
5. We are left with choice B, which is the correct answer.

ESSENTIAL AND NONESSENTIAL ELEMENTS

Nonessential elements sound like a tricky grammar concept, but they aren't. A nonessential element is a clause or phrase that is not essential to the meaning of the sentence. We briefly discussed nonessential elements in Lesson 4. Remember that if we can remove a clause or phrase and still have a sentence that makes perfect sense and hasn't lost meaning, then that clause or phrase is a nonessential element. Let's look at some examples:

Example 4: The woman who is wearing the ugly hat is my English teacher.

Example 5: Mrs. LaPierre, who is wearing the ugly hat, is my English teacher.

In Example 4, the phrase "who is wearing the ugly hat" tells us *which* woman is my English teacher. The phrase is **essential** to the meaning of the sentence. Without it, the sentence would read, "The woman is my English teacher." That sentence does not help us to identify the English teacher.

In Example 5, the same phrase is **nonessential**. If we remove the phrase, the sentence would read, "Mrs. LaPierre is my English teacher." We don't need to know that she is wearing an ugly hat to know who the English teacher is – it's Mrs. LaPierre.

Notice that there are no commas around the essential phrase. Commas would separate the phrase from the sentence, and since the phrase is important, we don't want to do that.

When the phrase is nonessential, then we use commas to separate it from the sentence. This tells reader that the information contained inside the commas might be interesting, but is not vital to the sentence.

Usually, a nonessential element is set off by commas, but sometimes we might see other punctuation such as parentheses. Although either commas or parentheses could be used, these punctuation marks serve different purposes.

PUNCTUATING NONESSENTIAL ELEMENTS

Notice that there are no commas around the essential phrase in Example 4. Commas would separate the phrase from the sentence, and since the phrase is important, we don't want to do that.

When the phrase is nonessential, as in Example 5, then we use commas to separate it from the sentence. This tells reader that the information contained inside the commas might be interesting, but is not vital to the sentence.

Usually, a nonessential element is set off by commas, but sometimes we might see other punctuation such as parentheses. Although either commas or parentheses could be used, these punctuation marks serve slightly different purposes.

Parentheses are used to de-emphasize or play down. They are also used to include information that seems just a bit out of place in the sentence (an aside, a clarification, or a commentary, for example), but that the writer wanted to include anyway.

Commas are far more commonly used. Because commas don't interrupt the flow of a sentence, we use them when the information is a natural part of the sentence and not some out of place comment.

Let's look at some examples:

<u>Example 6:</u> Greg, <u>who brought his metal detector on vacation,</u> spent the week searching the beach for buried treasure.

<u>Example 7:</u> Greg used his metal detector <u>(which uses a magnetic field to locate metal objects)</u> to search the beach for buried treasure.

Both of these sentences contain nonessential elements – if we were to eliminate the underlined portions of the sentences, both sentences would still communicate the same main idea.

However, the nonessential element in Example 6 provides information that helps the sentence to make more sense. Telling the reading that Greg brought his metal detector on vacation provides us with additional information that is relevant to the sentence. Since the nonessential element fits the flow of the sentence and adds relevant information, we shouldn't use parentheses, so we use commas.

In Example 7, the nonessential element is *really* nonessential: although it provides useful information, the information is completely unnecessary to the ideas being communicated in the sentence. Since the explanation of how a metal detector works is just an interesting aside, we place it in parenthesis.

ANSWERING NONESSENTIAL ELEMENTS QUESTIONS

Nonessential elements questions will ask us to determine whether a clause or phrase needs to be set off by punctuation and, if so, how we should punctuate it. When answering these questions, follow these steps:

1. To determine whether a clause or phrase is essential or nonessential, reread the sentence without the clause. If the sentence still makes sense and communicates the same main idea, the clause is nonessential and should be set off by punctuation. If the sentence no longer communicates the same main idea, the clause is essential and should *not* be set off by punctuation. Eliminate any answer choices that violate this rule.
2. If the clause or phrase is nonessential, determine whether it should be set off by commas or parentheses. If the clause or phrase fits the flow of the sentence and communicates relevant information, use commas. If it interrupts the flow of the sentence or communicates unimportant information, use parentheses. Eliminate any answer choices that violate this rule.
3. Nonessential elements need to be *set off* by punctuation, so there should be punctuation both before and after the element. If it is in the middle of the sentence, it should be surrounded by a pair of commas or parentheses. Eliminate any answer choices that violate this rule.
4. Examine the remaining answer choices and choose the one that best fits the flow of the sentence.

Let's look at an example:

Example 8: My grandfather <u>who is eighty years old</u> plays tennis every day.

A) NO CHANGE
B) (who is eighty years old)
C) , who is eighty years old,
D) , who is eighty years old

Let's follow the strategy:

1. If we eliminate the clause "who is eighty years old," the sentence reads, "My grandfather plays tennis every day." The main idea is still there, so the clause is a nonessential element. Since it needs to be properly punctuated, we can eliminate choice A.
2. The clause provides relevant information because the fact that my grandfather is eighty years old makes his daily tennis games more unusual. It also fits the flow of the sentence. Since it isn't irrelevant and it suits the flow of the sentence, we should use commas. We can eliminate choice B.
3. Choice D has only one comma. Since we know that a nonessential element needs punctuation at both ends, we can eliminate choice D.
4. This leaves us with choice C, the correct answer.

UNNECESSARY PUNCTUATION

The final type of punctuation error we will discuss in this lesson is unnecessary punctuation. These errors occur when an author includes punctuation that serves no real purpose in the sentence. By far the most common type of unnecessary punctuation error is overuse of commas.

One reason why it is important to remember the rules of comma use is so that we can identify the overuse of commas. To review the rules for commas, look back at Lesson 4.

The SAT will sometimes test our understanding of punctuation rules – particularly comma rules – by asking us to appropriately place or eliminate punctuation. Let's look at some examples:

<u>Example 9:</u> One of the smartest things a writer can do, is to learn how to use commas correctly.

In this example, the comma after the word "do" serves no function in the sentence. Remember that we should not use commas simply because it feels natural to pause at a particular place in a sentence. Commas must be used according to grammar rules.

<u>Example 10:</u> Eileen went to the store, because she needed to buy David a birthday cake.

This violates a rule we learned in Lesson 2: When a subordinating clause follows an independent clause, we do not use a comma.

<u>Example 11:</u> Rita scratched the dog's ears, and rubbed his belly.

This is a very common error because writers often feel a predicate that is separated by "and" should have a comma, just like two sentences combined by "and." When a sentence has a compound predicate – meaning two verbs that are being performed by the subject – the two verbs do not need to be separated by a comma.

Lesson wY13
Other Punctuation Errors
Learning to Swim

CONCEPT EXERCISE:

Directions: Correct the errors in the following sentences. Some sentences may have no errors.

1. Larry works full-time, collecting, and processing, customer complaints.

2. Sarah who was my best friend in college, moved cross-country to attend law school.

3. The company's leader was a former professor, he had wanted to apply his financial knowledge to the real world.

4. I was waiting for the bus to school, when I noticed that the sky looked ominously dark and gray.

5. Although, the two women had not seen each other in years, they were soon laughing and, chatting away as if they were back in high school.

6. He told me he didn't steal the cookies, still I don't believe him.

7. His father's friends knew him as a rebel, who wouldn't let outdated conventions weigh him down.

8. Henry, my brother, knows a good deal when he sees one. *No Error*

9. I'm seeing a movie this weekend, you can come if you don't mind driving there yourself.

10. His biggest, problem, wasn't his inexperience, rather, it was his indifference to the needs of the people?

11. Prolonged failure often stems from one of two things, lack of effort or a mismatch between one's skills and one's chosen field.

12. You may disagree, however, I am convinced everyone needs to take responsibility for the team's performance.

13. Maxine, the owner, does not mind if we stay a little longer.

14. These are your options: ignore the symptoms, try to treat them yourself, or see a doctor immediately. *N.E.*

15. I invited Sam, who I've known since grade school, Jerry, who I played soccer with in high school, and Alana, who I didn't meet until college.

16. His favorite subjects are English, French, and biology.

17. Parents, teachers, and staff all have a role to play in providing a positive educational environment for children.

18. The coworker, who helped me the most on the project, was a new hire named Thomas.

19. Sports, at least when they are played outdoors, are a very invigorating activity for me.

20. People, who know at least basic math, are better prepared for life.

9/24/16 Homework

Lesson wY13
Other Punctuation Errors
Diving into the Deep End

PRACTICE EXERCISE:

FDR

(1) <u>Franklin Delano Roosevelt, the 32nd president of the United States assumed the office</u> at a moment of great crisis for the nation. In 1929, the stock market had undergone the worst crash in its history, leading to the disaster historians refer to as the Great Depression. By the time Roosevelt entered the White House in 1933, unemployment (2) <u>had reached 24 percent and many more were underemployed or underpaid and unable to support themselves</u> or their families. Meanwhile, the agricultural sector was stuck in a deep depression that had begun long before 1929. Industrial production had also fallen dramatically, and new investment had nearly disappeared. Between the crash of 1929 and Roosevelt's inauguration, the gross national product—a measure of the nation's economic strength—had dropped by over 30 percent.

1. A) NO CHANGE
   B) Franklin Delano Roosevelt who was the 32nd president of the United States, assumed the office
   C) Franklin Delano Roosevelt, the 32nd president of the United States, assumed the office
   D) Franklin Delano Roosevelt the 32nd president of the United States assumed the office

2. A) NO CHANGE
   B) had reached 24 percent, and many more were underemployed or underpaid and unable to support themselves
   C) had reached 24 percent and many more were underemployed; or underpaid and unable to support themselves
   D) had reached 24 percent, and many more were underemployed, or underpaid and unable to support themselves

Alyson ♡ self-portrait

C2 education be smarter

All of these occupied **(3)** Roosevelt's mind in 1933. The most immediate task facing the new president was the unraveling of the banking system, which had become virtually paralyzed as a widening panic drained many banks of their reserves, leaving the public terrified. The banking crisis provided the ominous **(4)** backdrop, for Roosevelt's initial days in office. In his inaugural address, he tried to offer reassurance. "The only thing we have to fear is fear itself," he declared. But the new leader had few specific plans to offer the anxious public beyond his bold promise of "Action, and action now."

(5) Fortunately this soon changed and Roosevelt spent the first three months of his administration implementing one of the most ambitious programs of domestic reform ever undertaken in American history. This period is now referred to as Roosevelt's "First 100 Days." It began on his very first full day in office, when he ordered every bank in the nation closed—a "bank holiday," as he euphemistically described it. Later that week, Congress met to debate an emergency bill to save the banking system. The bill was quickly passed, and the president signed it the same day. Stronger banks **(6)** quickly reopened with promises of government assistance, weaker ones stayed closed until Treasury Department officials could assure their viability. This was a modest and essentially conservative step, but it worked as intended. Nearly three-quarters of the nation's banks reopened within three days of the measure's passage. The immediate panic had stopped.

3. Which of the following effectively combines the underlined portion of the two sentences?

 A) Roosevelt's mind in 1933, but the most immediate task
 B) Roosevelt's mind in 1933, therefore, the most immediate task
 C) Roosevelt's mind in 1933: But the most immediate task
 D) Roosevelt's mind in 1933— but the most immediate task

4. A) NO CHANGE
 B) backdrop for Roosevelt's initial days in office
 C) backdrop; for Roosevelt's initial days in office
 D) backdrop—for Roosevelt's initial days in office

5. A) NO CHANGE
 B) Fortunately, this soon changed and Roosevelt
 C) Fortunately, this soon changed, and Roosevelt
 D) Fortunately, this soon changed; and Roosevelt

6. A) NO CHANGE
 B) quickly reopened with promises of government assistance; weaker ones stayed closed until Treasury Department officials could assure their viability
 C) quickly reopened with promises of government assistance. While weaker ones stayed closed until Treasury Department officials could assure their viability
 D) quickly reopened with promises of government assistance; and weaker ones stayed closed until Treasury Department officials could assure their viability

(7) Of course Roosevelt knew that more needed to be done to restore the public's confidence in the economy. In an unprecedented act for a president, he took his message directly to the nation's voters, speaking to them over the radio in a series of broadcasts that became known as the "fireside chats." Roosevelt explained the provisions of the new banking bill in everyday terms, assuring voters that "It is safer to keep your money in a reopened bank than it is to keep it under your mattress." The fireside chats continued throughout Roosevelt's administration and remain one of his most enduring **(8)** legacies —he was the first national leader whose voice was a part of the nation's everyday life.

Despite these early successes, not all of Roosevelt's early decisions contributed to economic recovery. One **(9)** major reason for this stall, was that he and his advisers had only vague ideas of what had caused the crisis to begin with. This left them with no clear idea of how to fix it. Some believed the Depression was a result of producing too many material goods, which had driven down prices and launched a spiral of deflation.

7. A) NO CHANGE
   B) Of course Roosevelt knew, that more needed to be done
   C) Of course, Roosevelt knew that more needed to be done
   D) And of course Roosevelt knew that more needed to be done

8. A) NO CHANGE
   B) legacies, he was the first national leader
   C) legacies: he was the first national leader
   D) legacies; and he was the first national leader

9. A) NO CHANGE
   B) major reason for this stall was that he—and his advisers
   C) major reason for this stall, was that he, and his advisers
   D) major reason for this stall was that he and his advisers

C2 education
be smarter

(10) production was not the problem, rather it was underconsumption on the part of working people that prevented the economy from growing. Because those closest to him could not agree on the correct interpretation of the crisis at hand, Roosevelt ultimately settled on a set of fairly conservative compromise solutions that proved inadequate to the task of ending the depression. It was only years later that Roosevelt and his associates would come to accept the new ideas of Keynesian economics, which promoted aggressive public spending to generate economic activity during a recession. Ultimately, it was the unintentional application of Keynesian ideas **(11)** during World War II when government spending increased dramatically, that finally brought an end to the Depression that Roosevelt had fought for so long. Nevertheless, the president deserves immense credit for restoring Americans' confidence in their government, and many of the policies he championed—such as Social Security—remain foundational elements of American society even today.

10. A) NO CHANGE
    B) production was not the problem, rather, it was underconsumption
    C) production was not the problem: rather it was underconsumption
    D) production was not the problem; rather, it was underconsumption

11. A) NO CHANGE
    B) during World War II—when government spending increased dramatically— that finally brought an end
    C) during World War II, when government spending increased dramatically— that finally brought an end
    D) during World War II, when government spending increased dramatically; that finally brought an end

TEST EXERCISE:

Erbil

[1] The 100-foot-high, oval-shaped citadel of Erbil **(1)** <u>towers and soars</u> high above the northern Mesopotamian plain, within sight of the Zagros Mountains that lead to the Iranian plateau. [2] The massive mound, built up by its inhabitants over the last 6,000 years, is the heart of what might be the world's oldest continuously occupied settlement. [3] Other cities in the running **(2)** <u>include Damascus, Jericho, and Aleppo.</u> [4] Throughout its life, the city has been many things, including a pilgrimage site dedicated to a great goddess, a prosperous trading center, a town on the frontier of several empires, and a rebel stronghold. {3}

{4} A dense concentration of nineteenth- and twentieth-century houses **(5)** <u>stand</u> atop the mound, and these have prevented archaeologists from exploring the city's older layers. Because of this, almost everything known about the metropolis—once called Arbela—has been cobbled together from ancient texts and artifacts unearthed at other sites. "We know Arbela existed, but without excavating the site, all else is a hypothesis," says University of Cambridge archaeologist John MacGinnis.

1. A) NO CHANGE
   B) soars
   C) towers
   D) towers, and soars

2. A) NO CHANGE
   B) include: Damascus, Jericho, and Aleppo.
   C) include – Damascus, Jericho, and Aleppo.
   D) include Damascus Jericho and Aleppo.

3. Which of the following sentences should be removed in order to improve the focus of the paragraph?

   A) Sentence 1
   B) Sentence 2
   C) Sentence 3
   D) Sentence 4

4. Which choice most effectively establishes the main idea of the paragraph?

   A) Due to barriers blocking archaeologists' excavations, much about Erbil remains unknown.
   B) There have been many problems getting in the way of discovering more of Erbil.
   C) Despite the fact that Erbil has existed for so long, there is little known by historians about its past.
   D) Archaeologists have been studying and excavating Erbil for decades but have learned little.

5. A) NO CHANGE
   B) stands
   C) are standing
   D) stood

[1] Last year, the first major excavations began, revealing the first traces of the fabled city. [2] **(6)** Two large stone structures have been detected below the citadel's center that may be the remains of a temple dedicated to Ishtar, the goddess of love and war. [3] These finds are beginning to provide a more complete picture not only of Arbela's own story, **(7)** but of the growth of the first cities, the rise of the mighty Assyrian Empire, and the tenacity of an ethnically diverse urban center that has endured for more than six millennia. [4] At this temple, Assyrian kings sought divine guidance, and Alexander the Great assumed the title of King of Asia in 331 B.C. [5] Archaeologists are also searching for a massive fortification wall surrounding the ancient lower town, excavating an impressive tomb just north of the citadel likely dating to the seventh century B.C., and **(8)** doing an examination of what lies below the modern city's suburbs. {9}

6. A) NO CHANGE
   B) Two large stone structures have been detected below the center of the citadel that may be the remains of a temple dedicated to Ishtar, the goddess of love and war.
   C) Two large stone structures that may be the remains of a temple dedicated to Ishtar, the goddess of love and war, have been detected below the citadel's center.
   D) Detected below the center of the citadel was two stone structures that are the remains of a temple dedicated to Ishtar, the goddess of love and war.

7. A) NO CHANGE
   B) but also
   C) and
   D) also

8. A) NO CHANGE
   B) are examining
   C) an examination of
   D) examining

9. To improve the flow of the paragraph, Sentence 3 should be moved where?

   A) NO CHANGE
   B) After Sentence 1
   C) Before Sentence 5
   D) After Sentence 5

Located on a fertile plain, Erbil has been a regional breadbasket, a natural gateway to the east, and a key junction on the road connecting the Persian Gulf to the south. {10} Inhabitants fought back against repeated invasions by the soldiers of the Sumerian capital of Ur 4,000 years ago, witnessed three Roman emperors attack the Persians, and (11) suffered the onslaught of Genghis Khan's cavalry in the thirteenth century, the cannons of eighteenth-century Afghan warlords, and the wrath of Saddam Hussein's tanks only 20 years ago. Yet, through thousands of years, the city survived, and even thrived, while other once-great cities such as Babylon and Nineveh crumbled.

10. Which sentence, if added here, would best improve the coherence of the paragraph?

A) NO CHANGE
B) The fertile land, in addition to its geographic location, have created many problems for the city.
C) The combination of these factors has created a region plagued by turmoil throughout the centuries.
D) Geography has both helped the city and caused it trouble.

11. A) NO CHANGE
B) suffered and endured
C) underwent
D) experienced

Lesson wY13
Other Punctuation Errors
Race to the Finish

HOMEWORK EXERCISE 1:

Directions: Correct the errors in the following sentences. Some sentences may have no errors.

1. Kevin Judy and their two daughters went out to dinner at the new Thai restaurant.

2. The students gave their favorite teacher Miss Lyons a large bouquet of flowers.

3. The cousins decided to go on a ski trip to Park City, Utah, Killington, Vermont, or Aspen, Colorado.

4. The Smith family packed the cooler loaded the minivan and began the drive.

5. Everyone at school was very excited when a few, white, flakes of snow began to fall.

6. "Look at how pretty the sunset is" Danielle exclaimed.

7. The grueling drive continued: even though the road conditions were dangerous.

8. The strawberry-cheesecake was a hit at the surprise birthday party.

9. Ultimate Frisbee a sport that combines the rules of football, soccer, and basketball is one of the fastest growing sports in the world.

10. The principal told the teachers to fail any student – even a star athlete – if he or she did not complete all of the assignments for the class.

11. Eating a lot of vegetables fruit and lean meat is a good way to maintain a healthy diet and lifestyle.

12. After Kim waited months for her broken foot to heal; it was finally back to normal and she could dance again.

13. Most children agree, playing outside in the snow, is a great way to spend a snow day.

14. In the beginning, of the play, the audience witnesses a gruesome murder.

15. The players were ecstatic to learn that the disputed goal was to be accepted and they would win the game.

16. The swiftly, moving, current swept the toy boat down the storm drain.

17. Because Congress couldn't decide on the bill; it was tabled until they received new information.

18. Emily travels a lot for work: A photojournalist must go wherever an assignment takes her.

19. The date for the acquisition of the company would be December 15th, 2014, January 21st, 2015, or March 4th, 2015.

20. No one could believe that Jim was a basketball star, he was only 5 feet tall!

HOMEWORK EXERCISE 2:

Let's say you had **(1)** <u>an ordinary, run-of-the-mill, average</u> day. You got up, went to your challenging, college-graduate job, and worked hard all day. **(2)** <u>The fact that the day</u> is over, you're tired and a little **(3)** <u>stressed, you</u> just want to go home, eat supper, and go to bed. Then you remember you're out of food, so instead of going straight home, you head to the supermarket. Since it's rush hour, this takes far longer than it should. By the time you arrive, you're in a state of **(4)** <u>quiet, exhausted</u> rage.

When you go inside, you find the supermarket full of people who are just as **(5)** <u>weekend</u> and short-tempered as you are. After wandering all over the huge store's confusing aisles, you're eventually able to head for the checkout—where all the lines are insanely long. Then you have to walk out to the parking lot with the front wheel of your cart pulling maddeningly to the left, and finally you have to drive home through a rush hour full of SUVs with impatient drivers. {6}

1. A) NO CHANGE
   B) an ordinary, run-of-the-mill
   C) an ordinary and run-of-the-mill
   D) an ordinary

2. A) NO CHANGE
   B) Except that the day
   C) Now that the day
   D) Although the day

3. A) NO CHANGE
   B) stressed, and you
   C) stressed, but you
   D) stressed;

4. A) NO CHANGE
   B) quiet exhausted
   C) exhausted quiet
   D) exhaustedly quietly

5. A) NO CHANGE
   B) worn
   C) sleepy
   D) fatigued

6. In the context of the passage how does this paragraph function in the passage as whole?

   A) It provides a criticism of grocery stores and their employees.
   B) It disproves claims made earlier in the passage.
   C) It provides an example of an everyday, yet challenging experience that the students are bound to face.
   D) It illustrates the previously stated idea that life is full of suffering and only a select few people find a way out of it.

[1] That, however, is not my real point. [2] My real point is this: you have to choose what to focus your mind on, and if you don't consciously think about how to deal with frustrating circumstances, you're going to be angry and miserable every time you go shopping. [3] Blood-pressure-raising scenarios like this one in the supermarket have not yet been part of your actual life routine, but I guarantee you they will be. [4] This is true—and not just for shopping—because your natural, unconscious reaction is the certainty that everything is really all about you—*your* hunger, *your* fatigue, *your* desire to get home. {7}

Let me suggest that there are totally different ways to think about these kinds of situations. When you're stuck in traffic, bumper to bumper with all those other **(8)** vehicles, it's possible that the Hummer that cuts you off is being driven by a father who hates to drive this aggressively but needs to get his 5-year-old with a 103-degree fever to the hospital as quickly as possible. Or maybe the ugly lady screaming at her kid in the checkout line isn't usually like this. Maybe she volunteers at a nursing home two evenings a week, reading to the dozen or so Alzheimer's patients **(9)** whose child lives in another state and can't come out to see them very often. {10}

7. In order to create the most logical sequence for this paragraph, where should Sentence 3 be placed?
A) Where it is now
B) Before Sentence 1
C) Before Sentence 2
D) After Sentence 4

8. A) NO CHANGE
B) vehicles: it's
C) vehicles; it's
D) vehicles it's

9. A) NO CHANGE
B) whose child live in another state
C) whose children live in other states
D) their children live in other states

10. If the author were to describe a third example to illustrate his point, which of the following would be most appropriate in the context of the paragraph?
A) a teenager who is constantly in trouble with the law.
B) a kind elderly man who gives helpful advice to people he meets
C) a normally loving, compassionate pastor who argues with his wife in public.
D) a disobedient child who runs in front of the reader's car in the parking lot, causing the reader to slam on the brakes

Of course, none of this may be very likely, but all of it is certainly possible. It just depends on what you choose to focus on. If you learn to focus thoughtfully, you will—strange as it may seem—be able to experience unpleasant inconveniences as entirely meaningful. **{11}**

11. Which of the following sentences, if added here, would best conclude the passage?

A) There are, however, more important lessons to learn from this principle.

B) Otherwise, you'll discover that you can't focus on anything and will probably end up in adverse circumstances.

C) You might even find a little bit of joy in them.

D) They will only feel meaningful for a few minutes, though.

Lesson wY14
Possession Errors
Getting Your Feet Wet

Directions: The questions below are intended as a short diagnostic exam.

1. Ronald Reagan once said, "You can tell a lot about a <u>fellows character</u> by his way of eating jellybeans."

     A) NO CHANGE
     B) fellows' characters
     C) fellow's character
     D) fellow characters

2. France's famous general, Napoleon Bonaparte, wisely said, "Never interrupt <u>you're enemy</u> when he is making a mistake."

     A) NO CHANGE
     B) the enemy of you
     C) you are the enemy
     D) your enemy

3. The founder of one of the largest computer companies of the 1980s once said, "There is no reason anyone would want a computer in <u>they're home</u>."

     A) NO CHANGE
     B) their home
     C) there home
     D) they are home

4. Mark Twain coined the phrase "<u>Its not the size of the dog in the fight; its</u> the size of the fight in the dog."

     A) NO CHANGE
     B) It's not the size of the dog in the fight; its
     C) Its not the size of the dog's in the fight; it's
     D) It's not the size of the dog in the fight; it's

Lesson wY14
Possession Errors
Wading In

TOPIC OVERVIEW: POSSESSION ERRORS

The SAT tests our knowledge of possessives and plurals, which are frequently confused in writing. In addition, some plural and possessive words are often confused with contractions or adverbs, and such errors will also appear on the SAT.

TOPIC OVERVIEW: APOSTROPHES

Apostrophes first appeared in the English language in the 1500s as a way to indicate omissions. They are still used that way in contractions such as *can't* (for can *no*t). Over time, apostrophes came to serve new purposes. For example, today they are commonly used to indicate possession.

Most of the time, adding *'s* to a noun suggests possession, not plurality. This is a common error in writing. Let's look at an example:

Example 1: The sign at the grocery store read, "Banana's $1.50."

In this example, the sign was clearly intended to tell shoppers that bananas cost $1.50, but because of the apostrophe, the sign really says that a banana has $1.50.

A similar error can occur with verbs. For example:

Example 2: She fly's to Los Angeles regularly for her job.

In this case, *fly's* would mean "something that belongs to a fly." Instead, the writer should have written, "She *flies* to Los Angeles regularly for her job."

We'll discuss apostrophes and their role in possession and plurality in more depth later in this lesson.

TOPIC OVERVIEW: THEIR/THEY'RE/THERE

In addition to apostrophe abuse, possession errors will also test our understanding of possessive words like "their." *Their, they're,* and *there* are frequently confused words, but it's important to understand the specific uses for each version of the word.

Their is the possessive pronoun. This is always used to mean "belonging to them." For example:

Example 3: They had to take *their* dog to the vet.

They're is a contraction for "they are." This word is *always* used in this way. For example:

Example 4: *They're* worried that the dog might be seriously ill.

There is most frequently used to show the location or position of something. For example:

Example 5: The vet admitted the dog to the animal hospital and said he would have to stay *there* overnight for observation.

There is also often used to show the existence of something. For example:

Example 6: It turned out that *there* was nothing wrong with the dog.

TOPIC OVERVIEW: YOU'RE/YOUR

Another pair of commonly confused words is *your* and *you're*. Although these words sound the same, they have distinct meanings.

Your is possessive. It indicates that something belongs to you. For example:

Example 7: *Your* dog is so much better behaved than mine.

You're is the contraction for "you are." For example:

Example 8: *You're* going to have to tell me how you trained him to be so obedient!

TOPIC OVERVIEW: ITS/IT'S/ITS'

As we noted earlier, *'s* usually indicates possession, which is probably why *its* is so often confused with *it's*. This is an exception to the rule: *its* is possessive, while *it's* is a contraction that means "it is." *Its'*, which is also sometimes wrongly used in writing, is not actually a word and is never correct.

To determine whether we should use *its* or *it's*, the best method is to turn the word into "it is" and see if the sentence still makes sense. For example:

Example 9: Since <u>it's</u> going to be very hot this weekend, the hospital is having <u>it's</u> air conditioning unit serviced today.

If we replace both "it's" with "it is," this is the sentence we get:

Example 9 (again): Since <u>it is</u> going to be very hot this weekend, the hospital is having <u>it is</u> air conditioning unit serviced today.

When we use "it is," we see that the first use of *it's* is correct – "it is" makes sense, so the contraction "it's" should be used. The second use of *it's* is incorrect – "the hospital is having it is air conditioning unit serviced today" doesn't make sense. So the correct version of the sentence should read:

Example 9 (corrected): Since <u>it's</u> going to be very hot this weekend, the hospital is having <u>its</u> air conditioning unit serviced today.

TOPIC OVERVIEW: POSSESSIVE NOUNS

Adding *'s* to a noun makes it possessive, not plural. Adding an *s* or *es* makes a noun plural, not possessive.

The only exception to this rule is a noun that ends with *s*. To make a noun that ends with *s* possessive, it is acceptable to only add an apostrophe. For example:

Example 10: Kansas' statute was challenged in court.

If a noun is plural and ends in *s*, such as *apostrophes*, then you always add just an apostrophe and not an *s*. For example:

Example 11: The apostrophes' usage was incorrect throughout the essay.

If a noun is plural and does *not* end in *s*, such as *children*, then you add *'s*. For example:

Example 12: The children's hospital was in danger of shutting down.

Lesson wY14
Possession Errors
Learning to Swim

CONCEPT EXERCISE:

Directions: Correct the errors in the following sentences. Some sentences may have no errors.

1. Many people find English, especially it's spelling rules, very difficult to understand.

2. Even native speakers have trouble with the rule's for their own language.

3. Knowing exactly how to spell words in English is difficult because their not always phonetic. *they're*

4. That is, letter's in English are not always pronounced the same way in one word as they are in another.

5. Famously, the letters "ough" can be pronounced in over a dozen different ways, depending on the context.

6. Also, the letters in the word "ghoti" can actually be pronounced as if their spelling "fish." *they're*

7. Part of the reason for the weirdness of English spelling lies in the language's history.

8. English started out as one of the tongues most closely related to German.

9. In fact, it's still considered a Germanic language today.

10. However a thousand year's ago, the French lord William of Normandy invaded England.

11. With William's victory, French became the most important language in England.

12. Over time, many thousands' of French words and phrases became part of English.

13. If you say that you're entree was delicious at the hotel restaurant, you will have used four words that came into English from French.

14. Although English vocabulary grew, words' pronunciations stayed somewhat close to their spellings at first.

15. That began to change, however, as some letter combination's took on new sounds or simply stopped being pronounced.

16. Centuries ago, for example, you would have had to make a harsh sound in the back of you're mouth to properly pronounce "gh" in words like "light" and "eight."

17. Likewise, "a" used to be pronounced like the "ah" in "father" in words such as "romance" and names' such as "Andrew."

18. Finally, some choices of spelling are based entirely on a words language of origin, especially when that language is Greek.

19. For example, if a word has an "f" sound and originally came from Greek, chances' are good that the "f" sound is spelled with a "ph" like in "graph" or "telephone."

20. On the other hand, the letters "ch" are probably pronounced like a "k" if the word in which they make there appearance comes from Greek (like in "chrome") but probably not if the word comes from Latin ("chamber") or German ("chore"). *their*

21. Thus, knowing the backgrounds of words can often help you when you're trying to figure out how to spell a word.

22. Still, even knowing the origin's of a word won't always tell you the right spelling because even these helpful rules of thumb have exceptions.

23. It's this combination of many rules *and* many exceptions' that makes English more complicated to spell than most languages.

Lesson wY14
Possession Errors
Diving Into the Deep End

PRACTICE EXERCISE:

With **(1)** millions' of cameras and smartphones all over the planet pointed at the natural world, the chances that somebody might catch a new species or an unknown behavior have skyrocketed. And **(2)** scientist's are increasingly trying to tap into that vast pool of information. Wading into the billions of photos and videos shared on social media isn't easy—but if researchers can harness our cameras, they may be able to unlock a huge amount of information about our world.

But, **(3)** it's not just new species or behaviors that smartphones are documenting. Sometimes **(4)** photographs' with geotagged locations might be the only records of a species in that location. "I've come across blog posts that are making new geographic records, I've had tweets that are the first and currently only published records of some species," says Morgan Jackson, an entomologist at the University of Guelph.

These are the kinds of things that citizen science advocates dream of: collaborations between **(5)** amateurs and trained **(6)** scientist's that produce real, published results. But citizen science **(7)** projects are really hard to design—they have to be fun, interesting, and not too difficult for participants, while also being robust and scientifically useful.

1. A) NO CHANGE
   B) million's
   C) millions ⟲
   D) million

2. A) NO CHANGE
   B) scientists ⟲
   C) scientist's
   D) scientist

3. A) NO CHANGE ⟲
   B) its
   C) its'
   D) it isn't

4. A) NO CHANGE
   B) photographs ⟲
   C) photograph
   D) photograph's

5. A) NO CHANGE ⟲
   B) amateur's
   C) amateurs'
   D) amateur

6. A) NO CHANGE
   B) scientists ⟲
   C) scientists'
   D) scientist

7. A) NO CHANGE ⟲
   B) project's
   C) project
   D) projects'

(8) They're are more than eight million photos on Flickr tagged with the word "insect." Even if you try to drill down to things like "butterfly" or "spider," **(9)** you left with a crushing wall of photos, most of which aren't going to be useful. That's just Flickr. There is almost certainly useful data squirreled away in Twitter, Facebook, and YouTube. It's finding it that's the problem.

"You know how hard it is to find a certain Tweet—so trying to find one you don't know exists is nearly impossible," Jackson says. He thinks that if scientists can teach people just a little bit more about bugs—or any animal or plant, really—users could help filter some of the pictures they are taking.

And storing all this data will be crucial, too, another place where privacy and science might butt heads. If someone deletes his or her Instagram or Twitter account, and makes the conscious choice to remove that information from the web, can researchers still hang on to an archived copy?

(10) Its not just users that have some learning to do to make their photos helpful, though. Scientists also have to think to look to social media for information. Not many taxonomists would think to look through Facebook or Twitter hashtags.

If they can use it effectively, though, researchers could be on the verge of tapping into an incredibly valuable resource. **(11)** There are more than 500 million photos uploaded and shared every day. Some of those photos are bound to depict things nobody has ever seen before. It's just a matter of finding them.

8. A) NO CHANGE
    B) their
    C) theirs
    D) there

9. A) NO CHANGE
    B) your
    C) you're
    D) yours

10. A) NO CHANGE
    B) It's
    C) Its'
    D) It

11. A) NO CHANGE
    B) Their
    C) There's
    D) They're

HONEY

CUTE ♡

TEST EXERCISE:

Where Are All the Female Test Subjects?

In 1987, the National Institute of Health made a bold update to **(1)** their grant **(2)** guidelines: encouraging scientists seeking funding to include women and minorities in their clinical research. Six years later, the U.S. Congress took things a step further by passing a law that **(3)** mandates the inclusion of women and minorities in numbers adequate to allow for valid analyses of difference.

{**4**} Women still make up only one-third of all clinical trial participants. But, earlier along in the scientific pipeline, the disparity is even more pronounced. Test subjects in pre-clinical **(5)** studies those involving animals or human cells before human testing is conducted— are overwhelmingly male, which severely **(6)** skews the data.

1. A) NO CHANGE
   B) its
   C) his
   D) it's

2. A) NO CHANGE
   B) guidelines encouraging
   C) guidelines, encouraging
   D) guidelines. Encouraging

3. A) NO CHANGE
   B) mandate
   C) mandated
   D) mandating

4. Which of the following topic sentences best reflects the main idea of the paragraph?

   A) Inclusion and equality, however, are far from interchangeable.
   B) Males are not always exclusively utilized as test subjects.
   C) Women are becoming more included in scientific studies.
   D) However, many scientists still feel that sex does not play a role in research results.

5. A) NO CHANGE
   B) studies, those
   C) studies; those
   D) studies — those

6. Within the context of the passage, the underlined word most nearly means

   A) adjusts.
   B) warps.
   C) alters.
   D) curves.

The obvious issue is, if **(7)** <u>one is</u> only studying males, you don't know if that therapy is going to work in females. Research really needs to be conducted in both sexes.

Past research has suggested that the health benefits of aspirin, for example, may differ by sex, helping to prevent heart attacks in men and strokes in women. But, drugs are just the beginning. Sex differences have been found in pain receptors, liver enzymes, even the wiring of the brain.

So why do such **(8)** <u>harsh</u> differences still persist in basic science research?

7. A) NO CHANGE
    B) you are
    C) we are
    D) they are

8. Which of the following is the most precise replacement for the underlined word?

    A) damaging.
    B) stark
    C) plain
    D) rigid

Partly because of ignorance within the scientific community, which is something that prominent researcher Melina Kibbe has experienced. Kibbe's own interest in sex disparities in research subjects arose only after her professor asked if she had used rats of both sexes in her vascular therapy research. She hadn't.

[1] The reason Kibbe originally used only males—and the reason why male animals are vastly more common as test subjects in general—is one that presents a hurdle for those looking to level the scientific playing field. [2] Money, too, is a deterrent for many researchers; including animals or cells of both sexes means more subjects and more work to be funded. [3] The more dramatic hormone fluctuations of female animals mean that they're generally considered more difficult. [4] It's a variable that is not held constant throughout the experiment. {9}

[1]Recently, steps towards parity have grown increasingly larger. [2] Of the five journals surveyed in the *Surgery* study, three have since revised their author guidelines, requiring that researchers identify the sex makeup of their test. [3]Last year, they launched a program to provide supplemental funding to single-sex projects so that researchers could add subjects of the missing sex. {10}

(11) However, it's an exciting time for those who have been advocating for sex inclusion science. If we can fundamentally study the way sex influences biology, we're going to enter a whole new era of scientific work that's going to change our health.

9. Which of the following sentences should be removed to improve the clarity of the paragraph?

A) Sentence 1
B) Sentence 2
C) Sentence 3
D) Sentence 4

10. The author would like to include the following sentence: "In studies involving only one sex, researchers must provide rationale for excluding the other in order to be published."

A) before sentence 1
B) After sentence 1
C) After sentence 2
D) After sentence 3

11. A) NO CHANGE
B) Additionally,
C) Therefore,
D) Primarily,

Lesson wY14
Possession Errors
Race to the Finish

HOMEWORK EXERCISE 1:

Directions: Correct the errors in the following sentences. Some sentences may have no errors.

1. The word psychology gets it's name from Greek words for "study of the soul".

2. One of psychologys most important figures was Austrian Sigmund Freud, who created the field of psychoanalysis.

3. Perhaps the most well known of Freud's ideas was his splitting of the human psyche into three components – the id, ego, and super-ego – and defining there roles.

4. If Freud counseled you, he would likely tell you that the source of you're problems is rooted in your experiences as a child.

5. Many modern psychologists prefer behavioral or cognitive approaches that are based on scientific evidence to philosophical beliefs.

6. As advances in science have revealed more about the human brain, psychologists have had to adjust they're theories.

7. As a science, psychology makes use of experiments and studies to test its theories.

8. One of the most commonly studied experiments in psychology courses is Philip Zimbardos Stanford prison experiment.

9. Some experiment's, like the Stanford prison experiment, would be considered unethical in today's world.

10. If a person whose responsible for a crime is shown to have a mental disorder, he or she may receive a lesser punishment than would someone who does not.

11. In the "placebo effect", an individual who takes a pill claims to feel better because he or she is convinced of it's effectiveness, even if the pill has no medicinal properties.

12. Psychology is not always able to test its theories through experiments, so its sometimes reliant on individual case studies for information.

13. Case studies are informative because they're based on individuals who have experienced specific problems in their lives.

14. Phineas P. Gage was a railroad foreman who's life was changed when an iron rod was driven through his head.

15. Since he survived, psychologists studied Phineas behavior and discovered the function of the part of the brain the iron rod had damaged.

16. While you may not realize it, your actually taking advantage of a psychological principle when you teach your dog a new trick by rewarding it with treats.

17. A developmental psychologists field of study is the process by which people grow, and focuses on various life stages.

18. Many of the tests taken in schools today – including the SAT – were developed by psychologists.

19. Psychology is a broad field, with it's applications ranging from the artistry of therapy to the science of experiments.

20. Humans and animals throughout the world benefit from psychologists, and there work in understanding the brain.

HOMEWORK EXERCISE 2:

Fasting for Reform

    In 1968, **(1)** <u>when</u> the farmworkers' struggle to gain basic rights and relief from brutal mistreatment, Cesar Chavez didn't just march or strike or demonstrate – he fasted in order to raise awareness about his movement and highlight the importance of nonviolent resistance. Today, a new generation of activists is going without all food except **(2)** <u>water – this</u> time to bring attention to the urgent need for comprehensive immigration reform.

    {3} [1] I visited the fasters yesterday on the National Mall, where they are camped out in tents. [2] The tents were provided by a local non-profit organization that supported their cause. [3] I was moved by their conviction and their moral clarity. [4] They regard their discomfort as a mere inconvenience compared to the suffering of those living on the **(4)** <u>boundaries,</u> often separated from their families and stripped of basic dignity.

    One man **(5)** <u>whose been</u> fasting for 10 days told me: "This is a way to pay back my parents' sacrifices." Fasting, he explained, is "the only way I can look into my parents' and community's eyes and tell them I did everything I could to pass comprehensive immigration reform."

1. A) NO CHANGE
   B) while
   C) during
   D) instead of

2. A) NO CHANGE
   B) water; this
   C) water this
   D) water. This

3. Which of the following sentences should be removed in order to improve the focus of the paragraph?

   A) Sentence 1
   B) Sentence 2
   C) Sentence 3
   D) Sentence 4

4. A) NO CHANGE
   B) margins
   C) edges
   D) limits

5. A) NO CHANGE
   B) whos' been
   C) who is
   D) who has been

{6} With 11 million people living in the shadows, toiling in an underground, exploitative economy that depresses wages and working conditions for everyone, the immigration status quo is intolerable and unconscionable. Fixing it is a humanitarian and economic imperative

We are indeed a nation of immigrants. People who choose to come to America have always been one of our greatest sources of national vitality. They keep our economy strong and our communities dynamic. They are some of our greatest patriots. My parents, fleeing a repressive regime in the Dominican Republic, were embraced **(7)** from this country and taught us to love it in return. After my father served proudly in the U.S. Army, my parents settled in Buffalo, N.Y., and were able to live the American Dream. They taught **(8)** me and my four siblings to work hard, to aim high and also to make sure the ladder is down for others.

(9) Eliseo Medina's viewpoint, a stalwart of the labor movement who was an associate of Cesar Chavez and is now one of the leaders of this "Fast for Families" effort, has said: "I fast not out of anger or despair, but out of faith, of hope and love." For him and others, this fast is an act of empowerment, fueled by a belief that our nation's leaders will rise to this moment and give us an immigration system worthy of America and consistent with our values.

6. Which of the following sentences provides the most logical transition from the previous paragraph, considering the organization of the passage as a whole?

   A) People all over the world are beginning to learn about the fasters.
   B) Such reform has taken on increased importance in the face of present conditions.
   C) The "tent city" has grown far larger than officials expected.
   D) It is important that we allow more immigrants into this country.

7. A) NO CHANGE
   B) for
   C) through
   D) by

8. A) NO CHANGE
   B) my four siblings and I
   C) me and also my four siblings
   D) we five siblings

9. A) NO CHANGE
   B) Eliseo Medina believes immigrants
   C) Eliseo Medina
   D) Eliseo Medina's realization

"Paciencia y fe," my mother always used to say – patience and

faith. I believe, because of the passion and the resilience of the

fasters I met today, and so many others acting with courage and

conviction across our country, we will get there. {10} {11}

10. Considering the passage as a whole, which of the following best describes the perspective of the author relative to the fasters?

A) Uninformed insider
B) Interested observer
C) Passionate antagonist
D) Pessimistic outsider

11. Which of the following best summarizes the argument of the passage?

A) The problems faced by immigrants in the United States today are the same as those faced in Cesar Chavez's time.
B) Immigration reform has many supporters in Washington, D.C.
C) Fasting is a great way to promote causes that need support.
D) Immigration reform is a passionately supported and vital component of our nation's future.

Lesson wY15
Support and Focus
Getting Your Feet Wet

Directions: The following questions are intended as a short diagnostic exam.

[1] In the 1880s, the Great Red Spot resembled a huge blimp gliding high above white crystalline clouds of ammonia and spanned 25,000 miles across. [2] Nearly one hundred years later in 1979, the Spot's north-south length remained virtually unchanged, but its girth had shrunk to 15,535 miles. [3] Observations over the past 10 years indicate a continued steady shrinkage. {1}.

[4] If these figures prove accurate, we must wonder how long the Spot will continue to be a planetary highlight. [5] These figures also help to explain why the Spot has become more difficult to see in recent years. [6] The Spot has been paler than normal; this pallor, combined with a steady shrinkage, may explain why some amateur astronomers cannot even locate the Spot. [7] Higher-powered telescopes have improved astronomers' ability to observe phenomena like the Spot and Saturn's rings. {2}

[7] This may not be the first time the Great Red Spot has waned. [8] From 1713 to 1830, there are absolutely no observations or sketches mentioning the Spot. [9] In 1831, the Spot reappeared as a long, pale "hollow". [10] Was the "hollow" the genesis of a brand new Red Spot, unrelated to the one originally observed in 1665? [11] Or was it the resurgence of the same Spot?

1. Which choice would best provide support to the claim of the previous sentence?

   A) What will happen in the next 10 years?
   B) Other astronomers have argued it is getting larger.
   C) Still, the Spot is equally half the size of the Earth!
   D) The Spot now measures just 9,805 miles across.

2. Which of the following sentences should be removed in order to improve the focus of the paragraph?

   A) Sentence 4
   B) Sentence 5
   C) Sentence 6
   D) Sentence 7

3. In the third paragraph, which choice would provide the best support for Sentence 8?

   A) This gap proves that the Spot disappeared entirely.
   B) This could have been because the astronomers of the time were more interested in the moon.
   C) This suggests that the Spot goes through a growth and decline cycle.
   D) Some think that the Spot is dying down.

Lesson wY15
Support and Focus
Wading In

TOPIC OVERVIEW: SUPPORT AND FOCUS

The SAT Writing section doesn't limit itself to grammar rules. The test also examines our ability to revise text to improve content. Two of the question types that do this are Support questions and Focus questions.

TOPIC OVERVIEW: SUPPORT

Providing supporting evidence is a crucial skill in crafting a good argument. The Support questions on the SAT test this by asking which sentences are best added, removed, or revised in order to improve the claims made in the text. Use the following strategy to help answer Support questions:

1. Read the paragraph or sentence referenced by the question.
2. Determine the argument or main idea. This is much easier if you take notes on the passage as you read.
3. Look at each answer choice, asking if the information provided is specifically about the argument/main idea being referenced. Eliminate any answer choices that are irrelevant or only very loosely connected to the main argument or idea.
4. If the information in an answer choice is relevant, check if it supports the information in the passage or contradicts it. Eliminate any answer choices that contradict the main argument or idea.
5. Examine the remaining answer choices. Choose the answer that provides the strongest and clearest support for the argument or main idea.

TOPIC OVERVIEW: FOCUS

Paragraphs that contain a lot of unrelated or loosely related information are unnecessarily confusing and result in bad writing. Focus questions ask us to eliminate information that doesn't fit in its original location. Most Focus questions are easy to spot because they include the word "focus." Use the following strategy to help answer support questions:

1. Read the paragraph referenced by the question.
2. Determine the argument or main idea. As with Support questions, this is much easier if you take notes while reading the passage.
3. Without looking at the answer choices, try to identify the sentence that is the least related to the main idea or main argument.
4. Examine the answer choices. If the sentence you identified in step 3 is listed as an answer choice, that is most likely the correct answer. If not, proceed to the next step.
5. The answer choices narrow down the options for which sentence should be eliminated. Working through one answer choice at a time, reread the paragraph without the sentence identified by the answer choice. Select the answer choice that creates the clearest and most concise paragraph.

Let's look at some examples of these strategies:

More than 2,000 years ago, Hippocrates wrote of the use of silver in wound care; the Phoenicians stored water and other liquids in silver-lined containers to avoid contamination; and in World War I, infected wounds were treated using silver leaf. Silver did not fall out of widespread use until the introduction of modern antibiotics in the 1940s, and since then, antibiotics have become the primary means of fighting infection. **{1}** Amid concern over the rise of antibiotic-resistant bacteria, silver is enjoying a 21st century renaissance, with high-tech microscopic particles of silver embedded as antimicrobial agents in products from athletic clothing to food containers.

[1] Many researchers worry that we may be pursuing the benefits of silver nanotechnology without fully understanding its risks, both to the environment and to our health. [2] New studies have suggested that these tiny silver particles may be damaging plants and fish in ways that had not been seen with traditional silver exposure. [3] Other studies have shown that these silver nanoparticles can penetrate the protective outer layer of the skin, gaining access to plasma membranes and disrupting cell function. [4] There have also been some studies show that these same silver nanoparticles aid in wound healing, with some small studies suggesting that silver nanoparticles may even destroy cancer cells.

{2}

1. Which of the following, if added here, would best support the arguments in this paragraph?

   A) The most commonly prescribed antibiotics include Amoxicillin, Penicillin, Cipro, and Sulfa drugs, all of which are considered to be generally safe.
   B) As a result of this over-reliance on antibiotics, 23,000 people die each year as a direct result of antibiotic-resistant infections.
   C) The first antibiotic was discovered by Alexander Fleming, who found that a fungus called *Penicillium* killed a number of disease-causing bacteria.
   D) Louis Pasteur, who discovered the principles of vaccination and pasteurization, aided the development of antibiotics by theorizing that particular molds could be used to fight bacterial infections.

2. Which choice most effectively functions as the topic sentence of the paragraph?

   A) Sentence 1
   B) Sentence 2
   C) Sentence 3
   D) Sentence 4

For the first question, use the Support strategies:

1. Read the first paragraph.

2. Identify the argument or main idea. This paragraph imparts information about the medicinal uses of silver. It's main idea can be found in the final sentence: Because of fears over antibiotic-resistant bacteria, silver may be a better antimicrobial agent in some cases.

3. Now we examine each answer choice and eliminate any answers that are not closely connected to the main idea. All four answer choices discuss antibiotics, but C and D specifically discuss the *history* of antibiotics. The history of antibiotics has very little to do with the main idea of the paragraph, which focuses primarily on silver and only mentions the history of antibiotics once. We can eliminate C and D.

4. The information in choice A might be relevant because it discusses *current* use of antibiotics, which is referenced in the sentence immediately before the place where we are adding support. But choice A says that antibiotics are generally safe; the sentence that follows the place where we are adding support cites concern over the rise of antibiotic-resistant bacteria, suggesting a problem with antibiotics, so choice A does not support the main idea. We can eliminate choice A.

5. We are now left with choice B, the correct answer. Choice B establishes the dangers of excess use of antibiotics, thus supporting the idea that silver might be better than antibiotics in some cases.

For Question 2, we should use the Focus strategies.

1. Read the second paragraph of the passage.

2. The first sentence of the paragraph establishes the main idea: There may be environmental and health risks associated with silver nanotechnology.

3. Without looking at the answer choices, we should examine each sentence in the paragraph. The first sentence establishes the main idea of the paragraph, so we know we can't eliminate it. The second sentence discusses a study that claims that silver nanoparticles may be harming the environment. The third sentence discusses studies that show that silver nanoparticles may have health risks. The fourth sentence discusses studies that show health benefits. The fourth sentence doesn't fit.

4. It is clear that the fourth sentence, choice D, should be eliminated.

5. We did not need to complete step five.

11/18 HW

Lesson wY15
Support and Focus
Learning to Swim

CONCEPT EXERCISE:

Directions: Choose the sentence that should be removed to improve the coherency of each paragraph.

1. **[1]** Vincent van Gogh is perhaps one of the most famous artists of all time, with thousands of artworks in his considerable repertoire. **[2]** Some of his contemporaries included Georges Seurat and Henri Toulouse-Lautrec. **[3]** Within these works, one can find a wealth of portraits and still-life paintings as well as his famed landscapes. **[4]** The most recognizable piece in this artistic abundance, however, is likely *Starry Night* - depicting the view from his room in Saint-Remy-de-Provence asylum. **[5]** It was work of this style and caliber that would come to define Van Gogh's true legacy: the Post-Impressionist movement.

2. **[1]** In the course of World War II, one could point to any number of events as major turning points or important shifts in military or political direction. **[2]** However, it is not uncommon to view the attack on Pearl Harbor as one of the most influential events of that era in world history. **[3]** The implications of the attack and how it catalyzed the United States' entrance into the conflict would come to define the course of the war. **[4]** Although the attack was horrific, many consider the storming of Normandy to be a more tragic historical event. **[5]** It is not unfitting then that President Franklin D. Roosevelt would soon after declare December 7, 1941 would be "a date which will live in infamy".

3. **[1]** Attempting to compare different musical genres across a period of even a few years can be quite a difficult endeavor. **[2]** After all, the evolution of our musical pursuits has matched, if not even outpaced the technological advancements that marked the past century alone. **[3]** To this end, many would agree that music today is much better than that of the last decade. **[4]** As music became more intertwined with digital media, the possibilities for new media expanded with almost reckless abandon. **[5]** As unthinkable as it would have been in previous years, there are now even artists who literally cannot perform their music live since it exists only in the form of some audio file.

4. **[1]** If there is one name throughout the world that the average person will immediately associate with genius-level intelligence, it is that of Albert Einstein. **[2]** Einstein's famous equation, $E=mc^2$ has become a globally recognized representation of our scientific knowledge of the universe. **[3]** The popular belief that Einstein did not know how to tie his shoes has actually been proven to be a myth. **[4]** However, even he stood on the shoulders of intellectual giants such as Sir Isaac Newton. **[5]** One might thus wonder if the genius-level work behind these popular images is truly more justified than the previous momentous discoveries it built upon.

5. **[1]** Given the pervasiveness of the Internet today, it is nearly impossible to imagine how information could be spread without our modern technology. **[2]** Physical mail is becoming less prevalent as email takes its place as the standard mode of professional and personal contact. **[3]** Radio as well has been pushed to the brink in a fight to retain relevance – even then only being saved by a movement towards internet availability. **[4]** Even television has been through a tough time after having to deal with new consistent content providers like Netflix and Hulu. **[5]** One can only speculate as to how long these examples of previous generation media will be able to survive before being completely subsumed by the wave of their new digital iterations.

Directions: Read the passages below and answer the questions following them.

[1] Dante's *Divine Comedy* is widely considered to be one of the most prominent examples of Italian literature leading up to the Renaissance. **(6)** [2] Among the events of the story, one gets a glimpse of the religious philosophy and mythology of 14th century Christianity. [3] These ideals, laid out in such a clear and engaging poetic phrasing, would inspire innumerable other works for the next seven centuries. [4] Over the years, even though the religious minds of the time may not have agreed with the beliefs of the *Divine Comedy*, they continued to respect what Dante had achieved by outlining his theology in such a grand manner.

6. Which of the following, if added here, would best support the main purpose of the preceding paragraph?

   A) Other authors of the time could not combine religion and drama the same way Dante did.
   B) The poem chronicles Dante's experiences on his fictional journey beneath the medieval underworld, through Purgatory, and up through Paradise.
   C) The story even adds details of Italy's political struggles at the time of Dante's life.
   D) Much of the structure, especially of the setting itself, adheres to a rule of nines stemming from the Bible.

[1] In the pursuit of greater understanding scientists have always sought to categorize objects by similar qualities. [2] Such a breakdown of information allows us to focus on what characteristics truly define something rather than what may be common across multiple groups. [3] However, ensuring that this categorization still accounts for all possible examples of a group can be more difficult than it seems. [4] This usually leads to further stratification, such as the eight levels of our current taxonomical ranking system. **(7)**

7. Which of the following, if added here, would best support the main idea of the preceding paragraph?

   A) The breakdown involves a set of decreasingly inclusive groups that filter down to the individual level.
   B) Taxonomy is the science of defining and naming groups based on similar qualities.
   C) This demonstrates that the more groups we have, the easier it ends up being to understand the whole.
   D) Scientists are in perfect agreement about what the breakdown should be at this level.

[1] Horseshoe crabs are animals that can be said to have carried over from the ancient past. [2] In fact, they can trace their origins to around 450 million years ago. [3] Amazingly, the horseshoe crabs have hardly changed over such a long period. **(8)** [4] Indeed such evolutionary resilience is a testament to the ability of this species to endure changes on a global scale.

8. Which of the following, if added here, would best support the main claim of the preceding paragraph?

    A) These days, horseshoe crabs are finally reaching a point where they may be in danger of extinction.
    B) Though they may look like crustaceans, these crabs are actually more closely related to spiders.
    C) We now harvest horseshoe crabs for everything from their meat to their blood.
    D) Fossils reveal that the genetic makeup of 450-million-year-old horseshoe crabs is identical to that of those alive today.

[1] In recent years, some arguments have been made for the idea that astronomy may be the world's oldest science. [2] The ancient Greeks tend to be the most acclaimed of the ancient astronomers, but they were rather late by some historical standards. [3] Before it was studied strictly for science, many areas used the stars to tell the seasons or predict weather. **(9)** [4] Civilizations as far back as Mesopotamia have even provided the first written evidence of people purposefully watching the stars.

9. Which of the following, if added here, would best support the claim of the preceding paragraph?

    A) Ancient texts are discovered that prove that Chinese people used stars to predict when storms were approaching.
    B) Ancient Egypt as well asserted a particular focus on the sun and moon.
    C) This process of prediction for natural phenomena would be refined as the years went on.
    D) Of course, China had already developed the absolute best methods far earlier than most other areas.

[1] For the most part, if an entertainment production looks good to the audience, it is because the supporting staff has worked incredibly hard to make it that way. [2] In fact, one might even say that the easier the procession seems to flow, the more difficult it was to achieve such a level of finesse. [3] Events such as concerts or public festivals have so many moving pieces to keep track of that it becomes nearly impossible to keep everything running smoothly. [4] Everything from security, to audience seating, to media coverage must be organized and monitored from start to finish. **(10)**

10. Which of the following, if added here, would best support the claim of the paragraph?

   A) If the event is small enough, some of these elements can be cut out.
   B) The background work is remarkably unappreciated by those who attend these events.
   C) Thus, huge events like the 2014 World Cup can cost up to $2 billion to plan out and execute.
   D) Most of the man-hours are then spent cleaning up after the events.

Lesson wY15
Support and Focus
Diving Into the Deep End

PRACTICE EXERCISE:

Directions: Use the paragraphs below to answer the questions.

Silver and its Medicinal Uses

[1] Several years ago, a mosquito bite on Dr. Elizabeth Loboa's right leg became infected and refused to heal. [2] Mosquitoes can carry diseases such as encephalitis and West Nile virus. [3] Wary of antibiotic overuse, Dr. Loboa tried an alternative remedy: a new kind of bandage made with silver. [4] The bandage is inserted into a wound to encourage tissue growth, and the fibers of the bandage are coated with silver to fend off infection.   [5] Within days, the infection was gone. {1}

[6] More than 2,000 years ago, Hippocrates wrote of the use of silver in wound care; the Phoenicians stored water and other liquids in silver-lined containers to avoid contamination. {2} [7] Silver did not fall out of widespread use until the introduction of modern antibiotics in the 1940s, and since then, antibiotics have become the primary means of fighting infection. [8] Some common antibiotics include penicillin and tetracycline.   [9] Amid concern over the rise of antibiotic-resistant bacteria, silver is enjoying a 21st century renaissance, with high-tech microscopic particles of silver embedded as antimicrobial agents in products from athletic clothing to food containers. {3}

1. Which of the following sentences should be removed in order to improve the focus of the paragraph?

   A) Sentence 1
   B) Sentence 2
   C) Sentence 3
   D) Sentence 4

2. Which of the following, if added here, would best support the claim of the previous sentence?

   A) The Egyptians valued gold more than silver.
   B) Many civilizations created their currency from silver.
   C) Silver is valued highly around the world and used in jewelry and coinage.
   D) In World War I, infected wounds were treated using silver leaf.

3. Which of the following sentences should be removed in order to improve the focus of the paragraph?

   A) Sentence 6
   B) Sentence 7
   C) Sentence 8
   D) Sentence 9

[10] Many researchers worry that we may be pursuing the benefits of silver nanotechnology without fully understanding its risks, both to the environment and to our health. [11] New studies have suggested that these tiny silver particles may be damaging plants and fish in ways that had not been seen with traditional silver exposure. [12] Silver is often found with zinc, iron, and other ores. [13] Other studies have shown that these silver nanoparticles can penetrate the protective outer layer of the skin. {4} {5}

4. Which of the following, if added here, would best support the main purpose of the paragraph?

A) These nanoparticles can then gain access to plasma membranes and disrupt cell function.
B) Other metals do not penetrate the skin.
C) This may persuade you not to wear silver jewelry, but do not worry.
D) Silver is not usually comprised of nanoparticles.

5. Which of the following sentences should be removed in order to improve the focus of the paragraph?

A) Sentence 10
B) Sentence 11
C) Sentence 12
D) Sentence 13

[14] Traditional silver is considered a low-toxicity metal. **{6}**

[15] Silver nanoparticles, due to their astonishingly tiny size, don't necessarily behave in the same way. [16] A nanoparticle is an artificial item that is sized on the molecular level. [17] For example, silver has a tendency to bind with sulfur in the environment, forming a fairly inert and harmless silver sulfide compound. [18] Recent studies suggest that silver nanoparticles evade this bond. [19] Instead, these particles seem to be unusually reactive with oxygen molecules in water, encouraging the formation of hydrogen peroxide. **{7} {8}**

6. If added after the previous sentence, which of the following would best support the claim of the sentence?

A) It is infrequently worn because of this.
B) Other metals may have higher toxicities.
C) The metal rarely causes problems beyond mild discoloration of skin.
D) Toxicity means how dangerous the metal might be.

7. Which of the following, if added here, would best support the overall claim of the passage?

A) This chemical commonly used for cleaning purposes in the home.
B) This chemical can be poisonous to aquatic organisms.
C) Since both hydrogen peroxide and water have hydrogen, they are mostly analogous.
D) The silver nanoparticles thus create a new and interesting chemical.

8. Which of the following sentences should be removed to improve the focus of the paragraph?

A) Sentence 14
B) Sentence 15
C) Sentence 16
D) Sentence 17

[20] Use of silver nanoparticles in consumer products is not well regulated, despite the Environmental Protection Agency's best efforts. [21] Many companies avoid registering products using silver nanoparticles. {**9**} [22] Given the uncertainties regarding this emerging technology, many wonder whether the antimicrobial benefits outweigh the unknown risks associated with silver nanotechnology. [23] It is important to communicate with your doctor if you have any concerns about the treatment being used. {**10**}

9. Which of the following, if added here, would best develop the claim of the previous sentence?

A) This means that consumers are exposed to these particles without adequate information.
B) It is important to register all products that have health ramifications with the EPA.
C) The EPA was founded to regulate such sneaky maneuvers.
D) Such companies should be fined and punished.

10. Which of the following sentences should be removed in order to improve the focus of the paragraph?

A) Sentence 20
B) Sentence 21
C) Sentence 22
D) Sentence 23

11/19 STOP

TEST EXERCISE:

Directions: Use the paragraphs below to answer the questions.

Connecting Countries and Entrepreneurs

Purnima Voria's story is one of inspiration and achievement. Growing up in India, Voria **(1)** <u>will watch</u> her father build a successful company importing U.S. farm equipment. After several years and many business successes, her family came to the U.S. to pursue the American Dream. Inspired by her father's example, she merged her love for her native **(2)** <u>country, and her newly adopted country, developing</u> solutions to help U.S. business-owners bring high quality products overseas to India.

In 2005, Voria founded the National U.S. India Chamber of Commerce (NUICC), which leads trade missions and delegations to India. These missions began **(3)** <u>poorly,</u> with her using her family and social connections to help a fledgling U.S. textile machine manufacturer with embroidery computer software to **(4)** <u>access</u> the Indian market. Thanks to her connections and know-how, Voria was able to help the U.S. machine manufacturer connect with the top Indian textile maker, an exporter to major U.S. clothing stores. With only a handshake to seal the deal, Voria and the U.S. company sold 100 machines with software packages. Voria had found her niche. She quickly recognized the positive impact that she could have on both countries by serving as a mentor to U.S. businesses and entrepreneurs. {5}

1. A) NO CHANGE
   B) watches
   C) has watched
   D) watched

2. A) NO CHANGE
   B) country and her newly adopted country, developing
   C) country and her newly adopted country developing
   D) country, and her newly adopted country developing

3. In context, which choice provides the most precise meaning of the underlined word?

   A) NO CHANGE
   B) shyly
   C) humbly
   D) subserviently

4. A) NO CHANGE
   B) exploit
   C) employ
   D) interact

5. Which sentence, if added here, would provide the best evidence of the impact that the NUICC has had?

   A) The NUICC also offers courses to train business owners on overcoming cultural boundaries.
   B) Many Indian Americans have made their mark on U.S. commerce, including Satya Nadella, the CEO of Microsoft.
   C) To date, the NUICC has brokered over $300 million in deals between U.S. and Indian companies.
   D) India's economy has grown at a spectacular rate, with its GDP increasing by a factor of 12 in the past 20 years.

[1] Voria began NUICC at the request of the political and business leaders of the United States **(6)** <u>and the government and business leaders of India</u>. [2] India and the United States are the world's two largest democracies. [3] The membership of NUICC now spans across a wide spectrum of industries, with over 9,200 members worldwide. [4] NUICC's mission is to promote bilateral trade between the United States and India, cultivating business relationships and mutual profit. [5] NUICC also consults with small and large U.S. corporations to provide a road map for entering the Indian marketplace. {7}

Voria's efforts did not go unnoticed. In 2005, she was awarded a Congressional Medal of Distinction for her outstanding leadership in business and her contributions to the U.S. economy. {8} The Wall Street Journal also honored Ms. Voria as a "Business Woman of the Year."

6. A) NO CHANGE
    B) and the leaders of government and businesses in India
    C) and leaders of the same types in India
    D) and India

7. Which sentence from the previous paragraph is not essential to the paragraph's meaning and should be deleted?

    A) Sentence 2
    B) Sentence 3
    C) Sentence 4
    D) Sentence 5

8. Which sentence, if added here, would provide the most appropriate support for the paragraph?

    A) She has served as an economic advisor under both President George W. Bush and President Barack Obama.
    B) She has three daughters, each of whom is a successful businesswoman in her own right.
    C) She resides in Colorado, where the NUICC is headquartered, but she regularly travels to India.
    D) Organizations similar to the NUICC have since been formed to promote trade with other countries.

[1] Voria thrives in helping others succeed in business. [2] She spends much of her time advocating for minority-owned businesses that wish to operate internationally. [3] The member companies of NUICC **(9)** <u>spans</u> a variety of industries, from technology to agriculture. [4] During a recent roundtable discussion hosted at the U.S. Department of Commerce, she spoke on some of the challenges that businesses face when operating abroad. [5] During this speech, she also highlighted the valuable opportunities that await companies that are willing to seek out international relationships through organizations such as NUICC. {**10**}

As exemplified by her work with NUICC, Voria's business passion fosters growth, diversification, and transformation, **(11)** <u>making</u> her a true champion for the minority business community.

9. A) NO CHANGE
    B) span
    C) spanning
    D) span's

10. Which sentence in the preceding paragraph should be deleted because it is not relevant to the paragraph's main ideas?

    A) Sentence 2
    B) Sentence 3
    C) Sentence 4
    D) Sentence 5

11. A) NO CHANGE
    B) makes
    C) this makes
    D) OMIT the underlined portion

Lesson wY15
Support and Focus
Race to the Finish

HOMEWORK EXERCISE 1:

Directions: For each of the following paragraphs, choose the sentence that provides the best supporting evidence when added at the indicated point.

In Petén, the largest and northernmost region of Guatemala, villagers joke that the green color of the U.S. dollar comes from *xate*, a leafy ornamental plant they harvest for export to the United States. {1} Guatemalan communities earn more than $1 million each year from the plant, much of it grown in Petén. Now, more sustainable harvesting practices are ensuring that xate and other members of the plant kingdom contribute to building a better future for communities and individuals in the region.

1. Which sentence, if added here, would provide the most appropriate support for the paragraph?

    A) Most of Guatemala's population lives in the southern half of the country, which includes the capital, Guatemala City.
    B) The plants are popular in the U.S. for floral arrangements, especially for Easter celebrations, weddings, and funerals.
    C) The xate plant is also grown in some areas of Mexico and Belize.
    D) Guatemala's top exports, however, are coffee and sugar.

Petén is a region with a poverty rate above the national average. {2} To make matters worse, parts of the territory are threatened by illegal activity, including drug trafficking, illegal cattle ranching, and deliberate fires. Petén does have one thing working in its favor, though. The region is also home to 67 percent of Guatemala's protected areas, and to the Maya Biosphere Reserve, one of the largest areas of tropical forest north of the Amazon.

2. Which sentence, if added here, would provide the most appropriate support for the paragraph?

    A) Despite this, Guatemala does have the largest economy of any Central American nation.
    B) This is in a country where 13 percent of the population lives in extreme poverty and nearly 50 percent of all children under age 5 suffer from chronic malnutrition.
    C) The climate in the region is tropical and very rainy, with some parts receiving as much as 120 inches of rain each year.
    D) The Petén region also contains many important ruins of the Mayan civilization that ruled Central America hundreds of years ago.

These vast natural resources present an opportunity to address Petén's pressing challenges as well as the global challenge of climate change. Worldwide, approximately 12 percent of emissions that contribute to climate change are caused by forest loss. {3} The Maya Biosphere Reserve is the principal carbon reservoir in Central America, with more than a half million tons of carbon dioxide, enough to offset emissions from more than a million cars annually.

3. Which sentence, if added here, would provide the most appropriate support for the paragraph?

   A) Forests act as so-called "carbon reservoirs"—areas that store carbon dioxide and keep it from entering the atmosphere, where it is a greenhouse gas.
   B) The first paved road in the Petén region was not completed until 1982.
   C) The Maya Biosphere Reserve is home to a wide variety of species including several types of monkey, crocodiles, jaguars, and freshwater turtles.
   D) Other causes of climate change include the burning of fossil fuels and the release of air pollutants such as soot.

Creating a more sustainable future in the Petén region is an ongoing effort that can be traced back nearly 20 years to when Guatemala emerged from a bitter, decades-long civil war in 1996. As the government re-established control over the logging sector in Petén, it planned to hand concessions to outside logging companies instead of to the local citizens. {4} At the same time, desperate economic circumstances and ongoing insecurity led to rampant illegal logging, forest fires, slash-and-burn agriculture, and a wide range of criminal activity, including the looting of Guatemala's archeological heritage. Community leaders in Petén and their allies imagined a different future, and they fought for community control of natural resources as well as for the creation of the biosphere reserve.

4. Which sentence, if added here, would provide the most appropriate support for the paragraph?

   A) During the civil war, more than 45,000 Guatemalans from Petén fled to neighboring Mexico to escape the violence.
   B) Those who had lived in Petén—and depended on its resources for their livelihoods—for generations or, in many cases, centuries, were outraged by this choice.
   C) The local economy in Petén has become increasingly reliant on tourists who visit the region for its natural and archaeological wonders.
   D) The Petén region has a long history of independence, as it was home to the Itza people, the last independent native kingdom to be conquered by Europeans.

Community leaders persevered in the face of opposition and threats from a broad range of skeptics, including those who felt that communities would not be able to manage the forests effectively or sustainably. In 2000, 12 communities won a 25-year concession to nearly 84,000 hectares—an area slightly larger than New York City—in the multiple-use zone of the reserve. {5} The real work was just starting, however. Communities had to organize themselves, ensure they complied with government regulations, and prove that the concessions could be managed in a responsible yet profitable way.

5. Which sentence, if added here, would provide the most appropriate support for the paragraph?

   A) In addition to its wealth of xate, the area is also a major source of *chicle*, a tree sap used to make chewing gum, and *pimenta*, otherwise known as allspice.

   B) The population of the area, however, is far smaller than that of New York City.

   C) By contrast, many neighboring countries went ahead with plans to give concessions to loggers, resulting in widespread deforestation as well as increases in poverty.

   D) In practical terms, this meant that citizens now had the right to manage the forests around their communities and continue to make a living from the resources that surrounded them.

Directions: For each of the following paragraphs, choose the sentence that should be deleted because it contains unnecessary or irrelevant information.

Paragraph 1

[A] Xate has long been an important source of income for the region, but previously, most of the proceeds went to intermediaries. [B] They would come into communities and buy large quantities of the plant—of varying qualities—at a low price. [C] They then discarded whatever xate they could not sell, leading to large amounts of waste. [D] The slash-and-burn form of agriculture practiced by many in the region also produced large amounts of waste.

Paragraph 2

[A] The government concession to manage the reserve has enabled communities to cut out the middlemen, increase incomes, and reduce waste. [B] Now each community has approximately 10 *seleccionadoras*, women who sort through the xate as it comes in, focusing on the best-quality plants. [C] In Guatemalan culture, women typically wear distinctive patterns associated with their hometowns. [D] Other workers bundle up stems, wrap them in paper, and tie them with colored string to indicate the community that sold it.

Paragraph 3

[A] Xate leaves are prized by florists for their ability to last up to 40 days without water. [B] The communities have enacted measures to preserve the bounty of the xate plants well into the future. [C] Harvesters—about 20 per community—are paid only for the export-quality branches, and as a result, they cut fewer branches and have a lighter load to carry down the mountain. [D] Additionally, they are required to leave at least two stems on each plant to ensure that it will grow back quickly.

Paragraph 4

[A] From the community, the xate bundles are sent to a *bodega* (market) that collects the plant from five communities in Petén. [B] The xate is stored in a refrigerated container with water for up to a week. [C] Not all plant products should be refrigerated, however—tomatoes, for instance, degrade in texture and flavor when stored in cool temperatures. [D] The crop is then sent to Guatemala City, and from there to the United States.

Paragraph 5

[A] The community receives a percentage of the profits from xate sales and determines how to use it via a general assembly. [B] The two main priorities for these funds are education and health care. A particular point of pride is the community school, which now includes four years of high school and a staff of local teachers. [C] With more money for the community and an environmentally sustainable source of jobs, xate farming is a dream that many in Petén are only beginning to believe is real. [D] What dream would you like to come true for the good of your community?

HOMEWORK EXERCISE 2:

Directions: Use the paragraphs below to answer the questions.

A controversial literary quarrel **(1)** <u>had arose</u> in 2010, when bestselling author Jodi Picoult, peeved that the *Times* had given Jonathan Franzen's bestseller *Freedom* two glowing reviews in one week, gently **(2)** <u>chided</u> the paper via Twitter: "Is anyone shocked? Would love to see the NYT rave about authors who aren't white male literary darlings." Jennifer **(3)** <u>Weiner, the author of best-sellers like In Her Shoes, soon</u> weighed in on Picoult's side: "I think it's a very old and deep-seated double standard that holds that when a man writes about family and feelings, **(4)** <u>its</u> literature with a capital L, but when a woman considers the same topics, it's romance, or a beach book—in short, it's unworthy of a critic's attention."

1. A) NO CHANGE
   B) had arisen
   C) arose
   D) arisen

2. Within the context of the passage, which of the following would NOT be an effective replacement for this word?

   A) NO CHANGE
   B) commended
   C) scolded
   D) reprimanded

3. A) NO CHANGE
   B) Weiner; the author of bestsellers like *In Her Shoes,* soon
   C) Weiner – the author of bestsellers like *In Her Shoes,* soon
   D) Weiner, the author of bestsellers like *In Her Shoes*: soon

4. A) NO CHANGE
   B) these books being
   C) they are
   D) it's

(5) The *New York Times* really does review more fiction by men than by women - much more. **(6)** During that period, 101 books got two reviews – one in the daily *Times* and one in the paper's illustrious *Sunday Book Review*— and, unsurprisingly, 72 of them were by men. No matter how you spin them, these figures are disturbing. This bias extends further than the literary page of the *New York Times*, however. **(7)**

5. Which of the following sentences would provide the best transition between the previous paragraph and this one?

A) These accusations are not misguided.
B) Some might accuse Picoult and Weiner of acting persecuted.
C) A look at the sales figures tells a different story.
D) Recently reviewed by the Times are several memoirs, as well.

6. Which of the following would provide the best support to the claim in the previous sentence?

A) Many of the reviewers of the *New York Times* are male, thus they review more works by men.
B) Over about two years, the *Times* reviewed 545 works of fiction – 338, or 62 percent, were by men.
C) This is contrary to the finding that authors like Picoult and Weiner outsell male authors like Franzen.
D) How many female writers have been ignored by the *Times*'s discriminatory reviewing processes?

7. Which of the following would provide the best support to the claim in the previous sentence?

A) Many male authors don't believe that women are better writers than men.
B) Other newspapers tend to have less of a focus on reviewing fiction.
C) Bookstores such as Barnes & Noble and Borders fell on hard times.
D) Of the Pulitzer Prize for Fiction since 1984, 17 of the winners were men and only 11 were women.

[1] Is the *Times* **(8)** <u>entailing</u> books by women because those books are more likely to fall under the category of "commercial fiction," a category that critics are alleged to routinely ignore? [2] **(9)** <u>Fiction that is read for pleasure</u>, and often has no ambitions of 'making a statement' about life. [3] It seems to be that popular fiction by men might be "more likely to be lifted out of the 'disposable' pile, becoming the kind of cultural objects that the *New York Times* feels compelled to praise." [4] Just think of international bestsellers such as Stieg Larssen's *Girl with the Dragon Tattoo* series – why would this be more worthy of attention than a cracking good mystery by, for example, Patricia Cornwell? [5] It would be interesting to see how many books published per year are written by men, and how many are written by women. **(10)**

Indeed, Picoult and Weiner argued that genre matters more than gender: "The NYT has made it abundantly clear that they value literary fiction and disdain commercial fiction—and they disparage it regardless of race or gender of the author," Picoult said. "It would be as if the paper's film critics only reviewed tiny independent films and refused to watch a single moment of a star-studded romantic comedy, or if the music critics listened to Radiohead and **(11)** <u>refused</u> to acknowledge the existence of Katy Perry or Lady Gaga," Weiner said in an interview with the *Huffington Post*. "How seriously would you, as a reader, take a critic like that?"

8. Within the context of the passage, which of the following is the best replacement for the underlined word?

   A) NO CHANGE.
   B) withdrawing
   C) slighting
   D) impressing

9. A) NO CHANGE
   B) Reading for pleasure
   C) Commercial fiction being read for pleasure
   D) Commercial fiction is read for pleasure

10. Which of the following sentences should be eliminated in order to improve the focus of the paragraph?

    A) Sentence 1
    B) Sentence 3
    C) Sentence 4
    D) Sentence 5

11. A) NO CHANGE
    B) had refused
    C) refuse
    D) were refusing

Lesson wY16
Frequently Confused Words
Getting Your Feet Wet

Directions: The following questions are intended to serve as a brief diagnostic exam.

1. State law requires that all drivers <u>ensure</u> their vehicles.

    A) NO CHANGE
    B) assure
    C) insure
    D) reassure

2. The smells wafting from the kitchen <u>peaked</u> my appetite.

    A) NO CHANGE
    B) pricked
    C) peeked
    D) piqued

3. The <u>censor</u> on my computer automatically starts my webcam when I am seated at my desk.

    A) NO CHANGE
    B) sensor
    C) censure
    D) sensory

Lesson wY16
Frequently Confused Words
Wading In

TOPIC OVERVIEW – FREQUENTLY CONFUSED WORDS

Frequently Confused Words questions on the SAT will test your ability to recognize the misuse of pairs or groups of words that are commonly confused.

Recognizing Frequently Confused Words questions is fairly simple. If a question includes at least two answer choices that are very similar in spelling or pronunciation, the question is likely a Frequently Confused Words question. These questions require that we read very careful to distinguish between very similar words – it can be incredibly easy to make simple, silly mistakes on these questions.

Although it would be nearly impossible to provide a complete list of all commonly confused words, the following is a guide to some of the most frequently confused words:

accede exceed	**Accede** means "to agree or allow": Mom finally *acceded* to my request for a new phone.
	Exceed means "to go beyond": I had to pay a fee because my luggage *exceeded* the weight limit.
accept except	**Accept** means "to take willingly": Senator Deveron *accepted* the nomination.
	Except means "excluding": He was able to move everything *except* the blue couch.
adapt adept adopt	**Adapt** means "to adjust": It took the cats a week to *adapt* to their new home.
	Adept means "skilled": My cousin is *adept* at public speaking.
	Adopt means "to accept as your own": Though I was nervous, I *adopted* a carefree attitude.
adverse averse	**Adverse** means "unfavorable": The blizzard created *adverse* driving conditions.
	Averse means "unwilling": My teacher is not *averse* to offering extra credit assignments.
advice advise	**Advice** means "an opinion intended to be helpful": The counselor gave me great *advice* about applying to college.
	Advise means "to give advice": The counselor *advised* me about applying to college.
affect effect	**Affect** means "to influence": Unfortunately, the school schedule was not *affected* by the snow.
	Effect is usually a noun meaning "a result": Hunger can have an *effect* on your ability to concentrate.
alternately alternatively	**Alternately** means "taking turns": The author's most recent work is *alternately* prose and verse.
	Alternatively means "as an option: She debated whether to adopt a puppy, *alternatively* excited by the idea and worried about the responsibility.

among between	**Among** is used for things that are not distinct or individuals: Susan is choosing *among* her top four colleges.
	Between is used for things that are distinct or individual: She had trouble deciding *between* Cadence College and Uptown University.
assure ensure insure	**Assure** means "to guarantee": The salesman *assured* me that the car had been well maintained.
	Ensure means "to make sure": I decided to *ensure* the car's quality by bringing it to my mechanic.
	Insure means "to provide insurance against loss or injury": Since I got into an accident on the way there, I was glad I had already *insured* the car.
bare bear	**Bare** usually means "to reveal": When his private emails were leaked, the Senator was forced to *bare* his secrets to the world.
	Bear usually means "to carry": Now he must *bear* the burden of public shame.
breadth breath breathe	**Breadth** means "width" or "extent": The *breadth* of the internet security issues was revealed with the latest hacking incident.
	Breath means "the air that you breathe": I ran out of *breath* running up the stairs.
	Breathe means "to take air into your lungs": I couldn't *breathe* after doing the mile run.
censor sensor censure	**Censor** is to prohibit free expression: The editor of the school paper *censored* my article about the poor quality of school lunches.
	A **sensor** is something that interprets stimulation: Our security system includes a motion *sensor*.
	Censure means "to harshly criticize": The developer was severely *censured* for failing to meet her deadline.
complement compliment	**Complement** means "to make complete" or "to supplement": The new skyscraper *complements* the city skyline rather than competing with it.
	Compliment means "to express admiration": It made my day when he *complimented* my new haircut.
conscience conscious	**Conscience** means "knowing right from wrong": My *conscience* wouldn't allow me to cheat on a test.
	Conscious means "being awake or aware": I was absurdly *conscious* of the clock's constant ticking.
device devise	A **device** is an instrument used to complete a task: The *device* malfunctioned at a very inconvenient moment.
	To **devise** is "to create": I will *devise* a scheme to take over the world.
disinterested uninterested	**Disinterested** means "unbiased or impartial": They asked a *disinterested* third party to weigh in on their dispute.
	Uninterested means "not interested": I surmised by his snoring that Mike was *uninterested* in the play.
elicit illicit	**Elicit** means "to draw out": She purposely insulted me just to *elicit* a response.
	Illicit means "illegal or illegitimate": Do not try to sneak *illicit* produce past the customs officials.

emanate eminent imminent	**Emanate** means "to issue or spread": There was a noticeable smell *emanating* from his locker.
	Eminent means "prestigious": An *eminent* painter visited our art class today.
	Imminent means "about to happen": The tornado represents an *imminent* threat to the Dawsonville area.
explicit implicit	**Explicit** means "clear and direct": The author's argument is *explicitly* stated in his thesis statement.
	Implicit means "indirectly" or "implied": By contrasting blue skies and smog-filled skylines, the author *implicitly* argues for stricter air pollution regulations.
figuratively literally	**Figuratively** means metaphorical, not realistic or exact: To say that I am as happy as a clam is to speak *figuratively*.
	Literally means exactly as it happened: After all, how could I know if I am *literally* as happy as a clam since clams can't tell us how happy they are?
lay lie	**Lay** means "to set or put down flat": I *laid* the book on the table. OR Please *lay* the platter down gently.
	Lie means "to rest supine or remain in a certain place": I love to *lie* outside and look at clouds.
noisome noisy	**Noisome** means "disgusting, offensive, annoying": A *noisome* odor follows my baby brother around whenever his diaper is dirty.
	Noisy means "making a lot of sound": My baby brother is *noisy* when I have to change his diaper.
peek pique peak	**Peek** means to look quickly without someone knowing: I *peeked* under the bed to see if my presents were hidden there.
	Pique can either mean "to provoke" or "resentment": My parents exchanged a look that *piqued* my curiosity. OR Anne felt a bit of *pique* at the harsh criticism written on her essay.
	Peak means "the highest point": My family decided that it would be a bad idea to visit the amusement park during *peak* summer season.
perspective prospective	A **perspective** is a point of view: From my *perspective*, Hannah is clearly wrong.
	Prospective means "possible or likely to happen": The *prospective* employee did not help his chances by showing up to his interview twenty minutes late.
precede proceed	**Precede** means "to come before": The *preceding* paragraph clearly established the ideas that this paragraph is refuting.
	Proceed means "to move forward": Construction on the new building can *proceed* as soon as the permits are finalized.
restive restful	**Restive** means "impatient, nervous, or restless": My dog is very *restive* whenever a thunderstorm approaches.
	Restful means "full of rest, calm, quiet": My friends and I look forward to a long, *restful* vacation.
than then	**Than** is used to compare: My dog is smarter *than* your dog.
	Then is used to describe a time that is not now: First, add the eggs, and *then* add the milk.

It is a good idea to be familiar with the words on this list in order to easily and quickly recognize them on the SAT.

Here is a strategy for approaching Frequently Confused Words questions on the SAT:

1. Look for questions in which two or more answer choices are spelled or pronounced very similarly. This is a clue that the question is likely a Frequently Confused Words question.
2. Carefully read the sentence and come up with a word that would be appropriate for the underlined portion of the sentence.
3. Look at the answer choices. Quickly define each answer choice.
4. Eliminate any answer choices that do not fit the blank spot in the sentence based on the word you chose in step 2.
5. Carefully examine the remaining answer choices and select the one that best suits the blank in the sentence.

Let's look at an example:

Example 1:

The smoke billowing from the nearby volcano convinced residents that an eruption was <u>emanate</u> despite reports from scientists suggesting that an eruption would not occur for several weeks.

A) NO CHANGE
B) eminent
C) imminent
D) emphatic

Let's follow the steps:

1. Most of the answer choices are very similar in spelling and pronunciation, so we know to look carefully because this is likely a frequently confused words question.
2. Without looking at the answer choices, we should come up with a word to fill the blank in the sentence: The smoke billowing from the nearby volcano convinced residents that an eruption was <u>immediate</u> despite reports from scientists suggesting that an eruption would not occur for several weeks.
3. Now we quickly define each answer choice. A means "to spread"; B means "prestigious"; C means "about to happen"; D means "emphasized".
4. Based on the word we put into the sentence (immediate), we can definitely get rid of B and D. We can keep A only because the smoke is billowing, so A might possibly work.
5. Although A could potentially work given the billowing smoke, the underlined word refers to the eruption, not to the smoke, so C makes the most sense. C, imminent, is the correct answer.

Lesson wY16
Frequently Confused Words
Learning to Swim

CONCEPT EXERCISE:

Directions: Correct the errors in the following sentences. Some sentences may not have errors.

1. The Harry Potter series surprised many people with it's incredible popularity.

2. Many people thought the books were highly imaginary and loved reading about Harry's magical adventures.

3. I like everything on that restaurant's menu, accept their veggie burger.

4. When Jason shows up, be sure to complement him on his new outfit; he's very proud of it.

5. The disobedient boy always tried to flaunt his parents' rules and do what he wished.

6. Steve was distraught, for he had not expected to loose his bookbag on the first day of school.

7. First, I separated the egg yolks from the egg whites, than I mixed the yolks together in a bowl.

8. The principle gave detention to the vandals who had defaced the cafeteria wall.

9. Amelia was so bored that all she did was lay in bed all day.

10. The election worker poled all of the people in the area to determine which candidate was likely to win.

11. Try as I might, I was unable to illicit any response from the silent child.

12. Many days had past since I had seen my best friend.

13. I think that Illyana is trying to hard to impress the teacher.

14. When the sun raises in the morning, it is truly a beautiful sight.

15. For her birthday, Romilda got a lovely set of stationary from her aunt.

16. As Alice read the first few questions, she realized she was all together unprepared for the exam.

17. This writer is fond of making illusions to other texts, such as the Bible, Aesop's Fables, and Shakespeare's plays.

18. During a special emergency meeting of the City Counsel, the members discussed what to do about the flooding in the south area of town.

19. Mount Everest in the Himalayas is the tallest mountain in the world; very few mountain climbers attempt this dangerous assent.

20. The real estate developer toured the cite where his newest building would be erected.

Lesson wY16
Frequently Confused Words
Diving into the Deep End

PRACTICE EXERCISE:

Deep Impacts

Humans speak about 7,000 different languages, but those languages are becoming **(1)** <u>existent</u> faster than the earth's species, with a language dying out every 2 weeks. Now, researchers have pinpointed a major cause of linguistic extinction: economic development. Though economic growth had been found to **(2)** <u>deduce</u> language destruction on an individual basis, this is the first study to demonstrate that it is a global phenomenon.

Many environmentalists **(3)** <u>delude</u> to the plight of the polar bear, but few advocates tell of threatened and extinct languages such as Eyak in Alaska, whose last speaker died in 2008, says Tatsuya Amano, a zoologist at the University of Cambridge and lead author of the new study. It's known that economic growth or society's quest to achieve it can drive language loss—dominant languages are necessary tools for success in education and business. While specific case studies demonstrate how this kills individual languages, this is the first study to examine losses worldwide and rank economic growth above other potential threats.

Data about the few living, fluent speakers of endangered languages are scant, but Amano and colleagues used their best available resource—an online **(4)** <u>repository</u> called Ethnologue. The group was able to calculate the geographical range, number of speakers, and rate of speaker decline for languages worldwide and map that data. Although they found information about the range and number of speakers for over 90% of the world's estimated 6909 languages, they

1. A) NO CHANGE
   B) instinct
   C) extinct
   D) distinct

2. A) NO CHANGE
   B) induce
   C) reduce
   D) recluse

3. A) NO CHANGE
   B) elude
   C) allude
   D) lewd

4. A) NO CHANGE
   B) crematory
   C) depository
   D) depot

found few details about the rate of **(5)** <u>recline</u> or growth for 9%, or 649, of those languages.

Next, they examined the relationship between language loss and variables such as a country's industrialization, globalization, or gross domestic product. In addition, they examined environmental factors such as altitude, which might **(6)** <u>effect</u> language loss by influencing how easily communities can communicate and travel.

Of all the variables tested, economic growth seemed to have the strongest effect on language loss. The study showed language loss **(7)** <u>incurs</u> most frequently in two different types of locations. One was in economically well-developed regions such as northwestern North America and northern Australia; a second was in economically developing regions such as the tropics and the Himalayas. Certain aspects of geography seemed to accelerate or delay language loss, Amano says. For example, recent cases appear to happen more quickly in **(8)** <u>temperate</u> climates than in extreme climates or environments—perhaps because it is easier to travel in and out of temperate regions.

"This is the first fundamentally sound statistical study that shows the relationship between these factors that we suspected to be at fault and language decline," says Leanne Hinton, an **(9)** <u>imminent</u> scholar of linguistics at the University of California, Berkeley. Economics is not the **(10)** <u>singular</u> culprit, however. In the United States, for example, current attitudes toward endangered tongues are rooted in historical policies that forced young American Indians to lose their native tongues in order to learn English, she says. Generations of disease, murder, and genocide—both **(11)** <u>historical</u> and present-day—have also contributed but were not included in the new study.

5. A) NO CHANGE
   B) decrease
   C) incline
   D) decline

6. A) NO CHANGE
   B) affect
   C) infect
   D) defect

7. A) NO CHANGE
   B) concurs
   C) occurs
   D) recurs

8. A) NO CHANGE
   B) tempered
   C) tame
   D) template

9. A) NO CHANGE
   B) intermittent
   C) implement
   D) eminent

10. A) NO CHANGE
    B) sole
    C) soul
    D) alone

11. A) NO CHANGE
    B) historically
    C) historic
    D) history

TEST EXERCISE:

Shake it Out

       When dealing with an overstimulated child, many desperate teachers and parents still respond: "Sit still!" However, it might be better to encourage the child to do something physical. Recent research suggests that even short periods of exercise **(1)** <u>helps</u> kids to focus and improve their academic performance.

       It is common knowledge that diagnoses of attention deficit hyperactivity disorder are now common among American children: The label has been applied to about 11 percent of those between the ages of 4 and 17. Interestingly, past studies have shown a connection between the levels of **(2)** <u>aerobic fitness and paying attention.</u> {3}

       Discovering the answer was a goal of a study published last year in The Journal of Pediatrics. Researchers at the University of Illinois at Urbana-Champaign recruited forty 8-to-10-year-old boys and girls, half of whom had A.D.H.D. The children **(4)** <u>produced</u> a series of computerized academic and attentional tests. Later, on one occasion they sat and read quietly for 20 minutes; on another, they walked briskly or jogged for 20 minutes on treadmills. After **(5)** <u>each individual</u> task, scientists monitored the children's brain function as **(6)** <u>they repeated the original tests.</u>

1. A) NO CHANGE
   B) help
   C) helped
   D) is helping

2. A) NO CHANGE
   B) aerobic fitness and learning
   C) aerobically fit and paying attention
   D) aerobic fitness and attentiveness

3. Which best concludes the second paragraph and transitions to the third paragraph?

   A) But these studies did not answer the question of which comes first, the fitness or the attentional control.
   B) Of course, these studies did not answer a fundamental question about brain function.
   C) Nonetheless, the studies weren't producing enough data.
   D) However, there was not enough tested information to make a clear judgment.

4. A) NO CHANGE
   B) completed
   C) learned
   D) compiled

5. A) NO CHANGE
   B) every
   C) the
   D) this

6. A) NO CHANGE
   B) the children repeated them.
   C) the original tests were repeated by the children.
   D) the children repeated the original tests.

{7} Student performance did not change much after the quiet reading, but student scores **(8)** <u>raised</u> significantly in their math and reading comprehension after the exercise. More striking, the children with A.D.H.D. significantly increased their scores on a complicated test, not some simple task where performance could be due to chance or luck. Brain-wave readings showed that after exercise, the children with A.D.H.D. were better able to regulate their behavior, which helped them pay attention. They responded more effectively to small mistakes instead of getting distracted by them. In short, the children with A.D.H.D. were better students academically **(9)** <u>after exercise, as were the students without A.D.H.D.</u>

(10) <u>Despite this, rebuts Matthew Pontifex</u>, now an assistant professor at Michigan State University and the study's lead author, "You don't need treadmills." Just get restless children to march or hop or in some fashion be physically active for a few minutes. Having their peers join in makes the activity inclusive, and everyone receives the benefits.

Of course, even as it reinforces the assertion that exercise is good for brain activity, this short-term study leaves many questions unanswered: Does the length and stress level of the physical activity matter? Does it permanently lessen attentional problems? Does exercise have a direct effect on attention? In their study, the researchers speculate that exercise might help sharpen mental focus by increasing brain **(11)** <u>motion</u> in the frontal lobe. But understanding the neurological science might not be necessary for teachers and parents to consider using exercise to counter wandering attentions.

7. Which of the following best introduces the paragraph?

A) Administrators should cut P.E. classes based on these results.
B) P.E. classes should be extolled for their helping students to concentrate.
C) The results should make administrators question the wisdom of cutting P.E. classes.
D) The results still have not kept schools from cutting P.E. classes.

8. A) NO CHANGE
B) rose
C) razed
D) rise

9. A) NO CHANGE
B) after exercise, the students without A.D.H.D. were, as well.
C) after exercise as were the students without A.D.H.D.
D) after exercise; like the students without A.D.H.D.

10. A) NO CHANGE
B) Nonetheless, counters Matthew Pontifex,
C) In contrast, adds Matthew Pontifex,
D) What's more, adds Matthew Pontifex,

11. A) NO CHANGE
B) movement
C) activity
D) recreation

Lesson wY16
Frequently Confused Words
Race to the Finish

HOMEWORK EXERCISE 1:

Directions: Correct the errors in the following sentences. Some sentences may have no errors.

1. On September 14th, 1901, Vice President Theodore Roosevelt was on his way to a much needed vocation.

2. When he arrived at the train station, he was given most serious news: President William McKinley had died the proceeding night.

3. A special train was waiting to rush him back to the capitol of the United States, Washington D.C.

4. He could not except the fact that his mentor and friend was now dead.

5. The event was not a complete surprise, as the precedent had been shot on September 6th, 1901.

6. While it was believed that McKinley would make a full recovery, he took a turn for the worse as his injuries were exasperated by the bullet that was still lodged in his body.

7. The assassin, Leon Czolgosz, was an anarchist who had radical principles that motivated him to commit this ghastly crime.

8. Only a man with no morale fiber could attack such a beloved man.

9. Leon shot McKinley twice; one bullet was defected by a button, while the second one shot true.

10. The president tried to fight the injuries, but his wounds proved futile.

11. Roosevelt would soon assent to the position of President after a hasty inaugural ceremony.

12. There would be no brakes for him during the next few weeks as he tried to fill the position left behind by McKinley.

13. The entire country was deeply effected by the death of the president.

14. There was a brief period of morning held in memory of the recently departed president.

15. When the diseased president was buried, there was a five minute moment of silence in McKinley's honor.

16. Nine days after the president died, Leon Czolgosz was convicted in court.

17. Leon claimed that the American government was a despotic one, and that he was trying to insure America's freedom.

18. He inferred that McKinley was a dictator who was ruling the country with an iron fist.

19. After a bear half hour of deliberations, the jury found him guilty of murder.

20. No one who saw the stationery form of the President could forgive Leon for his crime.

HOMEWORK EXERCISE 2:

The Myth of Narcissus

(1) One of the most famous Greek myths is that of Narcissus. He was born of divine (2) parents, the River God Cephisus was his father and the nymph Lyriope was his mother. Narcissus was attractive and physically fit and was beloved and renowned for his beauty. There are only slight differences in the Greek and Roman versions of Narcissus. Where they (3) defer lies within the demise of our beloved character.

{4}

1. A) NO CHANGE
    B) The myth of Narcissus is a Greek myth that is one of the most famous of the myths.
    C) Narcissus's Greek myth is the most famous.
    D) Of all the Greek myths, one of the most famous myths is Narcissus.

2. A) NO CHANGE
    B) parents, and the
    C) parents, yet the
    D) parents; the

3. A) NO CHANGE
    B) differ
    C) are deferential
    D) differentiate

4. Which of the following choices best expresses the main idea of the preceding paragraph?

    A) To discuss the differences between the Greek and Roman versions of the myth
    B) To introduce the character Narcissus
    C) To highlight how Roman myths are just copies of Greek myths
    D) To clarify the need for myths in Greek culture

In the Greek myth, Narcissus is pursued by a young friend named Ameinias. However, Narcissus rejects the advances. Lacking the will to live without fulfilling these desires, **(5)** suicide is committed by Ameinias at **(6)** Narcissus's doorstep with a prayer that Narcissus would learn a lesson for his prideful ways and his cruel behavior. Upon seeing his own reflection for the first time, Narcissus becomes completely entranced and cannot look away from his own image in the lake. As time goes on, he grows weaker, and dies of starvation at the lakeside. **(7)** Narcissus, sent to the Underworld, sits, forever staring at his own reflection in the river Styx. {**8**}

[1] The Roman myth begins differently, with Narcissus walking through the woods when the nymph Echo spots him and immediately falls in love with him. [2] Echo follows him for some time before finally revealing herself to Narcissus. [3] Echo confesses her love to Narcissus after finally catching up to Narcissus. [4] He avoids her embrace and cruelly rejects her before running off. [5] Echo chases him again; however it was **(9)** in vain. [6] Heartbroken, she spends the rest of her sad life in valleys until only her voice, the echo, remains. [7] Nemesis, the Roman goddess of revenge, punishes Narcissus for his hubris by cursing him to fall in love with his own reflection. [8] Just as in the Greek myth, Narcissus eventually dies by a riverside while admiring his reflection. [9] This version, however, explains that he commits suicide when he realizes that he cannot ever attain the object of his desire: himself. {**10**}

5. A) NO CHANGE
   B) Ameinias will commit suicide
   C) Ameinias commits suicide
   D) Ameinias would be
      committing suicide

6. A) NO CHANGE
   B) Narcissuses doorstep
   C) Narcissus is doorstep
   D) Narcissu's doorstep

7. A) NO CHANGE
   B) Narcissus now sits in the
      Underworld,
   C) In the Underworld, Narcissus
      is sitting by the river Styx,
   D) He is, in the Underworld,
      sitting

8. Which of the following choices
   best describes where the
   following sentence should be
   added?

   "Later on, Narcissus happens by a
   lake where he stops to drink some
   water."

   A) Before Sentence 2
   B) Before Sentence 3
   C) Before Sentence 4
   D) Before Sentence 5

9. A) NO CHANGE
   B) in veins
   C) in vain
   D) in wane

10. Which of the following is the best
    way to combine Sentences 2 and
    3 in the preceding paragraph?

    A) Echo follows him for a while
       before she catches him, and
       then confesses to Narcissus
       that she loves only him.
    B) Narcissus is being chased by
       Echo, who is catching up to
       him to confess her love to him.
    C) Echo chases Narcissus for
       some time before confessing
       of her love for him.
    D) Echo, chasing Narcissus,
       confesses her love to him
       when she catches him and
       reveals him to her.

Narcissus is used as source of inspiration for writers, poets, and artists. There are several paintings of a beautiful young man staring at his own reflection, and many characters in literature tend to have narcissistic tendencies. His name is also attached to a flower, the narcissus, which, like **(11)** <u>its' namesake</u>, is only found on the banks of rivers and lakes.

11.A) NO CHANGE
   B) it's namesake
   C) their namesakes
   D) its namesake

Lesson wY17
Logical Comparisons
Getting Your Feet Wet

Directions: The following questions are intended to serve as a brief diagnostic exam.

1. The elephant performed <u>fewer tricks at this show</u>.

    A) NO CHANGE
    B) fewer tricks
    C) fewer tricks at this show than the dolphin.
    D) fewer tricks at this show than at last week's show

2. His singing is just as bad <u>as his mother</u>.

    A) NO CHANGE
    B) as his mother's
    C) as his mother when she sings
    D) as the singing of his mother

3. <u>Larry offered Hannah more pay than Susan.</u>

    A) NO CHANGE
    B) Larry offered Hannah more pay than Susan offered.
    C) Larry and Hannah offered more pay than Susan.
    D) Larry offered Hannah more pay from Susan offered.

Lesson wY17
Logical Comparison
Wading In

TOPIC OVERVIEW – LOGICAL COMPARISONS

Logical comparison questions on the SAT test our ability to recognize and correct incomplete, inconsistent, or unclear comparisons.

TOPIC OVERVIEW – INCOMPLETE COMPARISONS

At least two items are needed for a comparison to be complete. Incomplete comparisons will make the reader guess at which two things are being compared. For example:

Example 1: The high school has enrolled more students this year.

At first glance, this sentence might seem logical, but it doesn't complete the comparison: The high school enrolled more students than what? More students than it enrolled in another year, or more students compared to other schools?

Completed comparison:

The high school has enrolled more students this year *than in any year prior*.

Let's look at a trickier example:

Example 2: Eugene scored more touchdowns this year than anyone on the team.

In this example, the two things being compared are "Eugene" and "anyone on the team" – but since Eugene scored touchdowns, he's probably on the team, right? In this case, we're comparing Eugene to himself!

Completed comparison:

Eugene scored more touchdowns this year than *anyone else on the team*.

TOPIC OVERVIEW – INCONSISTENT COMPARISONS

Comparisons must also be consistent in that they need to compare apples to apples rather than apples to oranges. Let's look at an example:

Example 3: The animated feature films' awards got more coverage than the animated shorts.

If someone said this to you, you would know what the sentence meant, but in terms of proper English conventions, this sentence is incorrect. As written, this sentence compares an award to an animated short – this makes no logical sense.

Consistent comparison:

The animated feature films' awards got more coverage than *the animated shorts' awards.*

Inconsistent comparisons can often be addressed by simply making something possessive. For example, in the sentence above, it would also be correct to say:

The animated feature films' awards got more coverage than *the animated shorts'.*

TOPIC OVERVIEW – UNCLEAR COMPARISONS

Finally, comparisons must be clear. A reader needs to be able to tell exactly which two things are being compared. Let's look at an example:

Example 4: My dad plays baseball with me more than my brother.

In this example, the meaning is unclear. The sentence could mean that my dad plays baseball with me more often than he does with my brother, or it could mean that my dad plays baseball with me more often than my brother does.

RECOGNIZING LOGICAL COMPARISON QUESTIONS

Logical comparison questions can be identified by the use of key comparison words and phrases, such as:

- like
- less than
- that of
- as
- more than
- those of
- compared to
- other

You should also look for adjectives and adverbs in the comparative form (such as "bigger" or "longer").

ANSWERING LOGICAL COMPARISON QUESTIONS

The SAT presents logical comparison questions in two ways. Either the underlined portion will contain both items that are being compared, or the underlined portion needs to be altered to be logically compared to some other part of the sentence or paragraph.

Regardless of the presentation of the question, the process for finding the correct answer remains the same:

1. Identify the items that are being compared. Determine whether the error is the result of an incomplete, inconsistent, or unclear comparison.
2. If the comparison is incomplete, eliminate any answer choices that fail to logically complete the comparison.
3. Eliminate any answer choices that compare two items that are not similar. Look out for possessives because a seemingly inconsistent comparison can often be corrected by using possessives.
4. Eliminate any answer choices that create an unclear comparison.
5. Choose the best answer from the remaining choices.

<u>Example 5:</u>

The moderate candidate's speeches are different <u>from any other politician</u> in the race because they closely examine the nuances of the issues.

A) NO CHANGE
B) than any other politician
C) from those of any other politician
D) from any other speeches by other politicians

1. The moderate candidate's speeches are being compared to other politicians. That makes this an inconsistent comparison.
2. None of the answer choices are incomplete comparisons.
3. Answer choices A and B can be eliminated because they do not create a consistent comparison.
4. The difference between C and D is the way in which the information is presented. Though both provide consistent, clear, and complete comparisons, choice D is redundant and choice C is concise. Choice C is the best answer.

WRAP-UP

Logical comparison questions can be answered using the following steps:

1. Identify the items that are being compared. Determine whether the error is the result of an incomplete, inconsistent, or unclear comparison.
2. If the comparison is incomplete, eliminate any answer choices that fail to logically complete the comparison.
3. Eliminate any answer choices that compare two items that are not similar. Look out for possessives because a seemingly inconsistent comparison can often be corrected by using possessives.
4. Eliminate any answer choices that create an unclear comparison.
5. Choose the best answer from the remaining choices.

Lesson wY17
Logical Comparison
Learning to Swim

CONCEPT EXERCISE:

Directions: Correct the errors in the following sentences. Some sentences may not have errors.

1. In July of 1831, the island of Sicily in the Mediterranean Sea experienced an event unlike the past.

2. Compared to the day before, the ocean had become unusually bubbly.

3. Under the water, a volcano was erupting just like on land.

4. The lava spewed out for days, eventually building a new island that was four times larger than it had been before.

5. Countries soon began arguing over the island more than any island.

6. British representatives claimed the island faster than other countries, naming it Graham Land.

7. Unlike the British name, the Sicilians named the island Ferdinandea.

8. France and Spain thought their claims on the island were better than any other country.

9. The island was recognized as a more important trade post than any in the area.

10. Touring Ferdinandea became as popular as Sicily itself.

11. Unlike the sparring European countries, Nature's plans did not favor the new island.

12. The ocean waves wore away at Ferdinandea, whose volcanic foundation was weaker than Sicily.

13. In December of 1831, sailors passing Ferdinandea had a view very different from five months before.

14. In fact, the top of the island now sat ten meters lower than the surface of the water.

15. Similar to July, a dispute about the underwater formation's name occurred.

16. Now called Graham Shoal, the former island is considered a dormant volcano, rather than active.

17. Thinking the island would return, Italy sent divers to attach a plaque to the rock, claiming Ferdinandea before any country could.

18. Compared to the volcano, the marble plaque's strength was pathetic, and it was found shattered less than six months later.

19. The controversy surrounding this volcano has been greater than other submarine eruptions.

20. The volcano will likely erupt again, and if it does, France has said it will be less eager to claim the island than in 1831.

Lesson wY17
Logical Comparison
Diving into the Deep End

PRACTICE EXERCISE:

The Mysterious Mole Rat

At first glance, naked mole rats may look like mice. However, these creatures are larger and far less cute than **(1)** <u>the mice we know</u>. Wrinkled, hairless, and nearly blind, mole rats are actually completely unrelated to **(2)** <u>the genetics of either moles or rats</u>. Their peculiar physical and social traits have captured the attention of biologists for several decades and may provide clues to ways of improving the health of humans.

Despite the fact that mole rats are mammals, their social structure resembles **(3)** <u>that of ants</u>. One queen rules the colony, breeding with a few chosen males. The other, infertile males and females focus on building and maintaining the colony. Mole rats live underground in maze-like burrows. These they dig with their teeth, which protrude like **(4)** <u>a rat</u>. Each burrow can house from 20-300 individuals and cover an area as large as six football fields. Similar to **(5)** <u>a human's house</u>, tunnels connect chambers that each serve a specific purpose. This allows the mole rats to stay underground for almost their entire lives.

1. A) NO CHANGE
   B) the mice's we know
   C) mice.
   D) the bodies of the mice we know.

2. A) NO CHANGE
   B) either moles' or rats' genetics
   C) the genes of moles and rats
   D) either moles or rats

3. A) NO CHANGE
   B) ants
   C) those of ants
   D) the structure of ants

4. A) NO CHANGE
   B) rats
   C) those of rats
   D) a rat does

5. A) NO CHANGE
   B) humans' houses
   C) the hallways in a human's house
   D) the plan of a human's house

Living underground comes with its challenges, however. The oxygen concentration in the mole rats' burrows is far lower than **(6)** the concentration that most mammals need to survive. Naked mole rats have adapted to this through a gene mutation that allows them to be comfortable in the carbon dioxide-rich environment of the burrows and gives them a pain tolerance far higher than **(7)** any rodent. This tolerance, however, appears not to translate to extreme temperatures. Most mammals have the ability to self-regulate their body's temperature, which allows them to inhabit varied climates. Mole rats, **(8)** in contrast to these, cannot. Consequently, the burrow's ambient temperature cannot vary much from 86 degrees Fahrenheit or the mole rats will die. Luckily, the temperature underground does not fluctuate too much, so temperature regulation is rarely a problem.

If all goes well, naked mole rats can live to be about thirty years old, which makes the species the longest-living of all rodents by far. This longevity is at least partially due to the mole rats' apparent immunity to cancer. **(9)** Unlike other animals, cancer has never been observed in mole rats. Scientists have even gone so far as to expose the creatures to known carcinogens, without result. This trait has sparked considerable interest in the cancer research community. This fact alone could make mole rats more valuable to cancer research than **(10)** almost any rodents.

The naked mole rat may be ugly, but considering its potential for contributing to scientific research, it could prove to be one of the most important animals on Earth. Scientists in disciplines from biochemistry to behavioral psychology are turning to the humble mole rat for answers and inspiration. What they discover could help humanity become stronger and healthier **(11)** than even today.

6. A) NO CHANGE
   B) most mammals
   C) most mammals' concentrations
   D) the concentration of most mammals

7. A) NO CHANGE
   B) any other rodent
   C) any rodent before
   D) any other rodents'

8. A) NO CHANGE
   B) in contrast to this
   C) in contrast to other mammals
   D) in contrast to mammals

9. A) NO CHANGE
   B) Unlike other diseases
   C) Unlike other scientists
   D) Unlike other observations

10. A) NO CHANGE
    B) almost any other rodents
    C) any rodents
    D) almost no rodents

11. A) NO CHANGE
    B) than previously
    C) than it is today
    D) than today

TEST EXERCISE:

The television show *Deadliest Catch* depicts commercial crab fishermen in the Bering Sea. Another, *Dirty Jobs*, shows all kinds of grueling work; one episode featured someone whose job it was to go through caves and collect bat guano. These shows must fascinate us because such confrontations with physical realities seem **(1)** <u>exotic</u> as they are so removed from our daily lives. Many of us do work that feels "unreal." **(2)** <u>Working in an office, tangible results from your efforts are often difficult to see.</u> What exactly have you accomplished at the end of any given day? Is there a more "real," hands-on alternative?

There was a time when the trades were a viable career choice, but beginning in the 1990s, many high school shop programs and other non-academic programs were dissolved as schools began to prepare students to become "knowledge workers." In the 20 years since, visions of a pure information economy have made us act as if all students ought to be sent to college with the ultimate goal of working in an office.

[1] This vision ignores a fundamental fact: Now as ever, we require workers who can perform important services like **(3)** <u>fixing our cars, unclog our toilets, and building our houses.</u> [2] The downturn in demand for trade workers will pass eventually, and may already be over. [3] In fact, a car mechanics' trade association reported that repair shops saw business jump sharply during the recent recession. [4] During tough economic times, people fix the cars they have instead of purchasing new cars – bad for car manufacturers, but good for mechanics. **{4}**

1. Which of the following is the most precise replacement for the underlined word?

   A) NO CHANGE
   B) mysterious
   C) unimaginable
   D) unusual

2. A) NO CHANGE
   B) Working in an office, your tangible efforts are often difficult to see.
   C) Working in an office, you may often find it hard to see the tangible results of your efforts.
   D) Office work, you know, often leaves us with results that are tangible to see.

3. A) NO CHANGE
   B) fixing our cars, unclogging our toilets, and build our houses.
   C) fixing cars, toilets, and houses.
   D) fixing our cars, unclogging our toilets, and building our houses.

4. Which of the following sentences should be eliminated in order to improve the focus of the paragraph?

   A) Sentence 1
   B) Sentence 2
   C) Sentence 3
   D) Sentence 4

A gifted young person who chooses to become a mechanic rather than accumulate academic credentials is viewed as eccentric because **(5)** <u>many in society believes</u> that there is only one track to success for children: through a series of gates controlled by prestigious institutions. But my experience says otherwise. **(6)** <u>Because I have a master's degree</u> from a prestigious university and could do other work, I prefer working in the garage. The good life comes in a variety of forms, but this variety has become difficult to see; we have allowed our field of aspiration to be narrowed too much. {7}

5. A) NO CHANGE
   B) many in society believe
   C) many in society has believed
   D) too many in society believes

6. A) NO CHANGE
   B) In spite of my master's degree
   C) Though I have a master's degree
   D) In spite of the fact that I have a master's degree

7. Which of the following answer choices, if true, would best support the ideas in this paragraph?

   A) The economy does not determine what kind of future career a child will find satisfying and profitable.
   B) No matter what one's profession, acquiring a master's degree is a good way to increase one's knowledge of a specific subject area.
   C) Studies have shown that many workers in the trades enjoy better health and greater feelings of satisfaction than do knowledge workers with prestigious degrees.
   D) Eccentric children should be listened to, but for their own sake they should be encouraged to earn prestigious degrees.

The trades suffer from low prestige, but this is based on a simple mistake. Because the work is dirty, many people assume it is also stupid. This is not my experience. I have a small business as a motorcycle mechanic in Richmond, Va., which I started in 2002. I work on mostly older bikes with some "vintage" cachet that make people willing to spend **(8)** money on it. **(9)** I have found the intellectual challenges of the work to be equal to the academic work I was required to complete for my master's degree. **(10)** However, my decision to go into this line of work is a choice that seems to perplex many people.{11}

8. A) NO CHANGE
    B) money on them.
    C) money for it.
    D) money at them.

9. A) NO CHANGE
    B) No doubt, the intellectual challenges of the work have proven to be equal to the academic work
    C) I have found the cognitive demands of the work to be equivalent to the academic work
    D) I have found the intellectual challenges of the work to be equal to those of the academic work

10. A) NO CHANGE
    B) However, when I went into this line of work, I chose to
    C) However, my decision to do this kind of work seems to
    D) But why I decided to choose this line of work was something that seemed to

11. For the sake of the logical flow of this passage, this paragraph should be

    A) left where it is.
    B) placed between the third and fourth paragraphs.
    C) eliminated.
    D) placed between the second and third paragraphs.

Lesson wY17
Logical Comparison
Race to the Finish

HOMEWORK EXERCISE 1:

Directions: Correct the errors in the following sentences. Some sentences may have no errors.

1. Though he is the far worse equestrian, Andrew likes horses more than Rufio.

2. In competitions, Anuskha has proven time and time again to be the best swimmer of the two.

3. After receiving his doctorate in theoretical physics, Gordon was even closer to his goal of becoming better than any scientist.

4. Whereas English lessons in Asian countries focus primarily on rote memorization of syntax and grammatical rules, Western countries set aside grammar to focus on literary analysis.

5. My knowledge of post-modernism is even fewer than my knowledge of modernist art.

6. Because she was just a novice gymnast, Erika could not hope to outperform Theresa's flips on the vault.

7. Despite initial pleasantries, the class found Annie as strange, if not more so, than Kat.

8. Between Akhil, Sumil, and me, I believe I am the best test taker.

9. Michael's appetite, unlike Johnny, was insatiable; he never seemed to stop eating.

10. Lara prefers hiking alone in the wilderness to Nathan.

11. Personally, there were more reasons to apply to Northwestern than Stanford, though Stanford may be the better school.

12. Of the greats in cyberpunk literature, no one, not even William Gibson, matches the unique style of Neal Stephenson.

13. Club-Mate's taste, like that of most regional sodas, takes some getting used to after a life of more generic colas.

14. Mako and Raleigh were treated like an outsider by the other players after they lost the team the tournament.

15. Though I am no purist, I would pick using physical books over e-books any day.

16. Though the fixation on Frank Lloyd Wright was peculiar, the SAT work books were as good, if not better than, the ACT work books.

17. Tony has proven to be a much more charitable and straightforward person than Bruce.

18. The members of the boy band, like bands before them, eventually started quibbling over artistic differences and separated.

19. When comparing the two, Dave's art is better composed, but Eric is better at realism.

20. Steve Jobs may go down in history as more impactful than any technological innovator.

HOMEWORK EXERCISE 2:

Making the Invisible Visible

Roald Dahl once wrote a novel entitled *The BFG* **(1)** <u>where</u> the main character, a "big friendly giant," captures dreams in jars. Recently, at Pennsylvania State University, a professor in the engineering department captured something on film that was equally short-lived but **(2)** <u>more real</u>: a cough.

[1] The image was recently published online by The New England Journal of Medicine. [2] It would not have been possible without schlieren photography, which "takes an invisible phenomenon and turns it into a visible picture," said the engineering professor, Dr. Gary Settles. [3] This technique has also been used to reveal heat waves rising off the human body, thermal plumes surging from candles—or even to study the mass of microscopic particles. [4] Dr. Settles also enjoys schlieren photography for its artistic aspects. {3}

In German, the word "schlieren" means streaks; **(4)** <u>in this case it refers to</u> regions of different densities in a gas or a liquid, which can be photographed as shadows using a special technique.

Dr. Settles **(5)** <u>had mentioned</u> that the technique was frequently used in his lab. It is often used in other settings, like in supersonic wind tunnels, to simulate shock waves around high-speed aircraft.

1. A) NO CHANGE
   B) in which
   C) in that
   D) when

2. Within the context of the passage, which of the following is the most precise replacement for the underlined phrase?

   A) NO CHANGE
   B) more concrete
   C) more tangible
   D) more material

3. Which of the following sentences should be eliminated in order to improve the focus of the paragraph?

   A) Sentence 1
   B) Sentence 2
   C) Sentence 3
   D) Sentence 4

4. A) NO CHANGE
   B) however, where Dr. Settles' studies are concerned, it refers to
   C) in particular instances it means
   D) therefore it suggests

5. A) NO CHANGE
   B) was mentioning
   C) mentioned
   D) mentions

The process involves a small, bright light source, precisely placed lenses, a curved mirror, **(6)** <u>and a razor blade—to block part of the light beam.</u> **(7)** <u>Other tools created by scientists, some too specialized and intricate to mention here, also assist in helping to make it possible to see</u> and photograph disturbances in the air. In the world of gas dynamics, a cough is merely "a turbulent jet of air with density changes." Though coughs spread tuberculosis, SARS, influenza and other diseases, surprisingly little is known about **(8)** <u>them.</u> Settles said that our understanding of disease is better **(9)** <u>than our knowledge of how infections spread on air currents.</u>

{**10**} A healthy student provided the cough. The expelled air, traveling at 18 miles per hour, mixed with cooler surrounding air and produced "temperature differences that bend light rays by different amounts," Settles said.

6. A) NO CHANGE
   B) and a razor blade that blocks part of the light beam.
   C) and a razor blade blocking the light beam.
   D) and a razor blade, blocking part of the light beam.

7. A) NO CHANGE
   B) Other tools created by scientists, some very specialized and intricate, also assist in helping to make it possible to see
   C) Other tools, some too specialized to mention in this article created by scientists, also help in making it possible to see
   D) Scientists create other tools—some too specialized and intricate to mention here—to help researchers to see

8. A) NO CHANGE
   B) coughs.
   C) it.
   D) these diseases.

9. A) NO CHANGE
   B) than our knowledge of air currents.
   C) than air currents.
   D) than that of spreading air currents.

10. Which of the following best establishes the main idea of the paragraph?

   A) To map a cough, he teamed up with Dr. Julian Tang, a virus expert.
   B) Students usually volunteer as test subjects because it is required of them.
   C) Dr. Julian Tang, who had a wide variety of students to choose from, was chosen as Dr. Settles' research partner.
   D) Other researchers work with Dr. Settles because of their backgrounds in medicine.

Describing other ideas for experiments, Dr. Settles explained how two people could stand in front of a mirror talking, or how one might cough on another, which would allow researchers to see how air flow moves, and how people infect each other. One could also look at how coughing can spread airborne infection in a hospital. Dr. Settles strongly believes that the techniques used in wind tunnels can be used to study human diseases. {11}

11. Which of the following answer choices, if true, would provide the strongest conclusion for this passage?

A) Wind tunnels are also pervasive in the automotive industry.
B) Most medical professionals who were queried for this article disagreed.
C) Indubitably, scientists can learn much more about coughing.
D) Knowing more about the airborne paths of viruses would increase the knowledge of how disease is spread.

Lesson wY18
Quantitative Information
Getting Your Feet Wet

Directions: Use the paragraphs and figures to answer the questions.

{1} Like many other developed nations, Japan is experiencing a significant shortage of workers. This is due in part to the aging postwar generation and in part to low birth rates. With the shortage of workers in Japan reaching a crisis point, Japan's prime minister, Shinzo Abe, unveiled a sweeping economic plan that included, among other initiatives, longer maternity leave for mothers.

Though it may seem odd to address a worker shortage by giving large numbers of workers time off, it makes quite a bit of sense in the long term. Currently, 70% of Japanese women drop out of the workforce entirely after becoming mothers. {2} Abe is betting that providing women with longer maternity leave, which allows for greater job protection and an easier transition back to work, will help to bring more women back to the workforce.

Critics point out that longer maternity leave still forces women out of work for extended periods, thus promoting job discrimination and lessening the chances of women pursuing careers. Such critics point to countries like Sweden and Iceland, who have some of the highest female labor participation rates in the world. Their secret is not maternity leave, but paternity leave: Encouraging fathers to stay at home helps to reduce job discrimination against women and places male and female workers on more equal footing.

1. It can be inferred from the chart titled "Percent of Women Participating in the Workforce" and from the passage that

   A) Sweden and Iceland have successfully encouraged female participation in the workforce.
   B) Japan has policies in place that discourage female participation in the workforce.
   C) only about 30% of the workforce in Iceland is made up of male workers.
   D) well over half of the workforce in Sweden is made up of female workers.

2. Which of the following, if added here, would provide accurate support based on the charts provided?

   A) Addressing this problem could increase the percentage of women participating in the workforce by 70%.
   B) This is in contrast with Iceland, where 70% of women remain in the workforce after becoming mothers.
   C) As a result, the percentage of Japanese women participating in the workforce is lower than the percentage of women in the workforce worldwide.
   D) Worldwide, that number is closer to 50%.

Regardless of whether the answer is maternity leave or paternity leave, one thing remains undisputed: Countries with aging populations – which includes most developed nations – must find ways to encourage today's workers to have children (who will one day become workers themselves) while still remaining in the workforce. {3} The alternative is a severe labor shortage that could result in global economic collapse.

3. Which of the following, if added here, would provide the strongest support based on the charts provided?

A) Luckily, this is not a problem that the United States will face since the U.S. has a much smaller population over age 65.

B) Japan is certainly not alone: worldwide, the share of the population over age 65 is expected to double by 2050.

C) The problem of aging workers is not as bad in countries like Germany, where the share of the population over age 65 will only increase by about 11% between now and 2050.

D) The problem of aging populations is isolated to Japan, Europe, and the U.S.

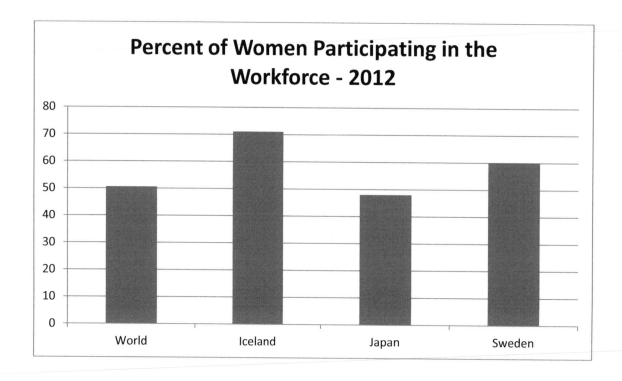

Percent of Women Participating in the Workforce - 2012

Share of the Population Aged 65+

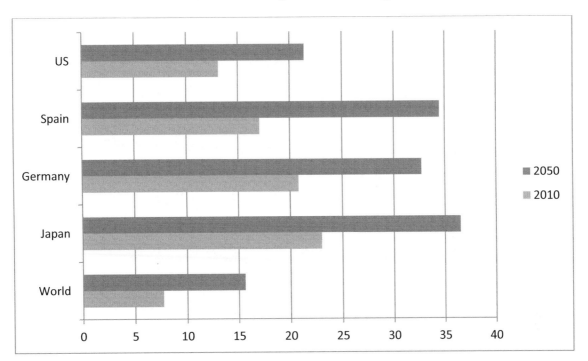

Lesson wY18
Quantitative Information
Wading In

TOPIC OVERVIEW: QUANTITATIVE ANALYSIS

The SAT Writing sections will often include graphics such as tables, charts, or maps along with the passages. Questions that accompany these graphics require that we use information from both the passage and the chart to arrive at the correct answer; this skill is called *synthesis*.

RECOGNIZING QUANTITATIVE ANALYSIS QUESTIONS

Questions that require the use of a graphic will always indicate this in the question statement. They will have phrases like "According to the graphic and the passage…" or "The passage and the graphic imply that…"

Some Quantitative Analysis questions ask us to add relevant information to the passage based on data from the graphic. Other Quantitative Analysis questions ask us what we can tell from both the passage and the graphic. In either case, it is likely that we will need at least some information from both the passage and the graphic.

ANSWERING QUANTITATIVE ANALYSIS QUESTIONS

One of the best methods for answering questions like these is elimination. It's often easy to quickly find answers that do not agree with the information in the graph. Here is an outline of a strategy to use:

1) Read the question and examine the graph carefully, paying close attention to the title and the scale and labels on each axis (if the graph is a line or bar graph).
2) Eliminate any choices that provide information that does not agree with the graphic. This includes answer choices that misinterpret what the graphic is measuring.
3) Eliminate any choices that provide information that does not agree with the passage.
4) If two or more choices remain, examine the remaining options very carefully. The test will sometimes include options that might seem as if they could be supported by the passage/graphic, but that really state information that is not supported. After carefully examining the remaining choices, choose the one that most closely reflects information from the passage and the graphic.

Below is a short passage and a graphic, followed by two questions and explanations of their answers:

Nearly 8,000 cases of pertussis, or whooping cough, were reported in the first half of 2014 in the state of California, and 94% of all cases reported involve children. Although whooping cough was once a national menace, killing more than 1,100 in 1950, decades of immunizations almost eliminated the disease; in 1995, only 6 people died of the disease. {1}

Experts attribute the resurgence of whooping cough to low vaccination rates in certain parts of California. L.A. County has had more cases of whooping cough than any other county in California; perhaps unsurprisingly, parts of L.A. County also have immunization rates that are comparable to rates seen in developing countries like Chad and South Sudan. Many are concerned that continued declines in vaccination rates may result in future outbreaks like this one.

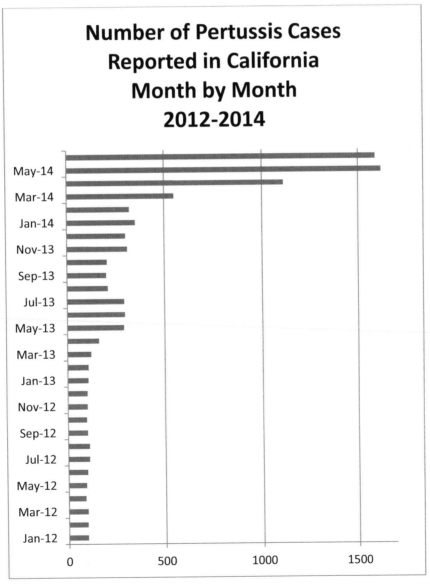

1. Which statement, if added here, would provide the most accurate and appropriate data, based on the graph at the end of the passage?

   A) 2014 has been the worst year on record for pertussis cases in California.
   B) Compared to recent years, the number of pertussis cases in California has grown at an alarming rate.
   C) Unfortunately, pertussis-related deaths have once again climbed to well over 1,000 in 2014.
   D) Although the number of pertussis cases in California in 2014 has been remarkably high, most experts believe this is an unusual occurrence that is unlikely to occur again.

   1. Notice that on our graph, the horizontal axis represents the number of pertussis cases in California, and the vertical axis represents the month and year in which the cases were reported.
   2. Start with choice A. Although the graph shows that 2014 as the worst year, the graph does not begin until January of 2012. To say that 2014 is the worst year *on record* is not supported by the graph because the graph only represents cases reported from 2012 to 2014. According to the graph, choice B is true – compared to cases reported in 2012 and 2013, 2014 has seen a very large number of pertussis cases. We can keep B. Choice C discusses pertussis-related deaths; although the passage notes numbers of pertussis-related deaths, the graph does not. Choice D does accurately note that the number of pertussis cases in California in 2014 has been unusually high, so we can keep D.
   3. We have narrowed our choices down to B and D. Nothing in the passage contradicts choice B, but the final sentence of the passage, which says that many experts fear future similar outbreaks, directly contradicts answer choice D. We can eliminate D.
   4. The only remaining answer choice is B, so this is the correct answer.

WRAP-UP

Use this strategy to answer questions that are accompanied by graphics in the writing section:

1. Read the question and examine the graph carefully, paying close attention to the title and the scale and labels on each axis (if the graph is a line or bar graph).
2. Eliminate any choices that provide information that does not agree with the graphic. This includes answer choices that misinterpret what the graphic is measuring.
3. Eliminate any choices that provide information that does not agree with the passage.
4. If two or more choices remain, examine the remaining options very carefully. The test will sometimes include options that might seem as if they could be supported by the passage/graphic, but that really state information that is not supported. After carefully examining the remaining choices, choose the one that most closely reflects information from the passage and the graphic.

Lesson wY18
Quantitative Information
Learning to Swim

CONCEPT EXERCISE:

Use the graphs below to answer the questions.

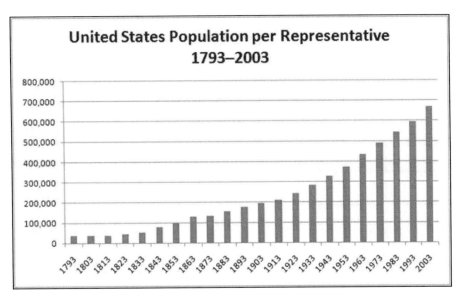

1. According to the graph, which of the following statements is true?

   A) The United States population per Representative has steadily decreased since 1813.
   B) The biggest jump in the population per Representative was between 1863 and 1873.
   C) The United States population was at about 600,000 in 1993.
   D) The United States population per Representative more than doubled between 1853 and 1913

2. Which of the following statements CANNOT be verified by the graph?

   A) The United States population per Representative increased every decade from 1813 to 2003.
   B) The United States population per Representative exceeded 600,000 in 2003.
   C) The United States total population increased every decade from 1793 to 2003.
   D) On average, each Representative represented about 500,000 people in 1973.

3. Based on the graph, is it reasonable to assume that in 2013 the United States population per Representative will be over 700,000?

   A) Yes because the population per Representative has increased every decade since 1813.
   B) Yes because the population per Representative has remained steady since 1793.
   C) No because the population per Representative never reached 800,000 between 1793 and 2003.
   D) No because 700,000 is the maximum number of people that can be represented per Representative.

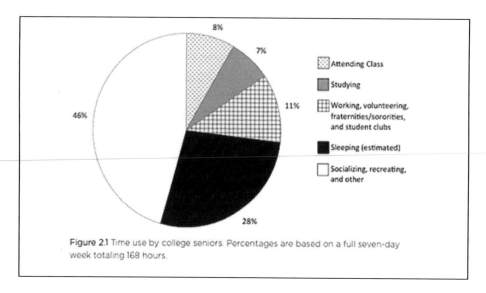

Figure 2.1 Time use by college seniors. Percentages are based on a full seven-day week totaling 168 hours.

4. According to the pie chart, which of the following statements is NOT true?

    A) The amount of time students spent attending class, studying, working and/or volunteering, and sleeping was about the same as the amount of time they spent socializing and recreating.
    B) Students spent about one-fourth of their time sleeping.
    C) Students spent more attending class and studying than they did sleeping.
    D) Out of the given categories, students spent the least amount of their time studying.

5. Which of the following activities COULD NOT be considered part of the "socializing, recreating and other" category?

    A) Attending musical events
    B) Shopping at malls
    C) Volunteering
    D) Attending sporting events

6. Which of the following is most likely to occur if the pie chart were to only account for days during which classes are in session (Monday through Friday)?

    A) The two largest categories would be reduced.
    B) The "attending class" category would be reduced.
    C) The "sleeping" category would be enlarged.
    D) There would be no change to the pie chart.

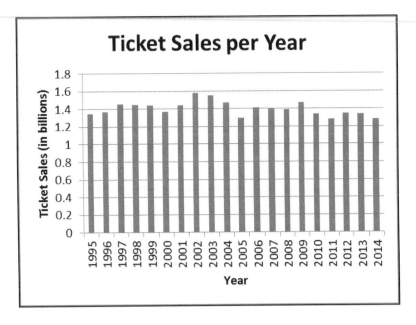

7. Which of the following statements can be made based on the graph?

   A) Ticket sales have significantly decreased since 1995.
   B) Ticket sales have significantly increased since 1995.
   C) Ticket sales since 1995 have steadily decreased then steadily increased.
   D) Ticket sales have remained about the same since 1995.

8. Which period saw a decline in ticket sales by year?

   A) 1995–1997
   B) 2003–2005
   C) 2005–2007
   D) 2007–2009

9. Based on the graph, which of the following statements is a reasonable prediction?

   A) Ticket sales in 2015 will exceed 2 billion.
   B) Ticket sales in 2015 will exceed 1 billion but not 1.6 billion.
   C) Ticket sales in 2015 will fail to reach 1 billion.
   D) Ticket sales in 2015 will be exactly at 1.28 billion.

Ratings of U.S. School Quality, Among Parents of Children in Grades K-12

	Excellent	Good	Only fair	Poor	Total excellent/good
	%	%	%	%	%
Independent private school	34	46	15	1	80
Parochial or church-related schools	18	54	18	3	72
Charter schools	19	42	24	3	61
Public schools	7	40	28	15	47
Home schooling	14	32	33	14	46

10. According to the table, which of the following statements is true?

    A) Charter schools were the most popular category among parents.
    B) Parents were more likely to rate schools as "poor" than as "excellent".
    C) Less than half of the surveyed parents rated public schools as either "excellent" or "good".
    D) The majority of parents rated parochial schools as "excellent".

11. According to the table, which type or types of schooling are parents most likely to be dissatisfied with?

    A) Private schools, parochial schools, and charter schools
    B) Public schools and home schooling
    C) Charter schools and public schools
    D) Private schools

12. Which of the conclusions can be drawn from the table?

    A) Students prefer private schooling to home schooling.
    B) Home schooling is gaining popularity among parents.
    C) Parents have similar opinions about parochial schools and charter schools.
    D) Parents are more satisfied with charter school teachers than they are with public school teachers.

Lesson wY18
Quantitative Information
Diving into the Deep End

PRACTICE EXERCISE:

Ancient Dry Spells Offer Clues

Scientists have unearthed new evidence about ancient dry spells that suggest the future could bring even more serious water shortages. New **(1)** <u>research that indicates</u> the ancient Meso-American civilizations of the Mayans and Aztecs likely amplified droughts in the Yucatán Peninsula and southern and central Mexico by clearing rainforests to make room for pastures and farmland.

Converting forest to farmland can increase the reflectivity of the land surface in ways that affect precipitation patterns. Farmland and pastures **(2)** <u>absorb slightly less energy from the sun than the rainforest</u> because their surfaces tend to be lighter and more reflective. This means that there's less energy available in the climate system to create precipitation.

The researchers used a high-resolution climate model to run simulations that compared how patterns of vegetation cover during pre-Columbian (before 1492 C.E.) and post-Columbian periods affected precipitation and drought in Central America. The pre-Columbian era **(3)** <u>seen</u> widespread deforestation on the Yucatán Peninsula and throughout southern and central Mexico. **{4}** During the post-Columbian period, forests regenerated as native populations declined and farmlands and pastures were abandoned.

1. A) NO CHANGE
   B) research indicates
   C) research: it indicates
   D) research; it indicates

2. A) NO CHANGE
   B) from the sun absorb slightly less energy than the rainforest
   C) absorb slightly less energy than the rainforest from the sun
   D) absorb than the rainforest slightly less energy from the sun

3. A) NO CHANGE
   B) has seen
   C) saw
   D) sees

4. Which statement, if added here, would support the paragraph's argument using accurate information from the figures and the passage?

   A) Northeastern Mexico, by contrast, experienced little deforestation, although it had few forests to begin with.
   B) This deforestation was particularly acute during the height of the Mayan empire around 800 to 950 C.E.
   C) In addition to logging, climate change is likely to contribute to the shrinking of the world's forests.
   D) Many other ancient civilizations, such as those on Easter Island and in Israel, also experienced heavy deforestation.

Cook's simulations include input from a newly published land-cover reconstruction that is one of the most complete and accurate records of human vegetation changes available. The results are unmistakable: Precipitation levels declined by a considerable amount—generally 10 to 20 percent—when deforestation was widespread. In the Yucatán, precipitation records from stalagmites—cave formations that paleoclimatologists use to deduce past climate **(5)** trends—because they are affected by moisture levels, agree with Cook's model results.

The effect is most noticeable over **(6)** the Yucatán Peninsula and southern Mexico, areas that overlapped with the centers of the Mayan and Aztec civilizations and had high levels of deforestation and the most densely concentrated populations. Rainfall levels declined **(7)** significantly, for example, over parts of the Yucatán Peninsula between 800 C.E. and 950 C.E. {8}

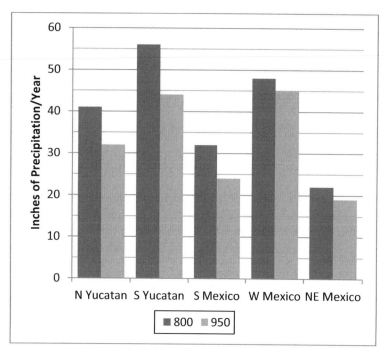

Figure 1: Estimated precipitation decline in Central America, 800 C.E. to 950 C.E. It was during this period of time that the Mayan civilization reached its peak population and abruptly collapsed.

5. A) NO CHANGE
   B) trends because they are affected—by moisture levels, agree
   C) trends because they are affected by moisture levels—agree
   D) trends, because they are affected, by moisture levels—agree

6. Which choice best matches the data shown in Figure 1?

   A) NO CHANGE
   B) the Yucatán Peninsula and northeastern Mexico
   C) the Yucatán Peninsula and western Mexico
   D) southern and western Mexico

7. Which choice provides the most precise and accurate supporting information from Figure 1?

   A) NO CHANGE
   B) by more than just a few inches per year
   C) by over 15 inches per year
   D) by as much as 44 inches per year

8. Which sentence, if added here, best utilizes the data in Figure 1 to provide context for information mentioned earlier in the paragraph?

   A) These declines, however, were slightly less notable in other parts of the Yucatán Peninsula.
   B) By comparison, rainfall levels remained steady in Europe during this era.
   C) Precipitation rose to its prior level in the years after the Mayan Empire's collapse.
   D) This compares to declines of only a few inches per year in other regions of Mexico.

During the peak of Mayan civilization between 800 C.E. and 950 C.E., the land cover reconstruction Cook based his modeling on indicates that the Maya had left only **(9)** <u>a tiny percentage</u> of the forests on the Yucatán Peninsula intact. By the period between 1500 C.E. and 1650 C.E., in contrast, after the arrival of Europeans had decimated native populations, natural vegetation covered nearly all of the Yucatán. **(10)** <u>Unfortunately, modern clear-cutting practices have led to deforestation nearly on par with that of the Mayan era.</u>

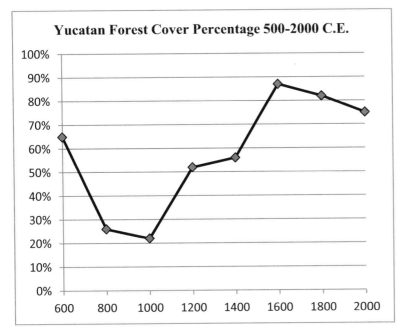

Figure 2: The estimated percentage of the Yucatán peninsula covered in forest at different points in history.

The researchers caution that this does not prove deforestation causes drought or **(11)** <u>being entirely responsible</u> for the decline of the Maya. However, the results do show that deforestation can bias the climate toward drought and that about half of the dryness in the pre-Colonial period was the result of deforestation. This provides a warning to governments around the world already struggling with global climate change: restrict deforestation or risk even more damage.

9. Which choice provides the most precise and accurate information, based on Figure 2?

A) NO CHANGE
B) a bit more than half
C) a few
D) around twenty-five percent

10. Which choice best characterizes the trends seen in modern times, as shown in Figure 2?

A) NO CHANGE
B) In modern times, deforestation has affected some areas, but a majority of the region's forests remain intact.
C) Since then, forest cover has continued to rise on the peninsula; it is currently at its highest recorded level.
D) In modern times, deforestation has vacillated wildly depending on local laws and customs.

11. A) NO CHANGE
   B) entire responsibility
   C) its entire responsibility to be
   D) that it is entirely responsible

TEST EXERCISE:

Over the last five years, inventors and investors in the United

States **(1)** <u>has</u> delivered significant progress in developing and

deploying clean energy technology. Our cars and trucks go farther on

a gallon of gas, saving families money at the pump. In 2012, US

carbon pollution fell to **(2)** <u>their</u> lowest level in nearly 20 years.

(3) <u>The simple fact is that clean energy technology costs are</u>

<u>continuing to decrease,</u> and these technologies are producing more

American energy than ever before.

From 1980 to 2012, installed wind capacity and cumulative wind

deployment **(4)** <u>increased only slightly.</u> Furthermore, the cost of wind

power during that same time period, measured by cents per kilowatt-

hour, **(5)** <u>greatly decreased.</u> This growth in wind deployment has

spurred more US manufacturing. According to the American Wind

Energy Association **(6)**<u>: by 2012</u> there were well over 80,000 students

employed in wind-related jobs in the US.

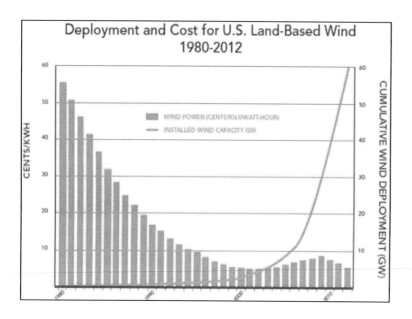

1. A) NO CHANGE
   B) had
   C) have
   D) were

2. A) NO CHANGE
   B) they
   C) those
   D) its

3. Which of the following best fits
   the style and tone of the passage?

   A) NO CHANGE
   B) Energy technology costs are
      coming down faster and faster,
   C) The monetary value for energy
      technology has been steadily
      diminishing,
   D) Prices are basically going
      down for energy technology
      every day,

4. Which choice best completes the
   sentence with accurate data based
   on the charts provided?

   A) NO CHANGE
   B) increased significantly.
   C) decreased slightly.
   D) decreased significantly.

5. Which choice best completes the
   sentence with accurate data based
   on the charts provided?

   A) NO CHANGE
   B) remained steady.
   C) decreased by just a bit.
   D) went up, then back down
      again.

6. A) NO CHANGE
   B) — by 2012
   C) by 2012
   D) , by 2012

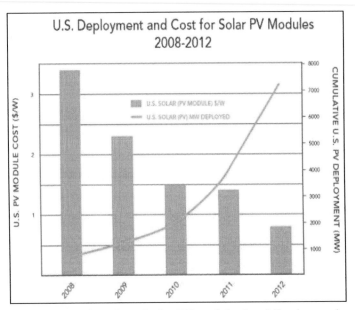

Since 2008, the price of solar PV modules has fallen by nearly

(7) $2 and solar installations have increased by a factor of 13.

Administration support **(8)** helps launch some of the tiniest solar

projects in the world, and renewable energy projects on federal public

land have gone from virtually zero to nearly 50 approved solar, wind,

and geothermal utility, scale projects. {**9**}

(10) Because of investors and fuel economy standards that

control how much fuel each vehicle uses, we have a more fuel-

efficient vehicle fleet that will continue to improve. For example,

during the first eleven months of 2013, Americans bought more than

87,000 plug-in electric vehicles, nearly twice as many as they did

during the same period in 2012. Prices are falling and export markets

are opening up. Since 2008, the cost of electric vehicle batteries has

dropped by 50 percent.

The US has made great strides in clean energy over the last five

years. At the same time, **(11)** those are producing more oil and natural

gas as we reduce carbon pollution. More clean energy. Greater energy

security. Less carbon pollution. Those are the facts.

7. Which choice best completes the sentence with accurate data based on the charts provided?

A) NO CHANGE
B) $1
C) $1 per W
D) $2 per W

8. A) NO CHANGE
B) will help
C) can help
D) has helped

9. Which of the following, if added to this paragraph, would add additional relevant data to the passage?

A) Sadly, most will fail.
B) These projects may hopefully one day have an impact in the US.
C) Unfortunately, public opposition has forced most of these projects to be closed down.
D) These projects add up to more than 13,300 megawatts—enough energy to power 4.6 million homes.

10. A) NO CHANGE
B) Due to donations given by investors and better fuel economy standards
C) Thanks to investments and fuel economy standards
D) With more money and better standards

11. A) NO CHANGE
B) we
C) they
D) these

Lesson wY18
Quantitative Information
Race to the Finish

HOMEWORK EXERCISE 1:

Directions: For each question, select the option that contains correct grammar and usage and accurately reflects the information in the accompanying graph.

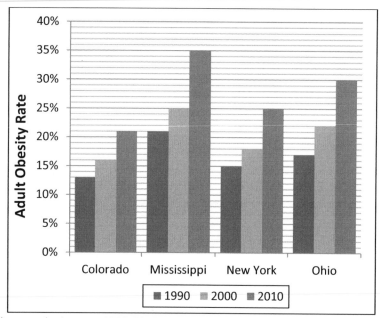

Figure 1: Adult obesity rates in 4 states, 1990-2010. In 2010, Colorado had the lowest obesity rate in the nation, and Mississippi had the highest.

1.
  - A) Colorado, it has long had one of the lowest obesity rates in the nation, also rates well in other health measures.
  - B) Colorado has long had one of the lowest obesity rates in the nation, it also rates well in other health measures.
  - C) Colorado, which has long had one of the lowest obesity rates in the nation, it also rates well in other health measures.
  - D) Colorado, which has long had one of the lowest obesity rates in the nation, also rates well in other health measures.

2.
  - A) Mississippi's 21% obesity rate in 1990 is the same as Colorado's 2010 obesity rate—the lowest in the U.S.
  - B) In 2010, more than one-half of adults in Mississippi were obese.
  - C) Mississippi's obesity rate has skyrocketed, but it was once lower than Ohio's rate.
  - D) Despite its small population, no state has more total obese adults than Mississippi.

3.
  - A) Frighteningly, the obesity rate has doubled in several of these states in just 20 years.
  - B) Even worse, each state saw a larger increase from 2000-2010 than in the previous decade.
  - C) Unfortunately, only one state had managed to keep its obesity rate under 20% by 2010.
  - D) Despite this alarming trend, one state has managed to actually cut its obesity rate.

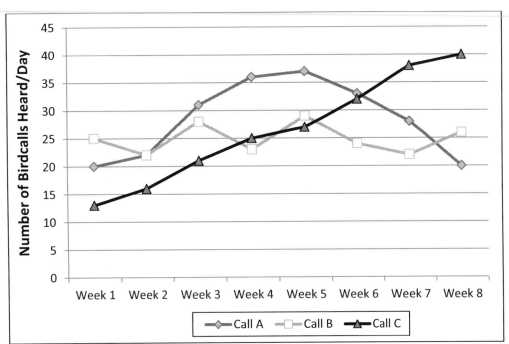

Figure 2: Robin calls heard per day. An ornithologist observed the birdcalls made by robins in a bird sanctuary over the course of 8 weeks, noting each of the bird's three main calls.

4.

    A) As the mating season reached its peak in Weeks 4 and 5, the number type A calls likewise peaked.

    B) As the mating season reached its peak in Weeks 4 and 5, the number of type C calls likewise peaked.

    C) As the mating season reached its peak in Weeks 4 and 5, the number of type A calls declined.

    D) As the mating season reached its peak in Weeks 4 and 5, the number of type B call declined.

5.

    A) Call B, the most stable of the three calls during the study.

    B) Call B was the most stable of the three calls during the study.

    C) Call B was the most stable than the other two calls during the study.

    D) Call B was stable during the study, it was the most of the three calls.

6. *Assume that the study took place during the spring and that each week, the average temperature rose.*

    A) Unlike the other two calls, the frequency with which Call C was heard tracked closely with the average temperature.

    B) Unlike the other two calls, the frequency with which Call B was heard tracked closely with the average temperature.

    C) Unlike the frequencies of the other two calls, the frequency with which Call C was heard tracked closely with the average temperature.

    D) Unlike the frequencies of the other two calls, the frequency with which Call B was heard tracked closely with the average temperature.

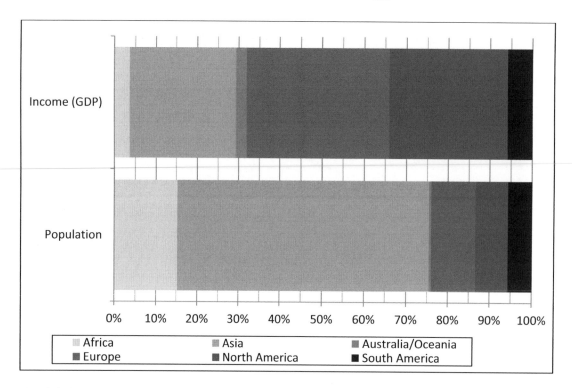

Figure 3: Global Income vs. Population, by Continent.

7.

    A) More than two-thirds of the world's population lives in the Americas, but less than one-third of the world's income is from those continents.

    B) Less than one-third of the world's population lives in the Americas, but more than two-thirds of the world's income is from those continents.

    C) More than two-thirds of the world's population lives in Africa or Asia, but less than one-third of the world's income is from those continents.

    D) Less than one-third of the world's population lives in Africa or Asia, but more than two-thirds of the world's income is from those continents.

8.

    A) Europe and North America have similar populations and they have similar incomes, too.

    B) Europe and North America, which save similar populations, they have similar incomes, too.

    C) Europe and North America have similar populations and similar incomes.

    D) Europe's population and its income are both similar to North America.

9.

    A) The continent that comes closest to having an income proportional to its population is South America.

    B) The continent that comes closest to having an income proportional to its population is North America.

    C) The continent that comes closest to having an income proportional to its population is Africa.

    D) The continent that comes closest to having an income proportional to its population is Asia.

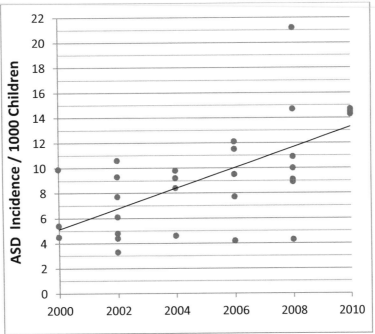

Figure 4: Autism Spectrum Disorder (ASD) Incidence since 2000. Every 2 years, a number of studies measured the rate of ASD diagnosis among 8-year-olds. The results from each study, as well as the trendline for the data, are shown above.

10.

    A) Of all the years in the study, 2002 had by far the least amount of variance among its data points.
    B) Of all the years in the study, 2006 had by far the least amount of variance among its data points.
    C) Of all the years in the study, 2008 had by far the least amount of variance among its data points.
    D) Of all the years in the study, 2010 had by far the least amount of variance among its data points.

11.

    A) The biggest outlier among any of the data points occurs in 2004.
    B) The biggest outlier among any of the data points occurs in 2008.
    C) The biggest outlier among any of the data points occur in 2004.
    D) The biggest outlier among any of the data points occur in 2008.

12.

    A) The lowest measured rate in every year of the study is close to 4 out of every 1,000 children.
    B) The highest measured rate in each year was higher than that of the previous year.
    C) Though there is a lot of variability in the data, the trend shows a steady increase in ASD incidence.
    D) According to the data, ASD incidence appears to have peaked in 2008, and it will likely decline after 2010.

HOMEWORK EXERCISE 2:

Using Social Media to Make Lebanese Citizens' Voices Count

Historically viewed as a bastion of free expression in the Arab world, Lebanon is a country with **(1)** a confusing media landscape that mirrors the complexity of its politics. Since Lebanese media outlets are aligned with political parties, covering issues through a narrow political lens rather than a focus on the public interest, the voice of citizens **(2)** gets diluted. For non-governmental organizations (NGOs), the media environment makes it difficult to advocate for solutions to the country's problems on a non-partisan basis.

Enter social media, which is providing an unfettered space for dialogue. Despite a weak Internet infrastructure, the Lebanese have joined the digital revolution *en force*. **{3}** This makes Lebanon one of the five Arab countries with the highest rates in this measure. Even better, **(4)** Lebanon has nearly as many male users as its neighboring country, Jordan. This allows NGOs to easily get both genders involved in social action, an important requirement for groups that value equality.

1. A) NO CHANGE
   B) an intricate
   C) a large
   D) a wicked

2. A) NO CHANGE
   B) getting diluted
   C) got diluted
   D) had gotten diluted

3. Which statement, if added here, would be most consistent with the information in the figure?

   A) For example, nearly half of all Lebanese adults are active on Facebook.
   B) In fact, about two-thirds of Lebanese adults use Facebook.
   C) More Lebanese citizens use Facebook than any other social media site.
   D) Facebook use has caught on rapidly in Lebanon, rising almost 50% in just a few years.

4. Which choice most effectively incorporates information from the figure to support the paragraph's argument?

   A) NO CHANGE
   B) Lebanese women are nearly as likely as men to use Facebook, an unusual breakdown among male-dominated Arab nations.
   C) Most Lebanese Facebook users are also active on other networks, such as Twitter.
   D) Lebanon's rate of Facebook usage is growing, and could easily reach 50% soon.

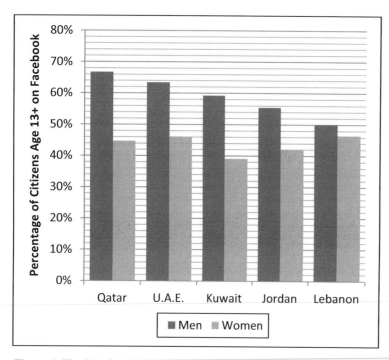

Figure 1: The 5 Arab countries with the greatest rates of Facebook use.

This data bodes well for NGOs engaged in digital campaigns against government injustices. **(5)** They have the potential to reach vast numbers of Lebanese men and women rapidly and at low cost. One such digitally active **(6)** NGO, Nahnoo, a youth-led group championing better public space policies. The issue is especially relevant in urban centers such as Beirut, where the average area of greenery per capita is just 0.8 square meters, far below the minimum of 9 square meters recommended by the World Health Organization.

Nahnoo documents its work on its website, Facebook, Twitter, and YouTube. Nahnoo volunteers recently mobilized hundreds of citizens in events aimed at reclaiming neglected public spaces, using these online platforms to publicize offline actions. This **(7)** integration, and it was effective, of online and offline activism has turned Nahnoo into a reference on public space issues that is frequently **(8)** cited for its niche expertise by traditional media, decision-makers, and researchers. {9}

5. Which choice best replaces the underlined pronoun?

   A) The data
   B) Such efforts
   C) These injustices
   D) People of both genders

6. A) NO CHANGE
   B) NGO: Nahnoo, a
   C) NGO is Nahnoo, a
   D) NGO is Nahnoo; a

7. A) NO CHANGE
   B) integration, which was effective,
   C) case of effective integration
   D) effective integration

8. A) NO CHANGE
   B) sighted for its
   C) sighted for it's
   D) cited for it's

9. The paragraph's arguments would be most effectively supported if which of the following were added here?

   A) An analysis of data comparing the number of Nahnoo volunteers to those of other NGOs
   B) A story about how traditional media helped publicize a protest
   C) A list of other Lebanese cities and their green space per capita figures
   D) An example of an influential person or group referencing Nahnoo's work

[1] Thanks to the influence of groups like Nahnoo, some TV stations, radio stations, and newspapers have recently begun to more deliberately give platforms for citizens. [2] They need to cover the issues that matter to their citizens—like the lack of green space—in order to keep people watching, listening, or reading. [3] This trend could lead to a much more balanced and informative media landscape that all citizens can enjoy, not just **(10)** <u>social media activity</u>. {**11**}

10. A) NO CHANGE
    B) social media sites with active users
    C) those who are active on social media
    D) the landscape of social media activity

11. Where in the preceding paragraph would the following sentence be most logically added?

    These traditional outlets, seeing that a new generation of Lebanese is heavily engaged with social media, have made a realization.

    A) Before Sentence 1
    B) After Sentence 1
    C) After Sentence 2
    D) After Sentence 3

Lesson wY19
Effective Language Use: Style and Tone
Getting Your Feet Wet

Directions: Use the paragraph below to answer the questions.

Fabien Cousteau has broken his grandfather Jacque Cousteau's record of spending 30 consecutive days underwater by one day. Part publicity stunt to raise awareness for oceanic research and part research mission, Mission 31 took place at the underwater habitat Aquarius some 60 feet below the ocean's surface at the Florida Keys, where Cousteau and five other people spent the month. **(1)** <u>There was an oxygen feed to the</u> surface, where a support team hovered, and the underwater habitat Aquarius.

{2} The undersea lab is about 43 feet long and nine feet wide, which is minuscule compared with, for instance, a submarine (those are about 275 feet long and 30 feet wide).

Of course, Cousteau comes from a family of aquaphiles. His father Jean-Michel, his sister Céline, and cousins Philippe and Alexandra have all dedicated their lives to ocean exploration and advocacy. His famous grandfather Jacques-Yves Cousteau believed that one day humans would build and inhabit underwater cities. **(3)** <u>He built</u> the first underwater habitat, called Conshelf I for "Continental Shelf Station", in 1962.

Ocean scientists have made enormous strides in underwater research, but the 20th century's love affair with outer space means we know far more about the moon than we do about the sea floor. Cousteau sees Earth as a "little brown veneer," compared with the vastness of the sea—and he gets frustrated when people marvel at the Earth's oceans by saying that 70 percent of the planet is covered by water.

1. A) NO CHANGE
    B) There was an oxygen feed connecting the
    C) There is an oxygen feed connecting the
    D) An oxygen feed linked the

2. Which replacement for the second paragraph best matches the style and tone of the rest of the passage?

    A) NO CHANGE
    B) Compared to submarines, which are about 275 feet long and 30 feet wide, the undersea lab is miniscule, measuring only 43 feet long and 9 feet wide.
    C) Aquarius feels claustrophobic, measuring only 1/5 the size of a typical submarine.
    D) The undersea lab is about forty-three feet long and nine feet wide, compared to submarines which are usually two hundred seventy-five feet long and thirty feet wide.

3. A) NO CHANGE
    B) In fact, his grandchildren still occasionally use
    C) It was Jacques-Yves who built
    D) The elder Cousteau was responsible for building

Lesson wY19
Effective Language Use: Style and Tone
Getting Your Feet Wet

TOPIC OVERVIEW: STYLE AND TONE

When an author writes something, she uses a specific style and tone in order to best convey her meaning. Style refers to the way an author writes, including sentence patterns and word choice. Style might be formal or informal, depending on the writer's purpose. Tone refers to the emotion that an author conveys through writing. For example, the tone of a piece might be objective or passionate. Both style and tone are typically determined by the author's purpose. For instance, if an author is writing a persuasive article about a serious topic, she is likely to use a formal style (to convey the seriousness of the topic) and a passionate tone (to persuade the audience to agree with her).

RECOGNIZING STYLE AND TONE QUESTIONS

Style or tone questions will usually include the words "style" or "tone" in the question. For example, a question might ask, "Which of the following best suits the tone of the passage?"

Some style and tone questions might simply look like a conventions question: an underlined portion of a sentence (or sentences) and several options for revision. If you see a question like this and you cannot identify a grammar or mechanics error in the underlined portion, this may be a style or tone question. If it is, then one of the answer choices will closely match the style or tone of the passage.

ANSWERING STYLE AND TONE QUESTIONS

In order to match the tone of the author, it's helpful to know what the author's purpose is. Some possibilities are persuasion, exposition, or narration. An author who is writing to persuade is likely to be passionate about the subject matter, whereas an author writing to inform is likely to be objective.

We can determine the style of the passage based on close reading. An author who uses slang, incorporates the use of second person point of view, or avoids using high level vocabulary is likely using an informal style, whereas an author who uses technical terms, relies on the third person point of view, or incorporates higher level vocabulary is likely using a formal style.

Here is a checklist of things to look for when answering style and tone questions:

1) What is the author's purpose? To convince the reader of something, to explain a concept to the reader, or to narrate a story? This will help to determine the author's tone.
2) Does the author refer directly to him/herself or directly to the reader? This is an indication of a somewhat informal tone.
3) Is the writing straightforward or metaphorical? This helps to define the style.
4) Are the adjectives and adverbs used vibrant or dull? This helps to define the style.

Here is a strategy to answer style and tone questions:

1) Quickly examine the passage for clues to the passage's style and tone.
2) Eliminate any answer choices that are inconsistent with the style or tone of the passage as a whole.
3) Closely examine the remaining answer choices to select the one that best reflects the style and tone of the passage as a whole.

Let's use the strategy:

Like human bodies, languages come in a wide variety of shapes – but those shapes still retain certain similarities. Just as people tend not to sprout spare limbs, languages tend to veer away from certain forms that might be imagined by a fertile mind. For example, human languages tend to follow *duality of patterning*: meaningful linguistic units (such as words) break down into smaller meaningless units (sounds). For example, the words *rots*, *sort*, and *store* utilize different combinations of the same sounds, even though their meanings are completely unrelated.

It's not hard for you to imagine that things could have been otherwise. Theoretically, we could have a language in which sounds relate to meanings: a yowl might mean "paper," a bark might mean "light," a high-pitched cry might mean "carrots," and so on. But there are certain advantages to duality of patterning. **(1)** <u>A language based on any other system would be incomprehensible, which is why no one should attempt to deviate from duality of patterning.</u>

Until recently, linguists did not believe that such a language existed, so you can imagine their surprise at the recent discovery of Al-Sayyid Bedouin Sign Language (ABSL), **(2)** <u>a language that works much like the imaginary one we just described.</u> ABSL is a new sign language emerging in a village with high rates of inherited deafness in Israel's Negev Desert. Words in this language correspond to unique gestures, unlike other sign languages that create words by re-combining a small collection of gestures.

1. Which of the following revisions to the underlined sentence best suits the style and tone of the passage?

   A) NO CHANGE
   B) Despite the advantages, a language that completely avoids this common linguistic pattern would be totally unique in a very cool way.
   C) Once upon a time, our ancestors decided that our languages would follow this pattern, and since it has worked for tens of thousands of years, it's clearly the best system of language.
   D) Try inventing a language of tens of thousands of easily distinguishable noises and you might wish you could simply re-use different combinations of sounds.

Let's use the strategy:

   1) Based on a reading of the passage, we can see that the author is writing to inform an audience of non-experts about a unique linguistic find. The passage as a whole is informative and somewhat informal.
   2) Since we know that passage is informative, not persuasive, we can eliminate choice A, which tries to persuade us that duality of patterning is the ideal means of structuring a language. Although the passage is somewhat informal, the word choices and sentence structure in choice B are much too informal to suit the passage as a whole ("totally unique in a very cool way"), so we can eliminate B. Choice C is persuasive rather than informative, and the use of "once upon a time" does not fit the style of the passage, so we can eliminate choice C.
   3) Only choice D is informative and suits the style of the passage, so choice D is the correct answer.

2. A) NO CHANGE
   B) a language that significantly deviates from duality of patterning by relying on distinct gestural elements with holistic meanings.
   C) an awesome language that turns everything anyone ever knew about linguistics on its head.
   D) a new form of sign language that ought to replace American Sign Language due to its unique structure.

Although this question doesn't give us a hint that it's a style and tone question, we can figure it out because the answer choices don't contain English convention errors and because they all have distinct differences in style or tone. Let's use the strategy:

   1) We already completed step one when we did the first question – we know that the passage is informative and somewhat informal.
   2) We can't eliminate choice A because it suits an informative and somewhat informal passage. We can keep B because it is informative, although a bit on the formal side. We can eliminate C because it is too informal for the rest of the passage ("awesome," "turns…on its head"). We can eliminate D because it is persuasive rather than informative.
   3) This leaves us with A and B. Though both are informative, B seems too formal for the rest of the passage. A is the better answer.

WRAP-UP

Use these questions determine the tone and style of the passage:

1) What is the author's purpose? To convince the reader of something, to explain a concept to the reader, or to narrate a story? This will help to determine the author's tone.
2) Does the author refer directly to him/herself or directly to the reader? This is an indication of a somewhat informal tone.
3) Is the writing straightforward or metaphorical? This helps to define the style.
4) Are the adjectives and adverbs used vibrant or dull? This helps to define the style.

Use this strategy to answer style and tone questions:

1) Quickly examine the passage for clues to the passage's style and tone.
2) Eliminate any answer choices that are inconsistent with the style or tone of the passage as a whole.
3) Closely examine the remaining answer choices to select the one that best reflects the style and tone of the passage as a whole.

Lesson wY19
Effective Language Use: Style and Tone
Learning to Swim

CONCEPT EXERCISE:

The Necklace

The day of the ball approached and Madame Loisel appeared sad, disturbed, and anxious. **(1)** <u>Nevertheless her dress was nearly ready.</u> Her husband said to her one evening, "What's new? You have acted strangely for the past three days.

She responded, "I am distraught not to have any jewelry, not a single stone or ornament to adorn myself with. I will have such an impoverished look. I am dreading every last minute of this party."

He replied, "You can wear some fresh flowers. At this season they look very chic. For ten francs you can have two or three magnificent roses."

She was not convinced. "No," she replied, "there is nothing more humiliating than looking shabby in the midst of rich women."

Then her husband cried out, "How stupid we are! Go and find your friend Mrs. Forestier and ask her to lend you her jewelry. You know her well enough to do that."

She yelped with wild abandon. "It is true!" she said. "I had not thought of that."

The next day she took herself to her friend's house **(2)** <u>and told her her troubles</u>. Mrs. Forestier went to her closet with the glass doors, took out a large jewel-case, brought it, opened it, and said, "Choose, my dear."

She saw at first some bracelets, then a collar of pearls, then a Venetian cross of gold and jewels that was **(3)** <u>of admirable</u>

1. A) NO CHANGE
    B) Nevertheless, her dress was nearly ready.
    C) Yet her dress was basically done.
    D) Her dress was just about at the point of completion.

2. A) NO CHANGE
    B) and unveiled her tale of woe
    C) and had a heart-to-heart talk about her problems
    D) and related her story of distress

3. A) NO CHANGE
    B) really nicely made
    C) phenomenally well-crafted
    D) produced very admirably

workmanship. She tried the jewels before the mirror, hesitated, but could neither decide to take them nor leave them. Then she asked, "Have you nothing more?"

"Why, yes. Look for yourself. I do not know what will please you."

(4) <u>All of a sudden, she saw a really near necklace in a black satin box</u>, and her heart began beating fast with an immoderate desire. Her hands trembled as she took them up. She placed them around her throat against her dress, and **(5)** <u>remained in ecstasy while asking</u> in a hesitating voice, full of anxiety, "Could you lend me this? Only this?"

"Why, yes, certainly."

She fell into her friend's arms, embraced her with passion, then went away with her treasure.

When the day of the ball arrived, Madame Loisel was a great success. She was **(6)** <u>the very most pretty of all</u>, elegant, gracious, smiling, and full of joy. She danced with enthusiasm, with passion, intoxicated with pleasure, thinking of nothing, in the triumph of her beauty, in the glory of her success, in a kind of cloud of happiness that came from all this homage, and all this admiration, from all these awakened desires, and this victory so complete and sweet to her heart.

4. A) NO CHANGE
   B) Suddenly she discovered, in a black satin box, a superb necklace of diamonds
   C) In an extremely brief moment, she discovered a stupendously attractive necklace of diamonds lying in a black satin box
   D) Really quick, she saw a shiny necklace in a black satin box

5. A) NO CHANGE
   B) remained in ecstasy, before asking
   C) remained in ecstasy. Then she asked
   D) remained in ecstasy. She now asked

6. A) NO CHANGE
   B) more pretty than all of them
   C) the prettiest of every one of them
   D) the prettiest of all

Bats

Bats play an important role in our ecosystem. However, many people are not aware that they can also be dangerous to humans. In fact, several highly fatal diseases have been linked to bats, and **(7)** you'd better watch yourself or you might be the victim.

Rabies is perhaps the most well-known disease associated with bats. Along with animals such as dogs, foxes, raccoons, and skunks, bats are one of the primary animals that transmit rabies. An exposure to rabies most commonly occurs when a person is bitten by a rabid animal. When a person is exposed to rabies, timely administration of a vaccine known as post-exposure prophylaxis (PEP) can prevent infection. Once a person becomes infected and symptoms begin to occur, rabies is almost always fatal.

Histoplasmosis is another disease linked with bats. Its symptoms vary greatly, but the disease primarily affects the lungs. Occasionally, other organs are affected. When this happens it can be fatal if untreated. While most infected persons **(8)** seem like they're just fine, antifungal medications are used to treat many forms of the disease.

While rabies and histoplasmosis **(9)** can be found literally everywhere, some diseases associated with bats are found exclusively in certain regions of the world. Notably, research suggests that bats might be the source of several hemorrhagic fevers, which affect multiple organ systems in the body and often lead to life-threatening diseases. One of these diseases is Marburg hemorrhagic fever, which is found exclusively in Africa. Past outbreaks have shown that Marburg Hemorrhagic Fever kills up to 90% of those infected. While the natural host **(10)** was once unknown and had been for years, new

7. A) NO CHANGE
   B) individuals who are not careful can easily expose themselves to infection
   C) people need to be really careful so they can avoid getting hurt
   D) unless you know what you're doing, could become a victim yourself.

8. A) NO CHANGE
   B) don't appear to be suffering at all
   C) have no apparent ill effects
   D) look as healthy as a horse

9. A) NO CHANGE
   B) can be found all over the world
   C) can be found in any place you care to name
   D) can be found in so many places around the globe

10. A) NO CHANGE
    B) for years had not been known at all
    C) was previously unknown for many years
    D) had been unknown for years

research suggests that fruit bats are a natural source of this virus, and the virus has been isolated repeatedly from fruit bats in Uganda.

The same may be true for Ebola hemorraghic fever. The virus that causes this disease is often referred to as the "cousin" of Marburg virus, since they are the only distinct viruses that belong to a group of viruses known as filoviruses. Like Marburg, Ebola is highly fatal and is **(11)** <u>found the majority of the time</u> in Africa. Recent studies indicate that, as with Marburg, bats are likely to be a natural source of this virus, although no Ebola virus has been isolated from bats.

While bats pose serious potential dangers to humans, taking appropriate, reasonable precautions can minimize one's risk of a negative encounter. The most important precaution is to avoid areas where bats are known to congregate, such as caves. In many outdoor situations, the presence or sighting of bats is common and normal. However, this does not mean there are no dangers. If you live in an area populated by bats, one valuable precaution is to "bat-proof" your living space by installing screens or mosquito netting, and by sealing off any holes in the walls or roof of your home to keep out intruding animals. Children should be **(12)** <u>taught to never handle</u> live or dead bats, as contact with either could expose them to infection. By employing these and other strategies, humans can learn to coexist safely with these fascinating creatures.

11. A) NO CHANGE
    B) found in the majority of cases
    C) more often than not found
    D) found mostly

12. A) NO CHANGE
    B) taught to not ever handle
    C) taught to avoid ever handling
    D) taught to make sure never to handle

Lesson wY19
Effective Language Use: Style and Tone
Diving into the Deep End

PRACTICE EXERCISE:

"Two Different Worlds at Yosemite," adapted from "Yosemite-Grace Under Pressure" by William Least Heat-Moon, *National Geographic*

[1] In Yosemite Village is a soft-drink machine with a poster of a golfer about to tee up. [2] Large words proclaim: DISCOVER YOUR YOSEMITE. **(1)** [3] <u>In contrast to what a Ranger had just told me, "National Parks aren't for entertainment,"</u> within Yosemite are a golf course, an ice-skating rink, five ski lifts, snowboard runs, a kennel, and a sports bar with a big-screen TV. **(2)** [4] <u>The crowd around me was shod more in flip-flops than hiking shoes. [5] They wore halter tops instead of field shirts. [6] And they licked ice cream cones and munched tacos. [7]</u> Was I at a mall or in a valley renowned for its natural wonders and trails? [8] Close by were two hotels, a store, a jail, a post office, an ATM, 2,000 parking spaces, and more than 200

1. A) NO CHANGE
   B) A Ranger told me, "National Parks aren't for entertainment," but within
   C) Ranger just informed me "National Parks aren't for entertainment," and within
   D) Although I had just learned from a Ranger that "National Parks aren't for entertainment," within

2. Which of the following versions of sentences 4, 5, and 6 best keeps the style of the passage?

   A) NO CHANGE
   B) The crowd around me was shod more in flip-flops than hiking shoes, wore halter tops instead of field shirts, and licked ice cream cones and munched tacos.
   C) All around me, the vast crowd exhibited flip-flops and halter tops instead of hiking shoes and field skirts. Moreover, they licked ice cream cones while consuming tacos.
   D) The crowd around me didn't wear hiking shoes or field shirts. Instead they wore flip-flops and halter tops. And they licked ice cream and munched tacos.

miles of asphalt. **(3)** [9] <u>The Yosemite I wanted to discover had to be somewhere else, both in time and place.</u>

The National Park Service has created a plan that emphasizes a better balance of tourism and conservation. The plan is **(4)** <u>extreme.</u> At its core are two changes: moving facilities that do not need to be in the valley to other areas, and persuading tourists to use public transport to get around the valley. **(5)** <u>Shuttles have already reduced traffic in the valley. Unfortunately the shuttles</u> have not eliminated 2-mile-long lines of cars at peak hours.

In my quest to experience a Yosemite matching my expectation, I headed toward the heart of the park to a granite dome. **(6)** <u>I walked up what was once the floor of the Pacific Ocean, once rising magma, once the basement of numerous glaciers.</u> This place, so apparently solid and immobile, was moving: Pebbles carried up, boulders waiting

3. Which of the following sentences best fits with the style and tone of the rest of the essay?

   A) NO CHANGE
   B) This wasn't the Yosemite I came to see.
   C) With all of these amenities, Yosemite was not quite what I had envisioned Yosemite to be.
   D) The Yosemite you wanted to discover had to be somewhere else, both in time and place.

4. A) NO CHANGE
   B) comprehensive
   C) unworkable
   D) thorough and sensible

5. A) NO CHANGE
   B) Shuttles have already reduced traffic in the valley although they
   C) Shuttles have already reduced traffic in the valley, while they
   D) Shuttles have had some success reducing traffic in the valley. It is regrettable that the shuttles

6. A) NO CHANGE
   B) I walked up what was once the floor of the Pacific Ocean. At one point it was rising magma. Next it was the basement of numerous glaciers.
   C) I was walking on what was once the floor of the Pacific Ocean, rising magma, and the bottom of glaciers.
   D) I walked up what was once the floor of the Pacific Ocean, which was once a mass of rising magma that eventually formed the basement of numerous glaciers.

to roll down, **(7)** <u>and you knew the whole dome was still rising a foot per millennium</u> with the rest of the Sierra. Conifers had found small crevices and were drawing out a harsh existence, twisting themselves into hideous shapes.

    Then I arrived on top, prepared for the modern world to intrude again. But the view was **(8)** <u>contrary to what I had expected</u>: to the east the jagged tops of the Sierra and to the southwest the totem of Yosemite, Half Dome—**(9)** <u>but I saw the back of it instead of the front that people usually see.</u> I realized I had discovered my Yosemite. Through my climb I felt **(10)** <u>connected</u> to the past, but now I wondered what the view from the dome would be like in the future. How different would the experience be then? **(11)** <u>Do you think there will be still be crowds? Or will it be pristine wilderness once more?</u>

7. A) NO CHANGE
  B) and the whole dome still rising a foot per millennium
  C) and I knew the whole dome was still rising a foot per millennium
  D) the whole dome rising up a foot per millennium

8. A) NO CHANGE
  B) marvelously different
  C) in contrast to what I expected
  D) opposite of the anticipated

9. A) NO CHANGE
  B) but not its most commonly photographed side.
  C) but I saw the back instead of its photogenic side.
  D) but the back instead of the front.

10. A) NO CHANGE
  B) linked
  C) hitched
  D) joined

11. A) NO CHANGE
  B) Do you think there will still be crowds? Will the park even still exist?
  C) Will there still be crowds? Or will it be pristine wilderness once more?
  D) Will there even still be a Yosemite National Park? If so, maybe there will be no crowds.

TEST EXERCISE:

Riley v. California

[1] The issue of privacy has been central to American identity since the foundation of the country. [2] In our modern world, however, new technology is constantly raising unprecedented questions with regard to privacy rights. [3] The Founding **(1)** <u>Fathers'</u> extreme dislike for the unrestrained searches conducted by the British resulted in the Fourth Amendment, which protects people from "unreasonable searches and seizures." [4] One such question recently came before the Supreme Court in the case of *Riley v. California.* **{2}**

The case involved whether the police may, without a warrant, search digital information on a cell phone taken from an individual under arrest. California argued that this should be allowed in keeping with a rule that permits the police to search other items on a person under arrest. The Supreme Court, however, rejected this argument, maintaining that there is a **(3)** <u>visible</u> difference between searching a wallet or purse and searching the digital contents of a phone. Thus, the Court determined that, except in the case of an emergency, the police **(4)** <u>must get an official warrant before searching through and examining all the contents of a phone.</u>

1. A) NO CHANGE
   B) Father's
   C) Fathers
   D) Fathers's

2. For the sake of the cohesion of this paragraph, sentence 3 should be placed

   A) where it is now.
   B) before sentence 1.
   C) after sentence 1
   D) after sentence 4.

3. Which of the following is the most precise replacement for the underlined word?

   A) NO CHANGE
   B) detectable
   C) powerful
   D) substantial

4. A) NO CHANGE
   B) must go through the process of obtaining a warrant before they are allowed to look at the digital contents of someone's personal cell phone
   C) have to get a warrant to look at your phone
   D) must get a warrant before examining the information on a phone

{5} Although a physical inspection of a phone is permissible to ensure that it cannot be used as a weapon, the Court determined that the digital data stored on a phone pose no **(6)** <u>threat, and thus</u> police officers have no need to search it immediately. The Court also rejected the claim that a search is necessary to avoid the destruction of evidence. Although it is possible that data could be wiped from the phone remotely, simply turning the phone off or **(7)** <u>if you remove the battery it will</u> prevent this.

5. Which choice most effectively establishes the main topic of the paragraph?

   A) In arriving at its decision, the Court first considered whether such a search is necessary under ordinary circumstances.
   B) The privacy of the individual was the primary factor in the Court's decision.
   C) The safety of the police officers was the one serious objection that the Court addressed.
   D) Before the case was decided, the Court had to assess the influence of new technology on the daily operations of the police.

6. A) NO CHANGE
   B) threat; and thus
   C) threat thus
   D) threat,

7. A) NO CHANGE
   B) the battery can be removed to
   C) removing the battery can
   D) remove the battery to

The Court then considered how far a person's privacy is invaded by a search of his or her phone. Here, the Court enumerated the many functions of cell phones and **(8)** <u>had emphasized</u> their "immense storage capacity." {9} In his opinion for the Court, Chief Justice John Roberts wrote: "With all [cell phones] contain and all they may reveal, they hold for many Americans 'the privacies of life'. The fact that technology now allows an individual to carry such information in his hand does not make the information any less worthy of the protection for which the Founders fought."

8. A) NO CHANGE
    B) emphasized
    C) has emphasized
    D) was emphasizing

9. Which of the following, if added here, would best support the ideas in the paragraph?

    A) It stated that many of the features on cell phones are not relevant to the police, so it would often not be worth their time to search the phones.
    B) It pointed out that the data stored on a cell phone may give a more complete picture of a person's life than a detailed search of the person's house.
    C) It claimed that the Founding Fathers could not have imagined the amount of data stored in a cell phone, and thus it is difficult to apply the Founders' principles to this issue.
    D) It argued that if people are concerned about their privacy, they should be careful how much data they store on their phones in the first place.

Although the Court's ruling may seem to hinder a police officer's ability to do **(10)** <u>one's</u> job, the Court also made clear the limits of this ruling. It did not declare that the police could never search a person's phone, but simply that they must acquire a warrant before doing so. Still, the Court admitted that "privacy comes at a cost." **{11}**

10. A) NO CHANGE
   B) his or her
   C) their
   D) its

11. Considering the overall tone and purpose of the passage, which of the following would provide the best conclusion?

   A) Luckily, the Court knows that our privacy is the most important thing!
   B) However, the warrant provision is an essential component of the Court's Fourth Amendment jurisprudence and therefore must be strictly observed in accordance with previous precedents.
   C) In fact, this cost is so high that one wonders if the Court has really made a wise decision in *Riley v. California*.
   D) Nevertheless, this cost is one that the Founding Fathers believed was worth paying.

Lesson wY19
Effective Language Use: Style and Tone
Race to the Finish

HOMEWORK EXERCISE 1:

Anatomy of a Hurricane

The term "hurricane" has its origin in the indigenous religions of past civilizations. The Mayan storm god was named Hunraken. A god considered evil by the Taino people of the Caribbean was called Huracan. **(1)** <u>They're probably not really evil, and</u> they are one of nature's most powerful storms. Their potential for loss of life and destruction of property is tremendous.

Those in hurricane-prone areas need to be prepared for hurricanes and tropical storms. This includes inland areas, well away from the coastline, where residents can also **(2)** <u>experience destructive winds, tornadoes and floods from</u> tropical storms and hurricanes.

On average each year, 11 tropical storms, 6 of which become hurricanes, develop in the Atlantic Ocean, Caribbean Sea, or Gulf of Mexico. In a typical 3-year span, the U. S. coastline is struck on average five times by hurricanes, two of which are designated as major hurricanes.

Hurricanes **(3)** <u>get their juice from the hot parts of the ocean and air.</u> Powered by heat from the sea, they are typically steered, when they are south of 25° north latitude, by the easterly winds at low altitudes (between the ocean's surface and 8 miles high). South of 25° north latitude, they are generally steered by high-level westerly winds. The Atlantic hurricane season starts on June 1. For the United States, the peak hurricane threat exists from mid-August to late October **(4),** <u>but hurricanes are allowed to occur anytime up until November 30.</u> Over other parts of the world, such as the western North Pacific, hurricanes (or typhoons, as they are called in that region) can occur year-round.

1. A) NO CHANGE
   B) While hurricanes may not actually be evil,
   C) Because hurricanes can't be good or bad,
   D) Hurricanes are a symbol of evil in the world; nevertheless,

2. A) NO CHANGE
   B) have their homes blasted apart by the amazing forces of nature in
   C) lose their stuff or have it messed up by
   D) be completely obliterated by the monstrous winds and heavy rains that come with

3. A) NO CHANGE
   B) derive their devastating power from their manner of forming: an intricate interplay between the copious moisture generated by torrid oceans and the receptive atmosphere hovering above the vast expanses of seawater
   C) would be friendlier weather systems if there were no oceans supporting them
   D) are products of a tropical ocean and a warm, moist atmosphere

4. A) NO CHANGE
   B) although the official hurricane season extends through November 30
   C) ,yet they can continue to annoy residents and frustrate plans any time before November 30
   D) ,but the drop-dead date for new hurricanes to form doesn't come until November 30

region) can occur year-round.

There are three conditions required for a disturbance to form and strengthen into a hurricane. **(5)** First, <u>disturbances have to get enough heat and energy</u> through contact with warm ocean waters. Next, added moisture evaporated from the sea surface powers the seedling tropical storm like a giant heat engine. Finally, the seedling storm forms a wind pattern near the ocean surface that spirals air inward. **(6)** <u>Bands of thunderstorms form,</u> allowing the air to warm further and rise higher into the atmosphere. If the winds at these higher levels are relatively light, this structure can remain intact and further strengthen the hurricane.

The center, or eye, of a hurricane is relatively calm, with sinking air, light winds and few clouds. **(7)** <u>The last place you want to be is the eyewall</u>, the ring of thunderstorms immediately surrounding the eye. At the top of the eyewall (about 50,000 feet), most of the air is propelled outward, increasing the air's upward motion. Some of the air, however, moves inward and sinks into the eye, creating a cloud-free area.

5. A) NO CHANGE
   B) you have to have a significant combination of heat and energy
   C) disturbances must gather heat and energy
   D) disturbances churn and swirl, and they eventually harness enough heat and energy

6. A) NO CHANGE
   B) Thunder comes crashing down, while
   C) The wind and the rain join together in a complex, yet beautiful dance,
   D) A concatenation of events, catalyzed by the aforementioned heating of the ocean and vertiginous movement of the winds, then ensues,

7. A) NO CHANGE
   B) Unlike a human eye, the eye of a hurricane has an eyewall
   C) If you think of a doughnut, the eye is like the hole in the middle, while the part that you eat is the eyewall
   D) In contrast, the most violent winds and rain are found in the eyewall

The Progression of ALS

Amyotrophic lateral sclerosis (ALS) is a progressive disease that affects motor neurons, which are specialized nerve cells that are important for controlling muscle movement and strength. **(8)** The spinal cord and the brain are where these nerve cells have home-field advantage. ALS causes motor neurons to die over time, leading to problems with muscle control and movement.

There are many different types of ALS; these types are distinguished by their signs and symptoms and by either their genetic cause or their lack of clear genetic association. Most people with ALS have condition that is described as sporadic, which means it occurs in people **(9)** whose number never came up before in the genetic lottery. People with sporadic ALS usually first develop features of the condition in their late fifties or early sixties. A small proportion of people with ALS, estimated at 5 to 10 percent, have a family history of the condition. The signs and symptoms of familial ALS typically first appear in one's late forties or early fifties. **(10)** In rare cases, people with familial ALS develop symptoms in childhood or their teenage years. These individuals have a form of the disorder known as juvenile ALS.

The first signs and symptoms of ALS may be so subtle that they are overlooked. **(11)** If the disease is just starting out, you need to watch for muscle twitching, cramping, stiffness, or weakness. Affected individuals may develop slurred speech and, later, dysphagia (difficulty chewing or swallowing). Many people with ALS experience malnutrition because of reduced food intake due to dysphagia and an increase in their metabolism (their body's energy demands) due to prolonged illness. Muscles become weaker as the disease progresses, and arms and legs begin to look thinner as muscle tissue wastes away. Individuals with ALS lose their strength and the ability to walk. **(12)** Not surprisingly, most patients at this

8. A) NO CHANGE
   B) These nerve cells are found in the spinal cord and the brain.
   C) It's sad is that most of these cells can't exist outside the spinal cord and the brain.
   D) If you were an explorer and wanted to find motor neurons, the best places to look would be the spinal cord and the brain.

9. A) NO CHANGE
   B) whose families have long escaped the angry scourge of ALS
   C) who are very bizarre in their families, since they have the disease while their family members do not.
   D) with no apparent history of the disorder in their family

10. A) NO CHANGE
    B) Children and teenagers sometimes show signs of familial ALS as well, but this is usually an extremely rare thing.
    C) Some kids get familial ALS, too, but not very many.
    D) It is extremely weird for familial ALS to show up in children or teenagers.

11. A) NO CHANGE
    B) It may become necessary to consult a doctor if one observes
    C) The earliest symptoms include
    D) There are, however, some signs that are so obvious that you can't miss them:

stage of the disease are glad for the invention of the wheelchair. Over time, muscle weakness causes affected individuals to lose the use of their hands and arms. Breathing becomes difficult because the muscles of the respiratory system weaken. Most people with ALS die from respiratory failure within 2 to 10 years after the signs and symptoms of ALS first appear; however, **(13)** trying to compare individual cases of ALS is like trying to compare apples and oranges.

Approximately 20 percent of individuals with ALS also develop a condition called frontotemporal dementia (FTD), which is a progressive brain disorder that affects personality, behavior, and language. Changes in personality and behavior may make it difficult for affected individuals to interact with others in a socially appropriate manner. People with FTD increasingly require help with personal care and other activities of daily living. Communication skills worsen as the disease progresses. **(14)** It would be nice to know how the development of ALS and FTD are related. Individuals who develop both conditions are simply diagnosed as having ALS-FTD.

12. A) NO CHANGE
   B) Affected individuals eventually become wheelchair-dependent.
   C) The walking incapability is often absolute, with the introduction of a wheelchair commonly required for the patient to achieve any degree of mobility.
   D) Fortunately, there are millions of high-quality wheelchairs available that these patients can purchase.

13. A) NO CHANGE
   B) there is really no way to tell exactly how long a person who is diagnosed with ALS will have between the time that he or she discovers that he or she has the disease and the time that he or she succumbs to the effects of the disease
   C) there is no way on earth to determine a precise timeframe
   D) the disease's progression varies widely among affected individuals

14. A) NO CHANGE
   B) As of yet, no one has a clue
   C) It is a mystery inside of a riddle wrapped up in an enigma
   D) It is unclear

HOMEWORK EXERCISE 2:

The Invasion of Kudzu

[1]

They lurk along the highways and dusty back roads of the rural South. They creep silently through the shadows, overpowering and strangling anything that gets in their way. **(1)** Nowhere is safe from these invaders. A poet once wrote that in Georgia, you must close your windows at night to keep them out of your house. If this sounds like the plot to a horror film—or perhaps an episode of *The Walking Dead*—well, it's thankfully nothing quite so spooky. I'm talking about kudzu vines.

[2]

Kudzu is a plant **(2)** sometimes colloquially known as "the vine that ate the South." At least 14 states are now **(3)** inflicted with this pest. **(4)** Originally imported from Japan for use in ornamental gardens, kudzu's boosters didn't realize that it would begin to spread uncontrollably like a weed. Kudzu **(5)** grows until it kills other trees and shrubs and depriving them of sunlight and nutrients. Kudzu can overtake an abandoned building in only a few years; old barns entirely covered by the tenacious vines are a common sight along Southern byways.

1. Which of the following choices for the underlined sentence best suits to tone and style of the paragraph?

   A) NO CHANGE
   B) If you see them coming, you should run for your life!
   C) These versatile adversaries are known to ascend even the tallest trees and overtake entire structures.
   D) They are a group of plants in the genus *Pueraria*, in the pea family *Fabaceae*.

2. Which of the following alternatives for the underlined portion would best help the author to clarify the origin of kudzu's nickname?

   A) NO CHANGE
   B) so pervasive in the southeastern states that it is
   C) which, although not carnivorous, is
   D) in the vine family,

3. A) NO CHANGE
   B) inflicted by
   C) afflicted with
   D) inflected with

4. A) NO CHANGE
   B) When they originally imported it
   C) Being originally imported
   D) To originally import it

5. Which choice for the underlined portion results in the clearest and most precise sentence?

   A) NO CHANGE
   B) kills by starving
   C) overtakes
   D) grows more quickly than most plants, engulfing

[3]

(6) Kudzu has even managed to colonize the storied halls of country music. One singer tells of his lover, who "wrapped her song around my heart just like the kudzu vine." A particularly macabre ballad describes in humorous detail the gruesome demise of an unfortunate man who stepped into the path of a kudzu vine as it crossed the road. There are bands named the Kudzu Kings, the Kudzu Quartet, and the Kudzu Krooners.

[4]

Not every Southerner seems to think **(7)** that getting rid of the invasive vine is the appropriate response to the kudzu invasion. Some have embraced the plant, **(8)** cooking up kudzu recipes, using it to make sturdy baskets, and even baling and stacking it to build walls. There is even some evidence that a kudzu extract might help treat alcoholism.

[5]

Those determined to fight back against the onslaught have few options. Chopping it down or using herbicides doesn't **(9)** work if even one shoot survives, it will return with a vengeance the following year. The city of Chattanooga, Tennessee has, however, hit upon a successful counterattack method: goats. The city's parks and recreation department **(10)** deploy herds of goats to areas overrun by kudzu, and the vine is gone within three years. Perhaps one day, the South will be free of its great green scourge. {11}

6. Which choice for the underlined sentence provides the best transition between paragraphs two and three?

   A) NO CHANGE
   B) Kudzu is a subject that has inspired many musicians.
   C) Kudzu, while troublesome, has provided much fertile ground for entertainment.
   D) Perhaps because of its widespread presence, kudzu has even invaded Southern music.

7. A) NO CHANGE
   B) elimination or eradication
   C) reversing the vine's invasive and annoying spread
   D) eliminating the vine

8. A) NO CHANGE
   B) cooked up kudzu recipes, used
   C) by cooking up kudzu recipes, or used
   D) cooked up kudzu recipes, tried using

9. A) NO CHANGE
   B) work, but if
   C) work, and if
   D) work; if

10. A) NO CHANGE
    B) deploys
    C) deploying
    D) have deployed

11. The author is considering adding the following sentence to the essay:
    Kudzu has been proposed as a cheap source of biofuel.
    To which paragraph would this most logically be added?

    A) Paragraph 1
    B) Paragraph 2
    C) Paragraph 3
    D) Paragraph 4

Lesson wY20
Practice Section

LET'S CHECK IN

Congratulations! We've reached the end of this book!

Today's lesson isn't really a lesson – it's a checkpoint to see how far we've come since the first lesson.

On the following pages, you'll find a series of writing passages and questions. Each set is designed to reflect the types of passages and questions that are common to the SAT writing section. As you work through each passage, keep these tips in mind:

- No matter what kind of question you face, always eliminate any answer choices that do not suit the style or tone of the passage as a whole.
- If you find yourself struggling with a particular question, look at the surrounding sentences to see if there are context clues that might help you to eliminate additional answer choices.
- If you've eliminated every answer choice you can, and you still can't seem to decide which of the remaining options is correct, rely on your ear for the language. Read the appropriate part of the passage with each remaining answer choice inserted in the correct place and choose the answer that sounds best.

As you work through each practice set, be sure to mark any questions that you find particularly challenging so that you and your teacher can review them in greater depth when you've finished this lesson.

Lesson wY20
Practice Section

PRACTICE PASSAGE 1:

The Golden Record

On September 5, 1977, a historic day for mankind, the *Voyager 1* space probe was launched by NASA to study the outer Solar System and, possibly, whatever **(1)** lay beyond. All eyes looked upward as it shot into the sky, carrying with it a strange package. A 12-inch gold plated phonograph record, the Golden Record, containing sounds and images from across the globe selected to portray the **(2)** different nature of Earth life and culture, was securely fastened to the outside of *Voyager 1* along with the **(3)** vital equipment to play it. {4}

The Golden Record is, in essence, a flying time-capsule. **(5)** It is humanity's message to the stars and the aliens and to whatever entity that encounters it. The idea of an alien species discovering it is fascinating, but it is extremely unlikely that anyone will ever play it, for the *Voyager's* path travels through deep, empty space after it leaves the Solar System. However, when asked about the spacecraft in an interview, Dr. Carl Sagan, head of the NASA committee slated to select the message to the stars, **(6)** noting, "The spacecraft will be encountered and the record played only if there are advanced spacefaring civilizations in interstellar space. But the launching of this bottle into the cosmic ocean says something very hopeful about life on this planet."

1. A) NO CHANGE
   B) will lie beyond
   C) has lied beyond
   D) had lied beyond

2. A) NO CHANGE
   B) unique
   C) multifaceted
   D) varied

3. A) NO CHANGE
   B) indispensable
   C) necessary
   D) essential

4. Which sentence, if added to the end of the preceding paragraph, would provide the most effective transition to the following paragraph?

   A) This record is sure to explain humanity's existence.
   B) To think this is just an eccentric add-on would be folly.
   C) This record is a good ambassador of humanity.
   D) However, this unusual record is not simply a music album.

5. A) NO CHANGE
   B) It is humanity's message to the universe.
   C) It is humanity's message to the aliens that are sure to discover it.
   D) It is humanity's futile attempt to communicate with possible extraterrestrial life.

6. A) NO CHANGE
   B) noted,
   C) notes,
   D) has noted,

[1] This launch into interplanetary communication is **(7)** <u>embedded not only at</u> music but also images, spoken greetings, and even printed messages. [2] The NASA committee selected 115 images depicting diverse aspects of human life. [3] People are also portrayed from various parts of the globe performing different tasks or carrying on with routine, everyday activities. [4] Pictures of Earth from space and its moon precede pictures of the human race. [5] The first images of people begin with the biological depictions of the human anatomy, musculature, and reproductive cycle. [6] Other images display the various climates of different geographical regions, along with assorted images of animals, plants, buildings, vehicles, and **(8)** <u>images of human beings</u>. {9}

The sounds present on the Golden Record are just as eclectic as the images. The first sounds to be heard are spoken greetings in 55 different languages, starting with Akkadian and ending with Wu, recited by native speakers of those languages. Up next, the sounds of nature, such as the surf, wind, thunder, birds, whales, and other animals play, attempting to depict the sounds that would be heard by any extra-terrestrial visiting Earth. Finally, a 90-minute selection of songs from disparate cultures and eras plays, including Beethoven, Bach, **(10)** <u>Chuck Berry, music</u> from tribes in Australia, Europe, Africa, and Asia. With that, the message from Earth, the Golden Record, will fall silent. {11}

7. A) NO CHANGE
   B) embedded not only on
   C) embedded not only with
   D) embedded not only to

8. A) NO CHANGE
   B) human beings
   C) those of human beings
   D) human beings'

9. Which of the following choices best improves the coherency of the preceding paragraph?

   A) Leave as is.
   B) Move sentence 2 in front of sentence 5.
   C) Move sentence 4 in front of sentence 1.
   D) Move sentence 3 to the end of the paragraph.

10. A) NO CHANGE
    B) Chuck Berry, and music
    C) Chuck Berry; music
    D) Chuck Berry. Also, music

11. Which of the following would provide the best conclusion to the passage?

    A) Through such means, those outside our solar system will learn things about us.
    B) The Golden Record would sure make a great addition to any music collection!
    C) What will those who find this Golden Record think of us?
    D) The Golden Record is a chronicle of humanity and Earth, providing those who find it with all we have to offer.

Lesson wY20
Practice Section

PRACTICE PASSAGE 2:

Investing in Africa's Growth

[1]

President Obama's town hall today with 500 of Africa's most promising young leaders provided an inspiring window into what the future holds for Africa, and the world.

[2]

The 500 participants in the Washington Fellowship program were selected from nearly 50,000 applicants from across Africa, as part of the President's Young African Leaders Initiative (YALI). **(1)** <u>YALI began through</u> President Obama in 2010, as part of a long-term investment in the next generation of African leaders. It aims to sharpen their skills, **(2)** <u>refining their networks</u>, and strengthen partnerships between the United States and Africa for years to come.

[3]

The President announced during the town hall that the Washington Fellowship **(3)** <u>is called</u> the Mandela Washington Fellowship for Young African Leaders, in honor of the former South African President, Nelson Mandela. Mandela Washington Fellows represent the best and brightest from communities across Africa, and fields ranging from education to medicine, law, business, and beyond. These are the young leaders whose skills, passion, and visions for the future will help shape the fate of their countries and the world. It is in everyone's best interest to help **(4)** <u>them</u> prepare with the tools they need to build a healthier, more secure, more prosperous, and more peaceful Africa, which is why President Obama launched YALI in the first place. **{5}**

1. Which of the following is the most precise replacement for the underlined phrase?

   A) YALI was launched by
   B) Started by
   C) YALI initiated
   D) YALI, having been developed by

2. A) NO CHANGE
   B) refined their networks
   C) refine their networks
   D) refines their networks

3. A) NO CHANGE
   B) would be renamed
   C) had been known as
   D) will have been

4. In context, which of the following is the best replacement for the underlined word?

   A) Africa's best students
   B) governments
   C) other people
   D) fellowships

5. Which of the following facts would best support an idea presented in this paragraph?

   A) The Washington Fellowship was formerly known as the Kennedy Fellowship.
   B) Stability in Africa is vital to the economic welfare of other other continents.
   C) Africa's best and brightest students never work abroad.
   D) Africa is home to a diverse array of cultures.

[4]

President Obama also took today's opportunity to preview another historic event planned for next week. The U.S.-Africa Leaders Summit will be hosted in Washington, by President Obama, and will represent the largest gathering any American president has ever hosted with African heads of state and government. {6} The President pointed out today, "even as we deal with crises and challenges in other parts of the world that often dominate the headlines; even as we acknowledge the real hardships that so many Africans face every day – **(7)** <u>you have</u> to make sure that we're all seizing the extraordinary potential of today's Africa, the youngest and fastest-growing continent."

[1] YALI, in addition to other state programs, **(8)** <u>is</u> about capitalizing on the creativity and talent of Africa's young leaders by empowering them with the skills, training, and technology necessary to make lasting change, and meaningful progress back home. [2] We're joining **(9)** <u>with</u> American universities, African institutions and business partners like Microsoft and MasterCard Foundation. [3] And to do so, we are engaging public and private sector partners to create new Regional Leadership Centers across Africa to reach more young leaders. [4] Starting next year, young Africans can come to these centers to network, access the latest technology, and get training in management and entrepreneurship. [5] The first centers will be located in Senegal, Ghana, South Africa and Kenya - and will provide tens of thousands of young Africans the resources they need to put their ideas into action. {10} {11}

6. For the sake of the cohesion of the passage, which sentence best transitions between the fourth and fifth paragraphs?

   A) Still, the President is keenly aware that problems in our own country must come first.
   B) This gathering will dwarf attempts by rival nations to connect with Africa's economic and political leaders.
   C) The Leaders Summit will begin with a speech at the Washington Mall, followed by a reception at the U.S. Capitol Building.
   D) Like YALI, this summit will help foster growth and goodwill in a quickly developing region.

7. A) NO CHANGE
   B) we have
   C) he has
   D) they have

8. A) NO CHANGE
   B) are
   C) have been
   D) had been

9. A) NO CHANGE
   B) to
   C) together to
   D) in

10. Which of the following changes would improve the focus of the paragraph?

   A) Combine sentences 1 and 2
   B) Move sentence 2 after sentence 3
   C) Switch sentences 3 and 5
   D) Omit sentence 4

11. Which of the following best summarizes the main claim of the passage?

A) African countries need intervention by the United States in order to maintain peace and develop economically.

B) The brightest students in Africa have more potential than those from other continents.

C) While YALI is important to the United States' relationship with Africa, leader summits and other programs that work from a government-to-government perspective are more helpful.

D) YALI and other attempts to connect to and invest in Africa are major and important undertakings for the future of our country.

Lesson wY20
Practice Section

PRACTICE PASSAGE 3:

James VIII's attempts to retake the English crown had met with defeat time and time again, so it was left to his son, Prince Charles Edward Stuart, known to history as Bonnie Prince Charlie. A man of great personal **(1)** charm, the Prince was, unfortunately, not a strong military leader, and **(2)** had a tendency of hesitating when strong action was called for. This character failing would come to haunt him.

On 23 July 1745, Bonnie Prince Charlie came to Scotland. He was counting on support from the Highland clans who lived in the more mountainous areas of Scotland, but he also strongly believed that once he had begun his rebellion, he would get the popular support he needed to **(3)** expel the unpopular George II. What the Prince did not realize was that very few people were willing to accept a Catholic king, so the support he was hoping for never materialized.

(4) Though his army was initially successful – taking Perth, Edinburgh, and Manchester. Yet the English government, under George II, raised fresh troops while Charles sat and waited for additional support. Englishmen failed to flock to his banner. **{5}** Soon, Charles's army began to run low on food, supplies, and morale.

1. A) NO CHANGE
   B) charm, was unfortunately
   C) charm, unfortunately the Prince
   D) charm; the Prince was, unfortunately

2. A) NO CHANGE
   B) tending to hesitate
   C) hesitated with a tendency
   D) tended to hesitate

3. Within context of the passage, which of the following is the best replacement for the underlined word?

   A) NO CHANGE
   B) exorcise
   C) dethrone
   D) abdicate

4. A) NO CHANGE
   B) His army was initially successful – taking Perth, Edinburgh, and Manchester.
   C) An initially successful early army – taking Perth, Edinburgh, and Manchester.
   D) Though his army was initially successful: taking Perth, Edinburgh, and Manchester.

5. Which of the following would provide supporting evidence for the previous sentence?

   A) His troops from Scotland believed firmly in his cause.
   B) Only two hundred English recruits ever joined his army.
   C) He had not made many friends among the English people.
   D) He appealed mainly to the Catholic contingent of Englishmen.

Finally, on 16 April 1746 the hungry and exhausted Jacobite army met government troops under English General Cumberland at Culloden Moor. Charles's military advisors pleaded with him to withdraw; his army was in no shape to fight, and the terrain was against him. **(6)** He did not listen.

Culloden was a **(7)** complete and total defeat for the Jacobites. Cumberland's men overran the Prince's army. Cumberland ordered his men to spare no one; he wanted to completely crush the Jacobite cause, and by all accounts it was a success. The ferocity of Cumberland's men and the vicious reprisals that went on long after the battle earned the Duke the name 'Butcher'. {8}

The English government was determined to **(9)** assure that there would be no further Jacobite risings. To do that, **(10)** they needed to break the power of the Highland clans who had supported the Stuarts. They began to declare new laws aimed at changing the traditional clan structure and destroying Highland culture.

As a result, clan chiefs no longer had the power to make legal decisions. Their chiefs had their lands taken away. All weapons had to be surrendered to the government on pain of death. Even bagpipes, strangely classified as a weapon, had to be turned in. The wearing of traditional clan tartans was forbidden. The lasting effect of these measures was to change forever the traditional clan **(11)** structure, many Highlanders left Scotland and emigrated overseas.

6. Which of the following phrases provides the best transition to the following paragraph?

A) NO CHANGE
B) It is important to listen to more experienced advisors.
C) It was a difficult decision for Charles to make.
D) This would have been a wise idea.

7. A) NO CHANGE
B) complete, total
C) total
D) totally complete

8. Which of the following would provide supporting evidence for the previous sentence?

A) Such conflicts often end in violence, even against innocents.
B) A butcher has very bloody work.
C) This name has stuck with Cumberland over the following centuries.
D) His troops burned houses and crops, looted, and killed suspected Jacobite sympathizers.

9. Within the context of the passage, which of the following is the best replacement for the underlined word?

A) NO CHANGE
B) insure
C) ensure
D) reassure

10. A) NO CHANGE
B) it's needed
C) it needed
D) they were needing

11. A) NO CHANGE
B) structure; many
C) structure, yet many
D) structure: many

Lesson wY20
Practice Section

PRACTICE PASSAGE 4:

Veggies in Space

{1} New research finds that simulated Martian soil supported plant life better than both simulated moon soil and low-quality soil from Earth.

Humans have never attempted to grow plants on other worlds, but scientists from the Apollo project rubbed and dusted moon materials on plants to see if the soil was toxic. More recently, **(2)** <u>a Russian experiment</u> found that marigolds could grow and live in a simulated lunar soil.

Scientist Wieger Wamelink and his colleagues experimented with growing plants in soils that mimic extraterrestrial ones. Neither soil contains many **(3)** <u>nutrients, but</u> the mock Mars soil has low levels of organic carbon, which is non-existent on Mars. They also used a low-quality soil from earth to compare growth in our native soil.

The researchers planted more than 4,000 seeds from 14 different plants. Some of their experimental species are "nitrogen-fixers" which carry special bacteria that provide the plant with nitrogen compounds.

(4) <u>The Martian and Earthen samples were more successful and yielded much more production than the scientists originally expected.</u>

"I didn't expect many plants to germinate because I know there are a lot of heavy metals in the soils," said Wamelink. "On the Martian soil it went very well - much better than we thought. It was really a surprise to us."

1. Which of the following should be the introductory sentence for the passage?

   A) Producing food in space in the greatest challenge to NASA's scientists.
   B) Earth's botanists have focused their efforts on how to grow edible plants in space.
   C) How much food would it take to support an extraterrestrial colony?
   D) The success of an extraterrestrial colony could depend on explorers being able to grow their own food.

2. A) NO CHANGE
   B) Russian scientists
   C) the Russians
   D) Russian scientific experiments

3. A) NO CHANGE
   B) nutrients but
   C) nutrients, although
   D) nutrients; nonetheless,

4. A) NO CHANGE
   B) Originally, the Martian and Earthen samples yielded much more production than the scientists first thought.
   C) The Martian and Earthen samples yielded much more production than the scientists originally expected.
   D) The Martian and Earthen samples originally yielded much more production and were overall more successful than the scientists had previously expected.

However, the species grew poorly in the lunar sample, and most died before the end of the experiment. Wamelink attributes this to the soil's high content of **(5)** <u>aluminum, being toxic to plants.</u> Genuine lunar soil might fare differently.

Extraterrestrial soils are known to have large amounts of aluminum and other metals which can **(6)** <u>arrest</u> plant growth. This could be problematic if the vegetables absorb too much of the toxic nutrients. On the other hand, **(7)** <u>that</u> could also be helpful if the astronauts could harvest the metal molecules from the plants.

"Plants, besides feeding the astronauts, are going to be **(8)** <u>soliciting</u> nutrients from the exterior environment and bringing it into the habitat," said Robert Ferl, a botanist at the University of Florida in Gainesville. He noted that there is a distinct benefit to not forcing the astronauts to bring all these molecules with them.

Wamelink and his colleagues originally forgot to consider a major player in the plant life cycle: pollinators. **{9}**

"You need to set up a small ecosystem," said Wamelink. "It's much more complicated than we first thought."

Astronauts will also have to bring bacteria and fungi to fertilize the plants, said Wamelink. The astronauts could use their own waste as fertilizer, as well. **{10}**

To help future colonists survive, NASA is developing a self-contained greenhouse which they plan to send to the moon to learn about growing plants in actual lunar soil and reduced gravity. After a recent set of experiments, researchers **(11)** <u>propose</u> that a similar container be sent to Mars, but the project was not selected for the Mars 2020 mission.

5. A) NO CHANGE
   B) aluminum, which is toxic to plants.
   C) aluminum; which is toxic to plants.
   D) aluminum, but aluminum is toxic to plants.

6. A) NO CHANGE
   B) contain
   C) detain
   D) retain

7. A) NO CHANGE
   B) it
   C) the soil
   D) they

8. A) NO CHANGE
   B) drawing
   C) excavating
   D) stealing

9. Which sentence draws an accurate conclusion from the preceding sentence?

   A) He suspects astronauts would need to bring insects with them to pollinate crops.
   B) There were once natural pollinators in space, but not anymore.
   C) Without pollinators, the astronauts would die.
   D) He thinks there is no way to overcome this obstacle.

10. Which provides the best conclusion to the paragraph?

   A) Growing plants without fertilizers would be disastrous.
   B) Wamelink knows a solution will present itself.
   C) Transporting these items would be quite costly.
   D) Wamelink sees these as viable solutions to the problem.

11. A) NO CHANGE
    B) will propose
    C) proposed
    D) proposing

Lesson wY20
Practice Section

PRACTICE PASSAGE 5:

Farming in Modern America

Farming, in the American popular imagination, is **(1)** <u>something done by farmers, not machines.</u> But for decades now, the reality of American agriculture has been quite different: large, corporate farms dominate most of our rural landscape. A growing interest in such trends as local and organic food, farmers' markets, and community-supported **(2)** <u>agriculture; these things</u> might be able to reverse the trend toward fewer, larger farms. But to do so will require a new generation of farmers to run a new generation of small farms. So far, this generation has been slow to emerge, likely because of the many **(3)** <u>formidable</u> obstacles that young farmers face in entering the profession.

A few numbers serve to illustrate the difficulty of making a living as a small-scale farmer. The median farm income in 2012 was, amazingly, less than zero—negative $1,453 to be precise. As a result, 91% of farm households rely on multiple sources of income. In fact, **(4)** <u>only commercial farmers were not dependent on off-farm income to some extent.</u> Given these daunting numbers, is it any surprise that the average age of an American farmer is now 60?

1. Which of the following choices for the underlined portion provides the most relevant and logical introduction to this paragraph?

   A) NO CHANGE
   B) synonymous with a certain romanticized image of the small family farm.
   C) not at all like the world of big business.
   D) becoming more local and sustainable every day.

2. A) NO CHANGE
   B) agriculture
   C) agriculture are things which
   D) agriculture, and it

3. A) NO CHANGE
   B) sinister
   C) impeding
   D) nasty

4. Which choice completes the sentence with accurate information based on the graph at the end of the passage?

   A) NO CHANGE
   B) nearly half of all non-farm income earned by farms in 2012 was earned by residential farms.
   C) every non-commercial farm required off-farm income to be profitable.
   D) non-commercial farms received the vast majority of their income from off-farm sources.

The high up-front cost of land, infrastructure, and technology to start a **(5)** <u>farm mean</u> that young farmers need access to substantial **(6)** <u>credit, which is a challenge</u> in an era in which banks are hesitant to make large loans. Young would-be farmers, daunted by these harsh financial realities, are largely avoiding the profession altogether. {7}

A recent *New York Times* editorial on these difficulties bore the provocative title "Don't Let Your Children Grow Up to Be Farmers." **(8)** <u>Unlike this cynical perspective,</u> some farming advocates insist that enough resources exist to help young farmers get their start. Organizations such as the Future Farmers of America (FFA) provide mentoring and support to prospective farmers. With a little creativity, they say, there are ways to make a go of it that don't require colossal start-up costs.

5. A) NO CHANGE
   B) farm, meaning
   C) farm means
   D) farm would mean

6. A) NO CHANGE
   B) credit; challenging
   C) credit, this is a challenge
   D) credit are challenges

7. Which sentence, if added here, would support the author's claim that small farms are particularly disadvantaged compared to large farms?

   A) NO CHANGE
   B) Getting a start in farming is difficult even in the best of circumstances.
   C) Large corporate farms, meanwhile, are not similarly deterred, as they have the cash on hand to pay their substantial start-up costs.
   D) Who can blame them, given that the deck is stacked in favor of large corporations?

8. A) NO CHANGE
   B) Whereas
   C) Another perspective,
   D) Rejecting this cynical perspective,

[1] "The number one thing to realize," says Joel Salatin, pioneering organic farmer and author of *You Can Farm*, "is that you don't have to own the land to farm." [2] Some young farmers, says Salatin, are forming partnerships with older farm **(9)** owners; these particular older farmers are looking to retire or scale back their working hours. [3] Other young farmers have used engineering expertise gained in college to design and build innovative, inexpensive systems for things like irrigation. [4] In addition to gaining a rented plot of land, new farmers benefit in such an arrangement from a mentor who can teach them the intricacies of the business. **(10)** [5] How resourceful they are, their determination, and the ingenuity of many young farmers suggests that the small family farm may yet see a resurgence.

{11}

9. A) NO CHANGE
   B) owners; they
   C) owners; in particular, they
   D) owners who

10. A) NO CHANGE
    B) The resourcefulness, determination, and
    C) Their resourcefulness, their determination, and the
    D) How resourceful and determined they are, and the

11. In this paragraph, Sentence 4 would most logically be placed

    A) where it is now.
    B) after Sentence 1.
    C) after Sentence 2.
    D) after Sentence 5.

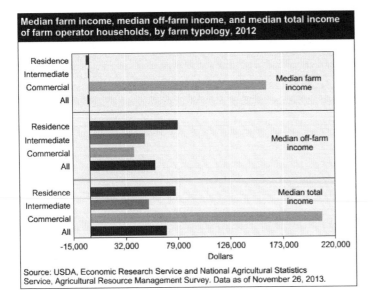

Median farm income, median off-farm income, and median total income of farm operator households, by farm typology, 2012

Source: USDA, Economic Research Service and National Agricultural Statistics Service, Agricultural Resource Management Survey. Data as of November 26, 2013.

Contributors

A Very Special Thank You to the following contributors

Ashley Zahn (HQ)

Brian MacNeel (HQ)

Chris Thomas (HQ)

Kyle Hurford (Johns Creek, GA)

Micah Medders (HQ)

Monica Huynh (Johns Creek, GA)

Sarah Plunkett (Cumming, GA)

Abigail Burns (Johns Creek, GA)

Alicyn Henkhaus (Palos Verdes, CA)

Ankit Rawtani (Bridgewater, NJ)

Anne Hellerman (Coppell, TX)

Benjamin Yu (Bridgewater, NJ)

Brent Cash (Germantown, MD)

Brett Vigil (Johns Creek, GA)

Brian Cabana (Paramus, NJ)

Brian Hester (Roswell, GA)

Caitlin Pancarician (Middletown, NJ)

Casey Lynch (Livingston, NJ)

Christopher Muyo (New York)

Christopher Woodside (Edison, NJ)

Danielle McMullin (Clifton, NJ)

David Rutter (Snellville, GA)

Drew McKelvy (Olney, MD)

Edward Helmsteter (Westfield, NJ)

Eli Aghassi (Northridge, CA)

Elizabeth Peterson (Centreville, VA)

Erica Schimmel (West Portal, CA)

Erin Lynch (Coppell, TX)

Erin Short (Palo Alto, CA)

Greg Hernandez (Rancho Cucamonga, CA)

Heather Kelly (Issaquah, WA)

James Kyrsiak (Old Alabama, GA)

James Wagner (Los Angeles, CA)

Jeffrey Pereira (Scarsdale, NY)

Jessica Loud (Palos Verdes, CA)

Jin Park (Frisco, TX)

John F. Callahan (Parsippany, NY)

Kaleab Tessema (Coppell, TX)

Katharine Galic (Palo Alto, CA)

Kyla Bye-Nagel (Sterling, MD)

Kyle Mesce (Chatham, NJ)

Lane D'Alessandro (King of Prussia, PA)

May-Lieng Karageorge (Lorton, MD)

Michael Fienburg (Calabasas, CA)

Michael Lupi (Paramus, NJ)

Morgan McLoughlin (Brentwood, CA)

Nicole Lampl (Calabasas, CA)

Peter Lee (Hamilton Mill, GA)

Rachel Becker (Burke, VA)

Rachel Tucker (Naperville, IL)

Richard Faulk (Fremont, CA)

Robert Jedrzejewski (Timonium, MD)

Sam Anderson (Paramus, NJ)

Sean Llewellyn (Lynnwood, WA)

Thach Do (Monrovia, CA)

Tina-Anne Mulligan (Paramus, NJ)

Qi-lu Lin (Parsippany, NY)

Zack Arenstein (Livingston, NJ)

Zafar Tejani (Little Neck, NY)